Renaissance Theatre Costume

and the sense of the historic past

Renaissance

and the sense of the historic past

Theatre Costume

STELLA MARY NEWTON

RAPP + WHITING
ANDRE DEUTSCH

First published 1975 by
Rapp and Whiting Limited
105 Great Russell Street London WC1

Printed in Great Britain by
Butler & Tanner Ltd, Frome and London

ISBN 0 85391 182 7

To Sir Martin Davies, KBE
with the gratitude of one of the
fortunate few to have watched
the discipline of his research.

Contents

List of Illustrations

The references to the illustrations are in square brackets in the text. Where no source reference is given the photograph has been supplied by the author

11

13

Very wisely indeed this earthly frame was called by many sages both ancient and modern the stage of the world, since while they are on it, men are treated as are the actors on the stage; for just as the players in tragedies and comedies or other poetic works are clothed by whoever directs them, one as a prince and another as a citizen, one as a soldier and another as a servant, and others still in more outlandish garbs, and then are sent on to the stage where each one plays as best he may the man he must imitate, and when the story is told, each one takes off his costume and returns to his former state, bearing with him either praise or censure according to whether he has played his part well or ill: so we see man to be clothed at his birth by Him who rules the Universe, where each one appears and plays his own part, as best he may, until life's story is at an end, and then, stripped, each one returns naked as he came, bearing with him praise or censure, or better, reward or punishment, according to whether he has acted well or ill in the state or in his calling.

LEONE DE' SOMMI C. 1565

Foreword

I do not know of any book on the costume of the Renaissance theatre; it has not, therefore, been possible to quote authorities on the subject and in consequence students of art history, of the theatre and of dress, all of whom may have felt the need of such a book, will inevitably find this brief study too elementary in parts. They may not all, however, agree as to which those parts are. Had the title not been rather long already I should like to have added 'outline' or 'aspects of' to it. As it is, the present book must be taken as no more than an introduction to the subject.

Since names for kinds or parts of clothing of the Renaissance have not been agreed even in any one language, I have tried either to avoid them or to explain those I have used. In translating passages from documents of the period, often written in naïve prose, I have tried to keep the character of the original without being absurdly literal; important passages, phrases or words are given in the original language in the notes. Where the form or the spelling of an author's name is in doubt, so far as possible I have reproduced the form used on the title page in the original edition in the Bibliography and subsequently used in the text a more or less accepted modern form.

I am glad to have this opportunity of thanking Miss Elizabeth O'Kelly MBE, Mrs Clare Sunderland and Miss Jane Bridgeman all of whom have helped with the more tedious tasks that a book of this kind involves. I am also greatly indebted to the photographic department of the Courtauld Institute. Miss Margaret Louttit has kindly allowed me to use some extremely valuable information she has discovered on the Netherlandish theatre.

STELLA MARY NEWTON
July 1972

CHAPTER 1

Introduction

With the *Passion* at Valenciennes in 1547 the theatre of the middle ages came
to an end. The theatre of the Renaissance had come into being long before
but such labels and dates are not only misleading but tiresome. Mediaeval
drama went on, as a matter of fact, even in Italy well into the seventeenth
century [1].

In using the term Renaissance theatre for the purpose of this study nothing
more precise is meant than dramatic entertainments which took place,
particularly in Italy, France and the Netherlands during the fifteenth and
sixteenth centuries. They were usually, though not always, performed by
men and boys. They included religious dramas, revivals of plays by

1. Rhetoricians' festival at Haarlem, 1606. *Entry of the Hazel-tree Chamber of Aedwaertswor:*
detail. The traditional Hell's Mouth marches between the Devil and Death; it is presented
as a blackened sack emitting smoke

Terence and Plautus, new plays based on classical themes, histories, pastorals,
mummeries, social satires and all the permutations of this kind of thing that
Polonius tried to enumerate, as well as buffooneries and little shows that
would have been beneath his notice, such as those put on by quack doctors
at country fairs.

The potency of the theatre has always been immense. Hence the alternating imposition and removal of censorship on what is performed in its name. Like the other arts, the theatre is rich in prophecy; under its aegis new ideas are perpetually presented to a public which finds them at first shocking, then gravely relevant or hilariously amusing and, finally, suitable to be incorporated into an acceptable commercial pattern.

The theatre has always behaved organically; dramatic forms have waxed and waned. The Church, once it had accepted the notion that religious drama could play an important part in its structure, fostered religious plays as a means of stimulating devotion and instructing the faithful but when, with the passing of time, religious dramas lost their early vitality and declined into a compound of extravagant spectacle and cynical mockery, both the Church and the governments of the day which supported it, combined to ban them. It was no accident that the final ban coincided, very often, with the Reformation. The prohibition of performances of sacred plays, however, merely freed the theatre for the development of other forms of entertainment which had already made their way on to the secular stage and, at the time that religious drama was falling into disfavour all over Europe, political satires, as dangerous to secular rulers as religious satire was to the Church, were themselves viewed with growing suspicion.

Whether the theatre struggles to evade censorship, is content to abide by its rules or is completely free from its restrictions, it speaks to a public which listens both with its conscious and its unconscious mind – a fact which the wise among the powerful have always understood. Carefully presented dramatic eulogies, especially when accompanied by music, dancing and pleasing spectacle inevitably raise the spirits. In the past when they were embedded in the 'joyous entry' of an unpopular prince, even though they might have been designed by men indifferent to his cause, they never failed to leave a surly populace a little less sceptical.

And nowhere can the current attitude to history be seen more clearly than in the theatre, where today, as in the past, not only new plays but standard classics and surviving literary curiosities are placed on the stage in front of audiences ignorant of the conditions that inspired them in the first place. Comparatively few can stand up to the test at all. Those that can receive very curious treatment which varies, naturally, according to prevailing taste; and this is not all, for when an author living in the past has written a history play then, when it is revived, we are faced with a double past – the author's and our own.

In some periods more or less scholarly attempts are made to reconstruct the simple, or if required, the double past in the presentation of these histori-cal dramas. At others, our own, for example, this is thought of as erecting a barrier between the author and the audience with the result that, today, such plays are either staged with no reference to the past at all or, alternatively, they are presented in settings and costumes which, reflecting a good deal of our own taste, make a sort of generalised reference either to the period intended by the author or to conventions which have come to represent in our minds the 'old days'. Settings and costumes of this kind are symbols; they depend not on scholarly recognition but on a visual language shared by the designer and the audience. It is a convention which was used in the theatre in the eighteenth century but not in the nineteenth, when scholarly reconstructions of places and clothing of the past were popular as were plays on historical themes which, speaking generally, the eighteenth century avoided.

Those who are not historians (and a good many who are), both despise and revere the past and it is not at all impossible to do both at the same time. The past, it is often thought, was brutish and ignorant and got us into our present mess: the past was wise, learned and upright – we are decadent: the past, though uninstructed, had an instinct for beauty and an apprehension of truth which we have lost: it was skilful, cunning, hypocritical and self-seeking – we are sincere.

These attitudes of mind do not, presumably, please us very much – hence our uneasiness at the concept called fashion; for fashion must imply that we too shall become the past – a disagreeable thought. We naturally prefer to believe that at last a stable point of view has been reached and one from which, apart from a few necessary modifications, we shall not be tempted to depart or, if we do shift, then only in the direction in which we are guided by common sense, untrammelled by the restlessness which is the basis of fashion. This belief is best nourished by maintaining the view that the past was either crudely ignorant or, if manifestly not, then directed only by a more or less accidental instinct towards wisdom. Among our more uncom-fortable moments are those in which, looking at an early photograph of ourselves or coming across a letter we once wrote, we discover that not only were we different then from what we are now, but different in the unattractive way that other people of that period were different. This we probably ascribe to some undesirable influence to which we were, at a weaker stage in our lives, submitted. Only if, in this intimate moment, we are subjected to the hilarity of a younger generation are we likely to defend that earlier period.

In this frame of mind we have been confronted through the ages with objects made in the past (including works of art and literature) and these we have preserved or destroyed (apart from those disposed of by God) in a more or less arbitrary way, but roughly in the ratio of our appreciation of the time at which they were made. Our opinion of the past is, therefore, based on survivals, since we soon cease to remember those things which have been destroyed. Thus surviving things, whether originally typical of their time or not, become its types from which we draw our conclusions.

The more or less random collections of man-made objects which have been allowed to survive from the past can, of course, be gathered together into groups according to their periods and each group will then be discovered to yield a recognisable perfume – its 'style'. Our ideas as to the nature of each style depend on our ability to read the evidence of the survivals. Those people who have interested themselves in the past and are able to recognise varieties in style disagree as to the exact characteristics of each, but the pressure of fashion sees to it that, on the whole, they disagree less with their contemporaries than with students of the same period living at times other than their own. Fashionable admiration at certain periods for particular earlier painters, Botticelli, Piero della Francesca, Caravaggio, for instance, is a good example of this. But, however inaccurate a picture of the past historians or art historians may have to content themselves with, their view is never as inaccurate as that of the average theatre-goer.

The theatre is normally concerned with communication (experiments in non-communicative entertainment are rare and though they may, from time to time, play a therapeutic part in the development of drama, they do not last). Decisions as to what aspect of nature to hold the mirror up to in putting on an old play for a new audience are, therefore, important. The choice depends not on the play but on the capacity of the audience to take it in.

Public taste in entertainment, like its taste in other forms of art has varied throughout history. There have been times when contemporary themes were not acceptable as serious drama. Without going back farther than to the time of Elizabeth I it is clear that, to Elizabethans, tragedies were to be concerned with people of the past while even comedies were usually removed to a different country, if not to a different period. Today, on the contrary, it is not easy to wring the heart with stories of people living far away or in other times; today, even plays written long ago are likely to stand a better chance if they are made to look up-to-date. In the theatre now, settings of historical plays, if they are meant to be urban are designed to look like three-dimensional non-figurative sculpture; if rural, abstract projections, often thrown on to mirrors, or mobile backgrounds, are devised. Either current dress, given a picturesque emphasis, is used for costumes or, where this produces too many anachronisms, the past is searched for fashions which look, superficially, rather like our own. These symbolise, but do not attempt to reconstruct, the past.

Despite today's unwillingness to attempt historically appropriate settings for plays written in the past, few people would question the modern stage-designer's ability to do so if he wanted to. But, it is generally thought, in the fifteenth, the sixteenth, or even in the eighteenth century, this would not have been possible, nor would it have appealed to designers to attempt such a thing if, indeed, designers existed at all. There are surviving paintings which certainly show, for example, David Garrick playing Macbeth in an eighteenth-century suit and there are fragments of documentation that seem to point to the fact that Shakespeare's plays were put on in the dress of his own day with a few added accessories to denote period or character. It is true that where the eighteenth century is concerned this theory seems to have applied to costumes rather than settings; there are works of art which show that early manifestations of the Gothic revival appeared as settings for drama and opera.[1] The Globe Theatre, on the other hand, is usually regarded as having been a very plain affair where anything at all ambitious in the way of settings would have been very difficult, if not impossible, to achieve.[2]

In the history of the Renaissance theatre, however, England is not representative. Although the great Elizabethan and early Jacobean dramas are unparalleled and English mystery plays have their own poetically pithy character, documentary records of methods of production in the fifteenth and sixteenth centuries are scanty and pictorial representations seem to be even rarer though not, perhaps, as rare as is usually supposed, as has lately been shown.[3] The scarcity of documentary records is not surprising; the atmosphere created by the dynastic Wars of the Roses was not conducive to upper-class cultural gossip. England lacked, moreover, the sort of conscientious diarist-chroniclers to be found in Italy and the Netherlands who busied themselves with recording the day-to-day doings at the princely court or the centre of state-government. There is no English equivalent to Charles le Téméraire's chamberlain, Olivier de la Marche, to the author of the *Diario Ferrarese* nor to Marin Sanudo of Venice. In spite of the likelihood that a good deal of sculpture and stained glass to be found in English mediaeval churches was based on incidents from theatrical productions which the men who executed them had actually seen, these works of art are not very plentiful. The huge areas of wall-painting eliminated by Cromwell's followers, which might have clarified the details of such performances, mean that compared with most European countries England is poor in pictorial art. Italy and the Netherlands, on the other hand, are rich.

The importance of pictorial evidence of theatrical costume can hardly be overestimated. Costumes themselves are fragile – they soon disintegrate and clothes that show signs of wear look too squalid at close quarters to be collected as antiques. Pepys in a visit back-stage was disgusted by what he saw in the way of shabby pieces of costume used in history plays.[4] Surviving clothes in our museums are those which were saved in the past because their condition was too good for them to have been thrown away; they are not the most representative nor the most interesting of their period.

But it is not only theatre costumes themselves which are perishable and have perished. The original designs from which they were made have almost all gone too. This is natural and it is probable that the majority of such designs as have survived – by Primaticcio, Vasari, Inigo Jones for instance – are those which for one reason or another were never used. Tailors and dressmakers are no respecters of designers; only the recent impressive prices in art sales rooms have persuaded modern workrooms to preserve designs which might fetch a good figure from the tea-stains, the marginal calculations and other scribbles, the pins attaching bits of textile to their various parts and from the cutting off of the head to pass to the milliner or the wigmaker and an arm to the sleeve-hand. Although mediaeval craftsmen were deprived of the pleasure of tea it is unlikely that they differed in other ways from their modern counterparts.

So information must be looked for elsewhere if the costume of the Renaissance theatre is to be understood and there are, indeed, apart from reports of spectators which, presumably most of the diarists were, a considerable number of inventories that list stage-properties, costumes and parts of costume preserved among various documents, the most important English ones being the *Great Wardrobe Accounts.*

Comparison between English and Italian inventories of the fifteenth century shows that both countries shared the same traditions where the costumes for at least some characters were concerned. Imitation-nude suits tailored from parchment for Adam and Eve, for instance, were used both in the north and in the south of Europe and devils' masks, which were made to last were, it appears from inventories preserved in several European countries, invariably kept from one production to the next. Indeed actors are reported to have become so fond of these fiends' masks that they had to be prohibited from wearing them off-stage except on certain days of the year.[5] Some of them have survived; they look exactly as one would expect and as they appear in many works of art. More fragile items mentioned in the inventories, however, have all disappeared and, from their descriptions, are impossible to visualise. What did a 'long garment of cloth of golde and tynsell for the Prophet' look like? And when, 'Itm xii garments of olde blew satten with scriptures of Romane letters' appears together with, 'Itm a long garment of crymson satten with ciphers embroudered' how are we to envisage it – where did the 'Romane letters' and the 'ciphers' appear? Pictorial evidence is essential before the costume of the Renaissance can be studied.

Since surviving designs for stage costumes are few and rather late in period – Leonardo's are, presumably, the earliest to be generally accepted – pictorial evidence of earlier as well as more varied forms of stage dress is not likely to be found in the form of original designs, it must be looked for elsewhere. In, that is to say, works of art in which it may be suspected that the artist, as a spectator in the theatre, had recorded theatrical costumes and used them in some of his paintings. In view of the interest in entertainments shown by diarists and chroniclers of the fifteenth century, it would be reasonable to suppose that artists, too, made records of spectacles by which they had been impressed and this did, in fact, happen in the case of the famous

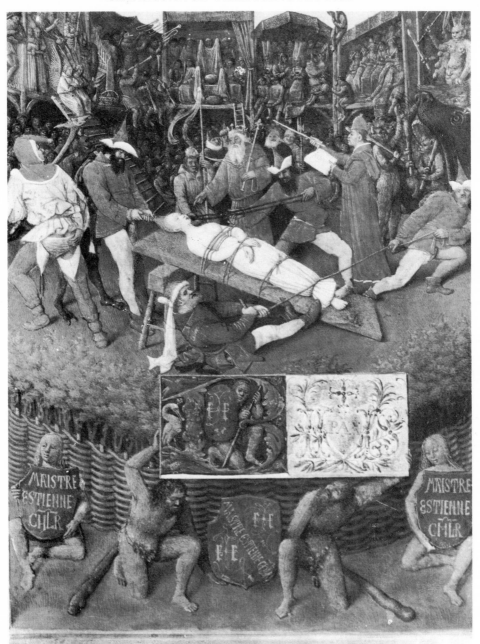

2. Jean Fouquet. *Heures de Etienne Chevalier: Martyrdom of St Apollonia.* The martyrdom is shown here as being performed as part of a religious play

miniature painting of the *Martyrdom of St Apollonia* by the French artist Jean Fouquet [2]. Here the scene is so manifestly a morality play in progress that this painting has become one of the most important sources of pictorial information on the mediaeval theatre, not only for the arrangement and behaviour of the actors but also for the disposition of the audience. It is, in fact, together with the equally famous 'frontispiece' to the *Térence des ducs*, widely reproduced because there is no doubt as to its authenticity as a contemporary eye-witness report.

These two unquestionable records of theatrical performances (and there are others much less known) are illustrations of a familiar episode in the everyday life of their respective periods. In the fifteenth century, public as well as semi-private entertainments occurred surprisingly often throughout the year and it would have been odd if no painter had thought of using one either as Fouquet did, both as a setting for his main subject and to amuse his patron or, as the unknown illustrator of the *Térence* did, as a frontispiece to a book of plays.

In the Fouquet miniature the costume is less spectacular than in the *Térence* painting (though as a record of the setting of a play it is extremely important). St Apollonia, in a shroud, is so tightly trussed up that its character can only be guessed at, the 'marshal', holding a white wand of office and a prompt-book, who directs the play wears the dress of an official councillor at a princely court, the Fool wears a conventional version of the traditional dress, the torturers, as minor characters wear the livery of their class in Fouquet's day with Jewish head-gear added and the Almighty and His attendant angels are so distant in the scene that their costumes are difficult to interpret, though the angels appear to wear, as was usual, albs. More interesting than his dress is the behaviour of the Fool which goes some way to explaining the Church's direction to the younger clergy not to attend miracle or morality plays performed outside the church building.

If the costumes in the Fouquet miniature are interesting but not particularly surprising, those in the *Térence des ducs* are astonishing and unlike anything to be found elsewhere at this period. Together with the illustrations to the plays themselves in the same manuscript they will be discussed in Chapter 3.

Books of Hours, expensively illustrated, of the kind to which the Fouquet manuscript belongs, though they were designed as aids to private meditation on the lives of the saints, almost always included pictorial comments on contemporary life meant to entertain as well as elevate the spirit. In Fouquet's manuscript, the *Heures de Etienne Chevalier*, worldly comment is emphasised. Devotion to St Stephen, the first martyr, is accompanied by an illustration in which the act of stoning him to death is directed by an enthroned official, just as the marshal directs the morality play of the death of St Apollonia. Indeed the two characters are very much alike and one might conclude that some minor official of Etienne's household was being mocked in a private joke between Fouquet and his master. Can the organiser of St Stephen's death really be meant to be Saul? In the St Stephen scene, however, although it, too, was probably derived from the performance of a play, Fouquet has appropriately opened up the landscape background to show the 'real' place where Stephen was stoned outside the city. But what could have inspired him to include that solid throne and the smart official who occupies it?

There is nothing in the least unusual, of course, in this mixture of the normal with the abnormal – painting during the middle ages and the Renaissance could not have got on without it – but the sudden representation of a theatrical scene, itself a representation of something else, presents us with another dimension and one which we might not have suspected as existing in works of art.

It is not the Fool that established Fouquet's *Martyrdom of St Apollonia* as a theatrical performance, Etienne Chevalier probably had a Fool, if not several, in his own household; nor is it the spectators, they could have assembled for any execution of a captive notorious enough to rate the erection of temporary grand-stands. What makes it absolutely certain that a play is being performed is the little group, not hovering in the sky but tucked into one of the boxes among the audience of God the Father and his angels, Hell's mouth – not very imaginatively constructed as a set-piece – on the right and the direction of the whole thing by the 'marshal' who holds the prompt-copy. The performance is being directed, in fact, not by the captain of the guard which an execution would have required, but by the manifestly civilian producer of a play wearing the equivalent of the respectable city suiting of a civil servant.

Since in Fouquet's St Stephen miniature, St Paul, in the disagreeable period of his life before his conversion, is also presented not as a captain of his troop but in this civilian aspect, the extra dimension, the confusion of the normal and the abnormal, appears once more, though more obscurely than in the scene of St Apollonia's martyrdom. At this point the whole question of the artist's source material comes to the surface.

There are, here and there, devout and simple people who believe that visions of the inhabitants of the heavenly regions for which they yearn are denied to them but granted (perhaps unfairly) to artists; but this is not the generally accepted view of the painter's privileges. The painter's problem of the identification of the characters in his pictures does certainly exist. How, for example, did a painter of 1431 differentiate between – say – the burning of a common witch such as Joan from Arc and the putting to death of the holy martyr St Apollonia? It is a problem which confronted the theatre, too, and confronts it today. At the present moment, when marks of nationality, rank, class and occupation are being discarded as rapidly as badges of temporary allegiances are being assumed, the difficulty is particularly awkward – off-duty the shoe-mender and the prime minister are indistinguishable. In the theatre, however, the author can see to it that the characters identify themselves in the words of the text, a device almost denied to the painter.

Since lucid or fairly lucid communication between painter and spectator or author and audience depends on the ability to read the painters' or the authors' symbols the intervention of fashion has to be reckoned with. If we feel a distaste for photographs of ourselves taken at earlier periods in our lives we also dislike the appearance of other works of art (and probably of literature and perhaps of music) made at the same periods. And this must always have happened. In due course Fouquet's torturers in their contemporary dress would have looked ridiculous while his Fool, his official and his Jewish hats would have remained valid for rather longer though they, too, must in time have ceased to perform as intelligible symbols. And now, with the lapse of centuries, the whole thing, no longer understood by the uninitiated, has passed into the realm of the art historian and the student of dress having, in the process, lost its power to inspire devotion to St Apollonia.

The terms in which painters (and stage designers) express themselves must lose their potency as fashion changes. What is exciting as a new creation becomes first flavourless then ridiculous and finally (relative to its aesthetic worth) permanently acceptable either as a quaint curiosity or as something more important. The kind of expression – the style – that one generation likes the next does not. If today we prefer the settings of our plays, like our paintings, either to reflect the life of our own moment or to be exercises in pure aesthetics, whereas the nineteenth century found most of its excitement in looking back into the past, it is reasonable to suppose that such fluctuations in taste have occurred throughout history. Because the eighteenth-century theatre presented its plays somewhat as we do now, dressed either in the fashion of the moment or else in formalised symbols of the 'old days', it does not necessarily follow that the fifteenth or the sixteenth centuries did likewise.

The view that artists of the past, though often geniuses, were ignorant, is an expression of the noble savage belief. Civilisation, according to this view, is to be mistrusted because it is regarded as cherishing too great a respect for the historic past (and therefore for changing fashion). In its acceptance of inspiration but rejection of inspiration's variable manifestations, this puritanical faith is a parallel to Unitarianism which, like the noble savage concept, was popular in the eighteenth century. Both concepts have existed throughout history under various labels; they have always been regarded by Western orthodoxy at least as heretical.

The veneration of the noble savage was very apparent in the fifteenth century when the jolly shepherd had become a hero of French satirical drama, especially in its more popular aspects. He opposed *Gens*[6] who represented what we call today the bourgeois values. A contemporary of the jolly shepherd in France was *Roger Bontemps*,[7] a mythical stage character who was frequently referred to but never appeared since he was always described as having died in the fourteenth century never to return. *Roger Bontemps*, like the shepherd, was a peasant, the antithesis of the wily lawyer or the bloated merchant. But if *Bontemps* was permanently dead and the clod-hopping shepherd played the hero on the popular stage of fifteenth-century France, in Italy a very different shepherd was beginning to appear in the great halls of the princely courts, a graceful decorative creature who came to assure the audience that the golden past, far from being dead, was yielding up the treasures of its civilisation for the enjoyment of the sophisticated modern world.

It would be wrong, of course, to see fifteenth-century France as dominated by the philosophy of the popular stage. Until his death in 1416, Jean, Duc de Berry, younger brother of Charles V of France was, like the king himself, an avid and discriminating collector of antiques and it is no accident that the

Térence des ducs was eventually acquired by him. The illuminated manuscripts he commissioned or bought were of the highest quality, but so were his antique gems and his goldsmiths' work, some of it from the classical periods and some from the early middle ages. During Jean de Berry's lifetime two Eastern emperors, members of the Paleologus family and their trains, travelled northwards and paid successive visits to Paris at the end of the fourteenth and the beginning of the fifteenth century in the hope of raising money and troops for the defence of Constantinople. Their arrival created an interest in the appearance and behaviour of people from countries of the Near East which was almost immediately reflected in illustrations to manuscripts.[8] Characters wearing strange and exotic costumes, unlike those which had been represented earlier, began to appear in these paintings and, perhaps, in the theatre itself; Eastern robes and hats noticed and recorded by eye-witnesses of the visits of the two emperors became, in all probability, standard source material for orientals in plays and paintings for years to come.

In Italy, later in the fifteenth century, Mantegna collected antiques and included them in his works; a habit he probably got from his master Squarcione, who had started life as a tailor and embroiderer and who brought back from travels in Greece and Armenia not only objects of antique art but also drawings of the clothes of the inhabitants of both countries. Both Mantegna and a fellow pupil, Marco Zoppo,[9] probably made use of them. The fact that Mantegna is recorded as having painted (and therefore naturally designed) the housings for a horse used in a joust is only one of the pointers to the probability that he worked in the theatre too, the favourite entertainment of his patrons the Gonzagas. As for the sixteenth century's interest both in the past and in the manners and dress of foreigners, not only was it a century of great historians and art historians but of the publication of a wealth of books of engravings of the clothes both of the past and of people of other countries. It would have been strange if none of these had been used by painters and stage-designers as sources of information and, indeed, they were.

The theatre of the fifteenth and sixteenth centuries has attracted considerable scholarly attention. Surviving texts of plays and fragments of plays have been collected and published, methods of production have been discussed and experiments have been carried out in reconstructing theatres and stages. References to troops of actors have been investigated. Little research apart

31

from listing its appearance in contemporary inventories has, however, been published on theatre costume. This is natural: pictorial representations of costumes that can be identified with certainty as theatrical are not very easy to find and, in any case, since the general opinion has been that the dress of the theatre differed only in minor details from the dress of the current fashion it could not be thought of as easy to recognise and would therefore be hardly worth looking for.

It must also be agreed that although both in the nineteenth century and recently, excellent general histories of the dress of the past have been published, very few studies that have dealt in any detail with the dress of a single country in either the fifteenth or the sixteenth century have appeared at all, and those that have, have usually contented themselves with such vague phrases as 'early in the century' or 'during the third quarter of the century'. Since fashions in dress changed during the Renaissance almost as rapidly as they do today, generalisations of this kind are not useful. Without an understanding of the normal fashion, stage costume, the abnormal, cannot be perceived.

Once the successive fashions of the fifteenth and sixteenth centuries can be distinguished (and this, though comparatively easy where Italian dress is concerned, is very much more difficult in the dress of France, Germany and the Netherlands), it becomes apparent that artists made use of clothing in their paintings to convey very subtle effects, nuances which would have been appreciated by their patrons and by members of the public who were their contemporaries, although they inevitably became imperceptible as fashions changed and details, once familiar, were forgotten. It also becomes clear that in paintings of these periods from all the countries of Europe, but especially those in the north, foreign dress and the dress of earlier periods was not infrequently attempted, though from the point of view of accuracy not always with success. Far from despising ephemeral fashions, painters made use of them to strengthen the narrative, explain the situation and emphasise character.

It is certainly noticeable that following the visits of the two Paleologus emperors artists changed their ideas as to how people from the East should look. And, furthermore, in paintings of biblical scenes the number of orientals increased, for not only subsidiary characters but also those who played leading roles in the story began to be represented in Eastern dress.

Although this did not extend to the main protagonists in the New Testament narratives, such as the Apostles, it soon became comparatively unusual for the three Magi, for example, to look like Gothic princes – the normal practice in works of art of the thirteenth and fourteenth centuries. At the same time as this new attitude to Eastern dress began to appear in paintings of the north of Europe, in Italian painting another kind of dress which was also manifestly no part of the current Western fashion, made its appearance. This, although perhaps slightly reminiscent of the East, cannot be explained by any political or social event but only by the fact that it was inspired by theatre costume.

There is nothing, of course, surprising about this. Even if he was not involved as designer (which on occasion he no doubt was) the Renaissance painter, like his contemporaries, was probably either a member of the audience at local dramatic spectacles or a part of the crowd that took part in them. He may have welcomed the visual experiences they provided which may have stimulated his imagination, but even if he did not welcome them they would be experiences difficult to escape in a period when almost all public communication, including entertainments, happened in the street. When, for instance, Florence dispatched couriers to Bologna to announce the ratification of peace by Alfonso of Aragon, the Bolognese senate thought the occasion important enough to justify sending out the city trumpeters to call attention to the news by marching three times round the main square blowing their trumpets.[10] Official games, races and mock-battles were arranged, as a contemporary diarist put it, 'to give pleasure to the people'.[11] Such pleasures could be mounted as a part of the celebrations at – say – an important wedding or, alternatively, they could be arranged to distract the attention of the public from unpalatable political manœuvres, but whatever the aim, the fun took place in the streets and the squares of the city. The municipal trumpeters of Florence were required to perform not only on every official and outstanding social occasion but also to give pleasure to the people on Saturday afternoons by playing in the *ringhiera* of the Palazzo Vecchio.[12] In the Netherlands poems were recited at public shooting-contests; in France, as elsewhere in Europe, quacks and actors performed on temporary platforms erected in the streets; it was not, in fact, until the sixteenth century that the theatre began to retreat systematically indoors. In the fifteenth century, although performances could on occasion be arranged

33

in the church or in the great hall of the palace, they were normally to be found as part of the city's outdoor life.

Nowadays when the news is spread not by the sound of trumpets but by newspapers, radio and television, all designed for consumption in the home, the life of the streets is disappearing fast but traces of these outdoor spectacles still appear from time to time. In England at the Opening of Parliament and on the election of the Lord Mayor of London: in Catholic countries religious processions still wind round the streets: Epiphany brings everyone in Rome out to buy fireworks in the Piazza Navona and to listen to Apuleian shepherds playing bag-pipes at every street corner: on Christmas Eve Swedes visit their cemeteries to place a lighted candle or a single flowering tulip on the grave of each friend or relative. As late as the beginning of the twentieth century bears still danced in the gutters of Herne Hill and much more recently Italians, turning the handles of their piano-organs, included as a part of their entertainment a monkey dressed in a cap and jacket. It would be strange if none of this kind of thing, of which only a shadow remains today, had found its way into the paintings of the Renaissance.

The idea that such chance appearances of the costume of the Renaissance theatre could provide material for study might be difficult to justify if no other evidence had survived to support it; fortunately, however, once the kind of dress which could only be theatrical has been recognised in works of art, documentary references to stage costume, which have hitherto been almost impossible to interpret, become much more comprehensible. And in works of art themselves dress which may be suspected of having been copied from theatrical costume begins to be seen to have a logic of its own instead of seeming a pure fantasy of the painters' invention – if the phrase 'pure fantasy' has any meaning which, where subject-matter in a work of art is concerned, is doubtful.

To discover evidence of theatrical costume in works of art without first understanding the kind of theatre which might have influenced the artist, and the type of organisation which lay behind it, is naturally impossible. In the European theatre the English mystery plays are famous but other texts from other countries have also survived – different in character but no less interesting – and it is not surprising that each country produced and developed its own type of drama as well as its own means of presenting it. Springing, everywhere in Europe, from dramatisations of the liturgy in the

34

early mediaeval Christian Church on the one hand, and on the other from high-spirited festivals of a less orthodox but perhaps even older origin – on which both the Church and society turned, on the whole, a tolerant eye – drama began, in the early years of the fourteenth century, to escape from the confines of the church building and to develop differently in different parts of Europe. By the beginning of the fifteenth century national characteristics in theatrical entertainment had become clearly defined. They will be discussed in the next chapter.

CHAPTER 2

The Structure of the Renaissance Theatre

While it would be true to say that in some parts of Europe feudalism survived until the French Revolution and that even today it can be found in a shrunken form here and there, by the end of the fourteenth century it was apparent that in progressive European centres feudal clusters were rapidly falling apart.

Although this was no doubt a sign of progress it needs very little imagination to see that it must have made life uncomfortable. With the disappearance of feudal paternalism even where the father had been a bad one, the wind must have felt cold. Despotism, even at its most unpleasant involves communication: those who freed themselves from it may have found that they were, though independent, in frightening isolation.

It is not surprising, therefore, that as feudalism declined, voluntary associations increased. With a number of varied aims, clusters reformed, the reasons for their existence being almost certainly less important than the fraternalisation they engendered. Some, religious orders for instance, had already been there for a long time and it is possible that the shadowy traces of other kinds of organisation that seem to be discernible mean that they, too, were already in existence, but in the thirteenth century religious orders themselves began to multiply and in the fourteenth an outbreak of lay confraternities occurred all over Europe. The most picturesque were the Orders of Chivalry which, though the dates of their foundation are often obscure, began to appear round about the middle of the fourteenth century in centres which seem today to have been surprisingly far apart.[1] These orders of knighthood, sometimes seen as an expression of feudalism, can more accurately be regarded as voluntary associations even though the founder's invitation to join might have seemed more like a command, and failure to accept might have led to disagreeable relationships.[2]

Since human beings find it impossible to invent anything completely new, orders of knighthood and other bands of people of common interests were, in character, not unlike the more recently formed of the religious foundations – the preaching friars. Although their vows were less strict (knights were free to marry) they undertook to devote themselves and their lives to their patron (not Christ but the prince), to make themselves available to go wherever they were sent and to follow a fairly detailed religious discipline. If this last undertaking was sometimes forgotten neither did monks and nuns always observe their vows.

And orders of knighthood, though more glamorous, were typical of the many other kinds of lay confraternity that increased in numbers as feudalism declined. Most confraternities that were not strictly religious served a 'king', a 'prince' or an 'abbot' who was given mock-honours on at least some days of the year. The various brotherhoods existed to perform special and limited functions and differed slightly from each other in the details of their organisation but there were certainly a great many of them. At the beginning of the sixteenth century in Florence, for instance, the son of a boiler-maker – having been sent to school to learn his abacus and to read and write and who was therefore able to keep his father's accounts – joined, during early manhood, no less than eight confraternities of a devotional nature. He finally founded one himself which, though it was limited to thirteen members, was organised under a *signiore*, a counsellor, a chamberlain and an official called a *sopportante*.[3] Fraternities of this kind existed – rather like the 'Friends' of modern institutions in need of support – to support the Church. They played an important part at various festivals, especially those of the patron saint of the confraternity, and walked in outdoor processions as required. In these they were allotted a position of honour according to their own importance and that of the procession in which they took part. The boiler-maker's son and one of the confraternities to which he belonged got up a subscription for a painted and inlaid decorative piece to embellish an altar in the church to which they were attached, but sometimes more ambitious works were commissioned, especially painted banners which led groups of the brethren in processions. Occasionally these banners were painted by distinguished artists or by painters who later became famous and sometimes they included portrait-groups of the members of the brotherhood, usually rather small in scale and crowded together kneeling at the feet of their patron saint.[4]

While communities of the kind to which the boiler-maker's son belonged did not, in all probability, include the presentation of plays among their activities, they probably took part on occasion in processions in which dramatic interludes were played. They could be called on to form a handy crowd of supers in approved religious entertainments, they added pomp to the grand trains of clerics accompanying a visiting cardinal or other prince of the Church and, when the Church and the State were closely interwoven, they could also be called on to increase the grandeur of a secular event. In Venice today it is not unusual to see the plimsoled feet of one's station-porter beneath a long gown in the procession of Corpus Christi.

Between the orders of knighthood committed by their statutes to hold regular chapters in which religious observance played an important part, and modest confraternities attached to local churches, the long gap was filled by a multiplicity of fraternal organisations of varying grandeur formed for various purposes. Although the boiler-maker's son's own confraternity – *l'Aquilino* – does not appear to have been attached to any established foundation it may well have been, for most of them were: sometimes, as in Florence, to the complex of a famous family or to a quarter of the city; sometimes, as in France, to a profession. In every country in the fifteenth century international chains of hospitals were run by lay-confraternities who supported, and worked together with, orders of monks and nuns and were responsible for many of the charitable activities of the hospitals, including the raising of money to maintain them.[5] In England, as in Florence, members of trades banded together – the English dramatic mysteries were performed by trade guilds.

The character of the organisations which included the presentation of plays among their activities influenced, of course, the sort of entertainment they offered and this character varied not only from one social group to another but also from country to country and often from town to town; and the taste of the community in which each flourished must also have played its part. So long as drama remained encased in the uniform liturgy of the European Church differences both in texts and in manner of presentation must have been comparatively unimportant. But once the theatre had spilt out into the life of the city or the village and had become the property of the laity, however religious its theme, drama was bound to develop local features and to become gradually quite different from its counterpart in other places: to develop as local schools of painting do, which while they are not totally uninfluenced by other artistic centres are, nevertheless, quite recognisably local in style. In the more fragmented European States influences may have come from outside the modern frontiers, as was also the case with painting, sculpture and architecture and, no doubt, minor eccentricities appeared in isolated places but, on the whole, there seem to have been fairly consistent patterns in France, Italy and the Netherlands about which it is reasonable to generalise.

Since generalisations can be based only on what has survived, it is wise to look first at those countries from which enough has survived for a satisfying, if not a satisfactory, picture to be extracted. In Italy, for example, though

41

works of pictorial and plastic art have survived in large numbers, texts of fifteenth-century plays, though many have been collected, are fewer than in France where an immense quantity of plays and fragments of plays have survived, together, in many cases, with some remarks which throw light on the people who performed them. Although, however, it appears that the French developed a popular secular drama earlier than the rest of Europe, it would be unsafe to assume that this was necessarily the case. Whether they were pioneers in the field of secular drama or not, the fact that French secular texts dating from the thirteenth century are known is important.[6]

The French are, not unnaturally, proud of their early pastorals by Adam de la Halle. His *Le Jeu de Robin et de Marion*, which is a true pastoral with songs, dances and musical accompaniment as well as a rural setting has, as its hero, Robin, a shepherd, and as heroine Marion, a shepherdess, who is carried off by a wandering knight. From references in the text it seems to have been written in about 1262 and in Arras but, since its author died in Naples in 1288 having followed Charles of Anjou, it may have been composed and was very likely played at the Angevin court there. Since it is recorded as having been produced in Angers in 1392, more than a hundred years after it was written, it certainly became a 'classic' and in the intervening time it seems unlikely that it had not become known in at least those parts of Italy which had ties with the Angevin court at Naples.[7]

Le Jeu de Robin et de Marion involving as it did two social classes — shepherds and a knight — means that characterisation was probably emphasised by appropriate costumes, though whether at this early date stage-shepherds were already dressed in the glamorous Arcadian clothes they certainly wore in the sixteenth century cannot be guessed at. When, however, it was produced in Angers in 1392, the actors who took part were described in a letter as *déguisés*[8] so that whatever they wore must have been recognised as theatrical.

Although 'Robin and Marion' can reasonably be described as a pastoral there is no point in trying to classify under precise headings the immense number of French dramas whose texts have survived or which are recorded as having existed.[9] Broadly speaking they can be divided into those which were purely religious, plays on the Passion, for instance, or 'miracle' plays usually based on the life of a saint as it was told in the Golden Legend: moralities which emphasised Christian ethics and which could have a theme that was

42

either overtly religious or, like our own *Everyman*, allegorical: fables which told a simple story without necessarily underlining its moral aspect: satires directed at, as a rule, any social or professional group which could be mocked at without involving the author or the players in too great a risk: finally, and these could be an ingredient in almost any of the above types of drama, there were the buffooneries or *sotties* which in their purest form were plays in which the whole of society was parodied and in which every character appeared literally as a Fool, in a hood with ears. Some of the *farces* are difficult to distinguish from *sotties* but the word 'farce', of ancient derivation, cannot be narrowed to include only one type of play. In the fifteenth and the early sixteenth centuries a farce is difficult to identify, it seems often merely to mean a comedy.[10]

In common with every other European country, France enriched its religious processions, its 'joyous entries' and its municipal and private festivities, with dramatic productions of various kinds, and although these cannot always be thought of as being strictly drama they were certainly theatrical and often dramatic.

The degree of professionalism in the mediaeval theatre and the theatre of the Renaissance has often been discussed. A professional theatre in the modern sense may not have existed in the fifteenth century, but although not necessarily inscribed as actors, it seems fairly certain that a good many people supported themselves entirely by acting or were kept by princes exclusively for the purpose of doing so. And even outside the princely courts those who acted seem to have appeared regularly with the same company or to have been lent by their 'own' company to another for special occasions. Acting companies existed as permanent organisations – as confraternities – and even if the actors performed their parts because they enjoyed doing so they were certainly expected to turn up regularly for rehearsals and to play when required whether they felt like it or not.[11] It would be reasonable to compare them to the tennis-players and cricketers of today who, whether or not they can actually be called professionals, can certainly become stars. The rather equivocal position of the modern sportsman reflects a recent change in the attitude of the public towards them and in the fifteenth and early sixteenth centuries the same sense of confusion seems to have existed towards the status of the actor. The final adoption of the idea of the professional theatre was marked not by the formation of a permanent theatrical company

43

– that had already existed for a long time – but by the granting of a permanent building in which the company could perform.

As in Italy and in England entertainments in France were regularly performed by students of law. In England the Inns of Court were compact enough to be thought of as confraternities. In France, in their theatrical aspect, legal clerks went under the name of *Basochiens* in whatever town they were to be found. *La Basoche* (the term seems to relate to the word basilica[12]) was by itself responsible for regular performances of plays, probably usually done indoors, but its members sometimes combined with those of other companies when an especially ambitious production was contemplated.

It is not surprising that the closed legal world should have produced for its amusement a prosperous and more or less permanent organisation to stage entertainments not only for its own members but for the general public too; French lay-confraternities, however, by no means stopped there. By the middle of the fifteenth century the concept of a free bourgeois society was sufficiently accepted for groups of people to band together with no closer tie than that of citizen. The *Connards* of Rouen,[13] the *Abbaye des Fous* of Auxerre, were among the numerous corporations, often several to a single town, that could be found all over France. In some of these the idea of a cultural academy was already beginning to appear; others were concerned purely with amusement or with political satire; some were a mixture of all three but all of them depended on a versifier if not on a poet for their material. In this connection the word *puy* – a platform – appears and often formed part of the official title of the company.[14] Meeting in or around the *puy*, usually in the open air, the players acted their shows and held their competitions before their elected 'Prince' to whom the *envoi* of their verses was personally addressed.[15]

Like the *Chambers of Rhetoric* of the Low Countries the various organisations with their *puys* existed on as many levels as society itself. The fifteenth century's freedom to present public entertainments that varied greatly both in quality and in kind can be judged from the fact that among the expenses of the *Confrèrie du Puy de Notre Dame* – which reformed itself in 1423 – salaries for actors, a poet and a preacher were included,[16] for sermons were often delivered from a *puy* by priests, and mock-sermons were preached not less frequently from the same platform by actors whose respect for the clergy was manifestly extremely limited. To ridicule the clergy was, however, very

44

different from mocking the Church itself, a practice that the fifteenth century indulged in comparatively seldom.[17]

Companies of the kind associated with a *puy* were usually too small to undertake large-scale productions elaborately staged, although their members were sometimes called upon to collaborate with larger groups who could. These included the rich trade guilds as well as one or two big companies of which the *Confrèrie de la Passion* of Paris was the most important and by far the most famous. The *Confrèrie de la Passion*, in a simple form, existed already in the fourteenth century when it played inside the Church, and in 1402 it was given letters patent by Charles VI which armed it with all the privileges of a corporation or guild. It was attached in the first place to the church of the Trinity and performed in the great open hall of the hospital belonging to the church. In 1518 Francis I, who was not pleased with the liberty allowed to the theatre in all its various forms by his predecessor Louis XII did, nevertheless, confirm the charter of the *Confrèrie de la Passion* and although in 1539 it had to quit the Hospital of the Trinity which the Church, somewhat chastened by the Reformation, felt should be returned to its proper charitable function, the *Confrèrie* was, by a happy combination of events, able to establish itself in the Hôtel de Flandres.[18]

From time to time large confraternities, the trade guilds and the *Basochiens* put on productions on a grand scale. The *Cordonniers* of Paris, for instance, commissioned the famous actor-producer-author Pierre Gringore to write a *Life of St Louis* for them which was subsequently often performed also by other companies at the beginning of the sixteenth century.[19] Below these important organisations came others, small but similarly well-founded and more or less permanent, which played usually in the open air and below these again there existed great numbers of small companies, generally referred to as *sociétés joyeuses* or *Enfants* of various kinds. No clear separation between these categories can be seen from this distance of time but in the eyes of the authorities of their own day they were probably very different from each other.

To us, today, the most curious aspect of the French theatre is the importance of the Fool. This character, who could be multiplied until the cast of the play could consist entirely of Fools, was descended on the one hand from the *stultus* of the mediaeval theatre which held its annual Feast of Fools, and on the other from the privileged private Fool of the princely or noble

45

household. In the fifteenth-century French theatre the Fool's province could be extended until, while he could in some contexts correspond to the low-comedian of today, he could both intervene in the actual texture of religious plays – as can be seen from the Fouquet miniature – and also play an even more important part in the comic interludes which were performed between the main episodes of religious dramas. The Fool could appear, wearing his motley and hood with asses' ears, by himself on a *puy* or, pushing his function even further, as the only sane character in a social satire. When all the characters of a play were represented by Fools they assumed over-garments appropriate to the members of society against whom their ridicule was directed but wherever they appeared they always wore the Fool's hood.[20]

Once he had been recognised as the wise clown the Fool's importance naturally increased, with the result that all over France certain confraternities incorporated the word *Fou, Folle* or *Sot* in their title and gave their leaders names such as *Prince des Sots* or *Abbé des Fous.* The most famous and the most fantastic company-leader was *La Mère Folle* of Dijon [3] who was, naturally, a man.[21] Confraternities of Fools came into the category of *société joyeuse* and played as a rule in the open air on a *puy.* The isolated Fool who appeared in

3. Reverse of the banner of the *Infanterie* of Dijon which was already in being in 1454, under Philip the Good

religious drama and, later, in plays with classical themes, was simply a member of a play-producing company chosen, no doubt, as being suitable for the part. However enigmatic the nature of the Fool he was certainly popular and his subtle role must have been understood by the contemporary audience.

In addition, therefore, to religious dramas, a well-established secular theatre already flourished in France in the fifteenth century. More than sixty texts of plays with a purely religious theme have survived and a larger number still of *moralités satiriques* as well as certain scripts of *pièces d'occasion* of a religious nature, written to celebrate a victory, a peace treaty or the entry of some potentate into the city. Although the farce is difficult to define it seems to be agreed that the most famous farce – *Pathelin*[22] – is true to type, and of plays that have been called farces at least a hundred and fifty dating from the fifteenth and sixteenth centuries have been published in France. In addition to these a great many *fabliaux* and *sotties*, about twenty monologues and as many *sermons joyeaux* have been collected so that, since an enormous number of texts must have been lost, the importance of the French theatre of the Renaissance can be seen to have been very considerable. There is a good deal of evidence from records kept by various companies that texts were not confined to the company that commissioned them but could be borrowed by others and some certainly continued to be played over a number of years.

The democratic side of the French theatre appeared in its history. In 1321 minstrels – *menestrels* – were permitted by the Prévôt of Paris to form their own corporation with approved statutes. Like other corporations they had their own church, St Julien le Menetrier, founded by two of their members, their own hospital for providing accommodation for foreign minstrels as well as for caring for the sick and, naturally, a system of apprenticeship and matriculation. Not only organisations, however, but the plays of political significance of the time designed to entertain and perhaps to comfort the ordinary citizen can also be seen as having a democratic significance. Most of these plays complained of the misfortunes of the times and, in fact, a character named *Temps* was often a member of the cast which could include also Merchant, Workman and Shepherd, the shepherd being cast as the happy man. Frequent references to the death or disappearance of *Roger Bontemps* mean that he was the antithesis of *Temps* – the present time. The *Sotties de Genève*, an entertainment written when Geneva was under the military occupation of the Duke of Savoy, had as its heroine *Mère Folie* who lamented that she was separated from her husband *Bon Temps*, at which point a messenger arrived with the news that *Bon Temps* would come back. 'Where, in that case, are the Fools' hoods?' was the cry, 'Lost or cut up.' 'In that case let us make new ones from the chemise of *Mère Folie*.' *Bon Temps* did not, of course, return and the company consoled themselves by going for a drink.[23] It is in plays of this kind that the equivocal character of the Fool can be seen most clearly.[24]

Equally common in the French fifteenth-century theatre were short plays of trickery, of quarrels between husbands and wives, of illicit love, of wicked misers, all obviously part of a tradition which reached its apotheosis with the curtain-raisers of Labiche in the Second Empire when the manners of the newly-rich were guyed in plots that combined a little pretty sentiment with a good deal of social satire. The pretty love-story was absent from the farces of the French theatre of the fifteenth century just as an ingredient that was popular then – a mixture of languages and of dialects as a comedy theme – was no longer present in the nineteenth-century theatre but in most respects they were remarkably similar.

Although they continued to be played in the sixteenth century, moralities, farces, fables and monologues were really fifteenth-century forms which, by the end of the century, showed signs of changing their characters in a direction that was bound to lead, eventually, to a complete metamorphosis. *L'Homme Pécheur*, a morality play presented in Tours in 1494 and in Orléans in 1507 for instance, included in its cast of sixty-seven, Adolescent, World, Charity, Good Angel, Reason and Free Will (*Franc Arbitre*), the latter being described as dressed as *Roger Bontemps*, urging Adolescent to do as he pleases.[25] This masquerading as a character hitherto thought of as representing the innocent 'old days' has subtle implications, among them the decline of the myth of *Roger Bontemps* as a dream of a lost golden age in the person of a simple peasant, although, as we have noticed, *Bontemps*[26] was still powerful enough to be invoked in his true character in the *Sotties de Genève* in the early 1520s.

Miracle plays developed in a different direction, for in these an increased emphasis was placed on those incidents in the lives of the saints, of characters from the Old Testament or from New Testament parables which best lent themselves to colourful and luxurious presentation. Mary Magdalene's early life was elaborated to the extent of introducing fashionable hunting-parties with crowds of liveried retainers, musicians and al fresco meals.[27] The same treatment was given to the riotous period in the life of the Prodigal Son.[28] When this kind of thing began to happen the end of the miracle play was, of course, in sight. Productions of this nature called for complicated settings as well as for rich costumes, both of which began to be the main attraction of the show, which partly as a result of the increased importance of the setting of the play called for a special building to house it. In the fifteenth century, although it is clear that large companies such as the *Basochiens* and the *Confrèrie de la Passion* normally played in their own premises indoors, they not only borrowed actors from each other but, when a particularly grandiose production was envisaged, especially one designed as a celebration of an important social or political event, they often played in the open air. To mark the Peace of Arras in 1482, for instance, the Cardinal Charles de Bourbon arranged for an entertainment to be staged in the courtyard of his Hôtel de Bourbon in Paris, but unfortunately on this occasion heavy rain not only damaged the specially-built scenery but also seriously injured his precious tapestries which formed part of it.[29] This may have been a semi-private affair but contemporary documents show that a great deal of drama was performed in the open and, furthermore, that the public could buy seats for the more ambitious productions. Where the audience simply stood round a *puy* to watch a short comedy the takings were probably donations of small coins for there appears to be no record of them.

As might be expected, open-air performances were even more usual in the south of Europe than in the north. In Italy, for example, grand and pro-longed productions of religious plays of the kind usually associated with the interior of a cathedral, where traditional and popular mechanical effects could easily be arranged were, instead, often presented in great public squares and even in the ideal setting of the Colosseum itself. Since dramas of this kind almost invariably included a *paradise*, required to open at an appropriate moment to reveal the Almighty surrounded by angels or other heavenly groups, when they were performed out of doors the *paradise* was usually situated high up in a convenient tower. In Siena, for instance, the tower of the Palazzo Communale housed the *paradise*;[30] for productions in the Colosseum a high piece of masonry was chosen.[31] Carried on a wire the archangel Gabriel could descend dramatically for a scene of the Annunciation, or a local saint, in Siena of course St Bernardino, could be carried up to heaven.

As early as the thirteenth century the Italians, with native ingenuity, were contriving stage-machines of considerable complexity and it is not surprising therefore that by the time the court entertainments of the later sixteenth century were fully developed immensely intricate scenic effects were always a part of the show. Throughout the fifteenth century in most Italian cities grand religious spectacles were produced, though not necessarily at regular intervals, and the many surviving documents that describe them in detail almost invariably refer to the appearance of God the Father grouped with angels, the risen Christ or simply single angelic *putti* standing each on a cloud high above the heads of the audience. To judge from the Fouquet miniature mechanical devices of this kind were not used to the same extent in open-air productions in France.

The political turmoils of the middle of the thirteenth century in Italy provoked an extraordinary manifestation in Umbria inspired, apparently, by an aged hermit, Ranieri Fasani, whose disciples formed themselves in 1258 into a confraternity, the *Disciplinati di Gesù Cristo*. In 1260 their example was followed by the founding of the *Flagellanti* of Perugia and, indeed, by the involvement of the whole community in a general frenzy of penitence which included the releasing of prisoners from the gaols. Before long, much to the disapproval of the Church, the fever had spread through the whole of Italy with the result that a great many people (the majority of the male population it has been suggested) were moved to gather themselves together into fervent companies devoted to religious discipline, penitence or praise.[32] After their first emotional outburst these companies of *Disciplinati*, *Flagellanti* and *Laudesi*[33] gradually settled down as lay propagandists of the faith and under their patron saints, whose banners they carried, began before long to be entrusted with the production and performance of religious dramas. In Italy these developed in two distinct directions: the first the type of grand spectacular production already referred to and the second, ambitious peripatetic processions through the city often of a dramatic nature and often, because its theme was so well suited to this kind of presentation, devoted to a re-enactment of the coming of the Magi.

By the end of the fifteenth century in Italy, as in France, grand religious spectacles became disturbingly elaborate. Scenes which gave an excuse for splendour were greatly extended and so were those which gave scope to theatrical engineers. The 'mansion' (still on the mediaeval pattern) which represented the Synagogue was made to fall to pieces before the eyes of the audience to reveal a vision of the Nativity, and instead of being carried into the mansion representing Hell's Mouth the damned now disappeared through a trap and literally descended from the scene to a world beneath.[34] Interludes were sandwiched into the action of religious plays; some of them on the French pattern were comic, but in Italy others took the form of ballets which seem, from contemporary accounts, to have appeared earlier there than in the religious dramas of France. Sometimes these ballets were danced by the dramatis personae themselves. An Italian play about Abraham, for instance, ended with a *laude* danced by Sarah and all the characters in the cast except Abraham and 'those two angels' – the one who had spoken the prologue and the one who had appeared on the mountain. This *laude* was sung as well as danced and when it had finished the angel of the prologue dismissed the audience with an appropriate verse.[35] When the ballets were woven into the action of the play itself they were often contrived to conceal or to distract the attention of the audience from minor scene changes or to give time for changes of costume.

From the middle of the fifteenth century until the seventeenth century at least, Italians were clearly passionately fond of ballet. It played an important part in earlier secular entertainments and its presence in both the early and the sporadic later productions of religious dramas shows that in Italian eyes the drama could hardly exist without it. Since all religious plays until well into the sixteenth century seem to have been performed by boys – *giovanetti* – ballets which were an integral part of the action would have presented no problem. The boys were usually junior members of confraternities, such as the *Laudesi* and others of a similar kind that followed them – the *Compagnia di Sta Lucia del Gonfalone*,[36] which played in the Colosseum, for instance – and were under the equivalent of the modern producer, the *Festajolo*. Texts of some religious dramas included a verse to be spoken by a member of the cast as an apology for the youth and inexperience of the actors and for the fact that since they had to play everything, including old people and women, they were ill-equipped for their parts and were acting in the play simply because they loved doing so.[37]

But not all drama was religious and in Italy, outside the jurisdiction of religious organisations, companies of youths banded together, drawn by common interests and high spirits. Among these clubs the Companies of the Stocking – *della Calza* – of Venice are remembered today partly because they survived into the nineteenth century, partly because they are described or referred to by many famous Venetian diarists and historians, and partly because it seems possible to identify the sparkling youths in the paintings of the life of St Ursula by Carpaccio as members of the *Compagnie della Calza*.[38] But although better publicised, these Venetian companies were not necessarily the prototypes of organisations of the kind which existed all over Italy.[39] Nor were they the only ones to wear a decorative stocking as a badge, for this was a common practice in the fifteenth century not only among youthful confraternities but also in noble households where a distinctive stocking could be worn as a part of the household livery issued to the middle-aged as well as to the young.[40]

The concept of a closely-knit band of young men prepared to stand together against rival bands in war or in sport has always been a basic feature in society. What distinguished the companies of youths in fifteenth-century Italy was the responsibility they assumed (or were given in exchange for the right to exist at all) for providing public entertainments and for taking part as compact bodies in tournaments and other important spectacles organised as special celebrations. Looked back on from this distance in time they seem more dashing, more elegant than their French and Netherlandish counterparts with their *sotties*, but this may be due simply to the stylish records of their appearance by the Gozzolis, the Signorellis and the Carpaccios. Whether or not this is true, that the young Italians certainly saw themselves as elegant can be judged from the names they gave their confraternities and the clothes they wore as members of them.

During his very temporary rule in Florence the Duke of Athens is said to have had a hand, in 1340, in constituting companies of young men, based on the city's various quarters and mainly for its defence.[41] Although this was no innovation, for such companies had already existed for some time, it may have given them a new status and a firmer organisation. The general name under which they were referred to in Italy is *brigate* and more specifically *signori festeggianti* or, and this applied only to Florence, *potenze*. The nickname *potenze* is exactly what might have been expected and sums up, in a light-hearted way, the *giovanetti*'s opinion of themselves. Like the confraternities of the north of Europe, the *brigate* organised themselves under their own 'kings', 'dukes' and 'councillors'.[42]

Although it boasted of its republican liberty, highly civilised Florence had become from the beginning of the fifteenth century, a prosperous mercantile community already ripe to produce a second crop of aristocrats from amongst its richest citizens, whose sons formed the members of the *brigate festeggiante*. Like the *Compagnie della Calza* of Venice whose splendour was so excessive that sumptuary regulations allowed them to indulge their tastes in dress to the full only when some particularly important foreign visitor was expected,[43] the *potenze* of Florence were drawn from middle-class families rich enough to provide their young sons with the silks and embroideries they chose to wear as their uniforms.[44] Companies responsible for presenting dramatic entertainments in Siena, on the other hand, were far more democratic in their structure. Their members could include knights and shoe-menders, priests, carpenters and lawyers. Like the companies of the north of Europe they wrote their own plays and they developed a character so distinct and lively that they endeared themselves to two successive Popes and were regularly invited to play in Rome.[45]

The Sienese *Compagnia dei Rozzi* published its plays as early as it was feasible to do so and from the earliest specimens of these the flavour of the Italian secular theatre can be guessed at. By the beginning of the fifteenth century Siena was already experienced in presenting grand religious spectacles in the Campo – from which the present form of the *Palio* derived[46] – and similarly elaborate productions continued to be put on side by side with secular plays of a humbler sort. Although the annals of the Rozzi and other similar Sienese companies date only from the early sixteenth century it is clear that if not these then other organisations very like them had existed earlier and possibly under the same names. Unlike the aristocratic titles of the Florentine *potenze* – *della Spera*, *del Fiore*, *del Diamante*, for instance – the Sienese companies underlined their less exclusive character by calling themselves *Rozzi* (the rough ones) *Insipidi* (the silly ones) *Intronati* (the thunderstruck ones) and so on. The Rozzi had as their badge a cork tree which, they explained, was ugly but which as it died at the top sent up fresh shoots from the roots.[47]

The Rozzi whose leader was called *il signore Rozzo* or simply *il Rozzo* included among their officers a *scrittore* to keep the records and a *lettore* to read aloud scripts submitted. Each member both wrote and acted under a sou-briquet related to his trade. Their scripts were licensed for performance only after approval by the whole company.[48] Those that have been collected from the earliest period show that almost all were 'eclogues' – pastoral or rustic plays – quite different from the corresponding sort of thing to be found in France. Instead of the Fool the inevitable member of every cast was the *contadino* or *villano*, a peasant of the most earthy kind usually cunning and dishonest, often stupid, but uttering, occasionally as the Fool could, pro-found wisdom in gross terms. In typical eclogues love-sick shepherds or shepherdesses (nymphs) and occasionally among them gods and goddesses appeared together with coarse countrymen. The plays of the Rozzi at the beginning of the sixteenth century show that a smattering of classical learning was already popular but although, while they were in the presence of a god or goddess, shepherds and nymphs spoke with a certain respect the *villano* continued to speak his mind.

The early traces of erudition which appeared among the Rozzi following the great revival of interest in classical themes at the courts of Ferrara and Mantua were typical of the care-free type of drama in which they specialised. In a Rozzi play of 1520 Dante, Homer, Bembo, Boccaccio, Cicero are all mentioned and at one point a *villano* exclaims, 'Seque romore, come disse Cato . . .'.[49] Equally typical, however, was a less pretentious play with a fifteenth-century flavour written by a tailor in which twelve *villani* together with their Mayor plan to murder Love. Apollo and Diana were often made to enter dressed as *villani* and in *Moti di fortuna*, a Rozzi play of 1517, two *villani* appeared together with Fortune, Apollo, Cupid, the King of Persia, the Sultan of Egypt and a singer. Rozzi plays of the early sixteenth century depend so much on rustic humour that they are less pointedly satirical than their French counterparts.

Meanwhile, in the princely courts of Italy, Terence and Plautus became increasingly popular and the immense success of Poliziano's *Orfeo* led modern poets to compose plays on classical themes. From the middle of the fifteenth century onwards all over Italy in centres where there were any pretensions to culture, plays by Terence and Plautus in Latin or in transla-tion were produced. Dukes and marquesses wrote to each other begging the loan of scripts[50] and the ingenuity which had been (and was still) employed in the production of religious spectacles was now directed to representing

Parnassus and the Castalian spring. At first the difference between the two forms of production was not great: plays about Abraham required a mount and Orpheus had to pursue Euridice into Hell's Mouth.

The religious processions through the streets in Italian cities in which the *brigate* were also required to take part, included companies that were of a different nature and not confined to the young. Not continually on the move, many of the processions stopped from time to time to play a short dramatic scene at an appropriate point in the parish. The traditional May time cavalcades were, naturally, elaborated during the later middle ages and the Renaissance so that the triumphal cars which still remained basically hay-wains and farm-drays (an essential part of country festivals) became works of art on which were built bowers of flowers and foliage or solid pediments, covered with brocade or carved and gilded. The cars were accompanied by musicians and dancers on foot. The *Maggio*[51] which in Florence lasted throughout the month of May inspired lyrics and poems that combined a joyous welcome to the spring with expressions of new and aggressive vigour. Tournaments and the performance of dramas with heroic themes of martyred saints or noble paladins belonged to this season of the year when, even in the present century, *Gerusalemme Liberata* was still played in Tuscany by boys in mock Roman armour.[52] Italy, of course, had no exclusive claim to the decorated car – the *trionfo*; it formed an important part of processions in cities and in the countryside all over Europe.

Singers and dancers, accompanying the 'triumph' or sometimes leading or following it, together with the car itself incorporated into a play, are referred to more and more frequently in Italian documents as the fifteenth century progressed and gradually, in letters from ambassadors, in chronicles and in diaries, these dances are given the name *moresche*, or a word related to it in other countries. As the century drew to a close the *moresca* itself began to change its form, sometimes to the extent of becoming a small mimed drama, always accompanied by music. Our morris dances are descended from the *moresca* in its rustic form and, in fact, a bucolic *moresca* set into a sophisticated drama could provide a piquant contrast.[53]

Letters sent home by ambassadors were particularly valuable to the courts which employed them since it was from them that princes and state departments could assess their own cultural standing in the European scene. Descriptions of festivities must have been known to be of extreme interest for they are usually long and detailed and, although the entertainments offered by small plebeian companies are seldom mentioned, anything in fashion at the moment was certainly reported immediately and, no doubt, soon copied at home. Since at the end of the fifteenth century the *moresca* was very much in fashion, in letters from most of the royal or princely courts it was frequently described, sometimes as being rather vulgar.[54] Naturally the eclogues and humble farces of the popular theatre were less infected by their counterparts abroad.

Controversies as to the rival claims of fashionable Italian cities (especially Florence) and the court of Burgundy as generators of new artistic ideas in the fifteenth century have been well aired and, since the theatre was an important part of the artistic life of the community everywhere, the same arguments could be applied, if not to the actual writing of plays, at least to the preparation of spectacles and the choice of themes. In considering the situation in the European theatre at the end of the fifteenth century it is worth noticing that Poliziano's first version of his *Orfeo*, written for the Marquess of Mantua, was first produced in 1471: that Terence's *Menechmi* was done in Ferrara in 1486 and in Florence in 1489: his *Eunuch* in Ferrara in 1499 and Plautus's *Golden Ass* produced there in 1500. It seems that permission was sought of Lorenzo de' Medici to produce a comedy by Terence in Florence as early as 1479[55] and it appears to have been put on privately earlier still[56], but from the enthusiastic reports of contemporaries the Ferrarese productions of Terence must have been thought of as innovations and the sort of sensation made by Poliziano's *Orfeo* would have been surprising if plays on similar classical themes had been written and produced earlier.

In the Netherlands the famous Feast of the Pheasant at Lille in 1454 included a series of scenes from the life of Hercules acted between the courses.[57] The Feast itself was arranged by the Duke of Burgundy to encourage his friends and supporters both to go themselves and to take contingents of their followers on a new Crusade to the Holy Land, a matter of extreme urgency after the fall of Constantinople to the Turk. The Labours of Hercules were a part, no doubt, of the general heroics of the occasion but whether these scenes can really also be thought of as a part of the revival of interest in the myths of classical antiquity is doubtful since the Duke claimed Hercules as an ancestor, a claim that had already been made by earlier members of his house. If memories of Greek myths came more easily to Italians than to north Europeans, it should be recalled that in the north the general reader would at least have been familiar with those that were included in the perennially popular *Roman de la Rose* and the other mediaeval romances that were still read.

Dramatic interludes at the court of Burgundy have been recorded in detail by faithful chamberlains to the dukes but most of them were seen only by a closed circle. The ingenuity and fantasy involved in the presentation of the great Burgundian jousts were designed to be enjoyed by a much larger crowd – perhaps by most of the local population although participation in them was reserved for those of noble, or at least gentle, birth. After the death of the last Duke of Burgundy the Burgundian court tradition was carried on by the Emperor Maximilian I, his son-in-law, who inherited Conrad Celtes, poet laureate, from his father, Frederick III. Celtes was the first German poet to write and publish dramatic pastorals in the Italian style; his *Ludus Dianae*[58] was performed in 1501 in Linz before Maximilian and his court. The woodcuts by Hans von Kulmbach which illustrate the first published edition of the *Ludus Dianae* show a familiarity with Italian engravings as well as with the theatre but neither Celtes nor von Kulmbach could be thought of as innovators on a European scale.

Apart, however, from the aristocratic entertainments at the Burgundian court, it is clear from the healthy state of the play-producing organisations that existed in all the towns and cities and even many of the villages, that the Netherlandish theatre flourished throughout the fifteenth century. Known as *Chambers of Rhetoric* [4], many of these confraternities had a long history; the most famous of them, the Chamber at Valenciennes was already well known in Froissart's day and it is unlikely to have been the only one. The Rhetoricians, who often gave their Chambers the names of flowers, emphasised the writing and declaiming of poetry and held regular competitions at which prizes were awarded for talent in a variety of fields. But they also produced plays, and many Chambers became associated with specific shooting-companies in order to provide formal entertainments after the shooting-contests which, at a period when skill in archery was still of importance in warfare, were greatly encouraged by the authorities.

Like the *sociétés joyeuses*, Chambers of Rhetoric organised themselves under elected officers. Sixteen members seem to have been the usual number in a chamber with, at their head, a 'prince' – who was addressed by title as

4. Rhetoricians' festival at Haarlem, 1606. The *Cartouche* of the Chamber of Rhetoric at Leyden called the *Orangie Lelie*

the first word in every ballade – a steward, a treasurer, a poet, a standard-bearer and a Fool. All the officers were elected every year. In Chambers of Rhetoric the Fool was responsible for providing innocent and witty buffoonery without malice or indecency – to honour, in fact, the principles of polished behaviour required in competitive festivals. In these contests the victor was awarded a silver crown of specified weight and all the contestants were given double portions of wine to cheer them up. Rhetoricians who appear in seventeenth-century paintings of Dutch low-life do not look as though they would produce major poets but it is clear from their history that these companies existed on all levels so that while some were no more than *sociétés joyeuses* others were the forerunners of academies of culture. There were usually several Chambers in the larger towns and at the contests

58

Chambers from other places were often invited to compete. These contests took into account not only the poems themselves – written on given themes – but also the general bearing of the competitors, their skill in solving problems, their wit, their artistry in the use of metaphor, their ability to render their poems dramatically and their poise. The larger festivals included competitions for the grandest and most original display of fireworks, for the most ingenious and effective water-battles and for the best productions of comedies.[59]

It is tempting to think of the Renaissance theatre as being sharply divided between presentations in the princely courts and plebeian entertainments which noblemen would have scorned to attend, but this is not correct. Grand productions of religious plays were not only done in open squares but could also form a part of the celebrations at the wedding of a prince when, no less public, they might be staged in a church or in the great hall of the palace. A good deal of princely entertainment was deliberately arranged to please the people. Those who have been present at traditional pageantry such as the race of the gondoliers in Venice or the *Palio* in Siena may not have noticed that whilst the populace is crowded along the course, at the windows above local aristocrats and their families watch with no less enthusiasm. Until the private carriage shut the upper classes away from the community they were divided, in the streets, not by inanimate barriers but by personal escorts. The young son of a wealthy house charging through a crowded thoroughfare on a lively horse might press the woodman and his donkey close to the wall or even kill a child or two but he was not shut away in a limousine. Popular or unpopular the local magnate was highly visible.

Enough paintings of performances have survived if not from the fifteenth certainly from the sixteenth, seventeenth and eighteenth centuries, to show that members of the audience grandly dressed and often seated on chairs brought out for them by their servants, enjoyed the show as much as the workmen and the beggars standing round or watching from the corners.[60] In France the first Terence play was put on in 1502, not in translation but in Latin, in the great hall of the archbishop's palace at Metz. It was performed by the younger clergy together with lay actors but the humbler members of the audience demonstrated against a language they could not understand and drove the actors from the stage. The following day the comedy was performed again but this time for clerks and men of the Church only. This striking example of the admission of the public to an experimental production is unlikely to have been unique.[61]

Political, religious and social changes in the sixteenth century resulted in changes in the organisation of the theatre – changes which did not, of course, coincide with the turn of the century itself but which began to be felt during the second and third decade. The capture of the papacy by the House of Medici led to the destruction of the vision of republican Florence for centuries to come and the ennoblement of other Medici by the first Medici pope, Leo X, meant that Tuscany became a dukedom with almost royal status, a fact that must have influenced the French theatre of the sixteenth century. But Leo X, who died in 1519, had still sent yearly for the democratic Rozzi of Siena to amuse his court in Rome and although the moral outlook of that court was not above suspicion, when Leo ordered a *moresca* to be danced by monks and friars it was most unlikely that this ridiculing of the religious orders was unpopular with the working classes who, if they did not actually see it happen, must certainly have heard about the scandal very soon. This particular *moresca* was performed on the same occasion as a comedy for which Raphael designed the scenery – a mixture typical of the Renaissance theatre.[62]

This very brief account of the theatre of the fifteenth century as it existed in one or two European countries has taken no account of the innumerable junketings that went on in universities and schools, of dramatic trifles done in country inns – perhaps, if the *Taming of the Shrew* can be believed, not so trifling – of country rites which included the acting-out of half-forgotten myths, nor of the offerings of small bands of wandering actors and musicians prepared to play in the servants' hall. By its nature a good deal of entertainment must have been done in contemporary dress and it would be unreasonable to expect to find every aspect of the theatre reflected in works of art but, at the same time, some entertainments were certainly performed in costumes that were exclusively theatrical and some theatrical costumes found their way into works of art.

Neither the Spanish nor the German theatre has been discussed here, partly because works of art of the fifteenth century from both these countries include so many strange and seemingly fanciful costumes that to discuss them usefully would involve a detailed analysis too long to be undertaken as part of a general study.

CHAPTER 3

Stage Costume in Works of Art of the Early Fifteenth Century

It is not unlikely that the comedies of Terence, of which Jean, Duc de Berry owned a lavishly illustrated copy, were actually performed at his court. Eccentricities that are totally alien to the spirit of their time often go unrecorded since they are too incomprehensible to seem worth mentioning and at the height of the International Gothic period plays by Terence would be difficult to fit in. All the same, since Jean de Berry was adventurous in his tastes, he may well have had them put on – for fun.

5. French School. *Térence des ducs:* frontispiece. Before 1416. *Above*, a theatrical entertainment is being performed. *Below*, Terence, in oriental dress, presents a book to Terentius whose costume is meant to be Roman

The remarkable miniature paintings which form a frontispiece to the *Térence des ducs*[1] [5] undoubtedly take stage-settings and costumes into account and so do, though in a more subtle way, the illustrations to the plays themselves. In the upper miniature of the frontispiece the artist has tried to reproduce the circular form of a Roman theatre, certainly from verbal descriptions since he has got it wrong and failed to accommodate the members of the audience who are not drawn in but simply indicated by the word *populus* in positions from which they would have been able to see little if anything of the action of the play. He has attempted a proscenium but neither of the right size nor in the right place.[2]

In the lower half of the same miniature the artist has fallen back more comfortably on an arrangement of mediaeval *mansions* – a little orientalised in design – within a city wall. The senator Terentius Lucanus, seated in state in the foremost mansion, receives homage from his enfranchised slave, the poet Terence, who presents him with a copy of his comedies.

Artists, even in the north of Europe where monuments and works of art surviving from classical antiquity were scarce, were surprisingly often able to make some attempt at representing armour from the classical period. When it came to civilian clothes, however, northern painters found themselves unable to discover any source on which to base them. Until the dissemination of Italian engravings towards the end of the fifteenth century they could not look to Italy for inspiration and even after engravings had begun to reach them it took some time for German and Netherlandish artists to absorb the information they contained. Many artists, as we have seen, relied for information on the dress of orientals on the successive visits of the two Eastern emperors to the north of Europe[3] and it was dress of this kind that they used not only to clothe orientals but Greeks too. This was not altogether illogical since the emperors of Constantinople not only followed the Greek Christian rite and must, therefore, have been thought of as in some respects descendants of the Greeks, but they were also descendants of the emperors of Rome.

Early forms of turbans and strips of linen with hanging ends, wound round close-fitting caps (without almost covering them as they did later): striped textiles – the stripes running horizontally: long white shirt-sleeves, emerging, usually, from short over-sleeves that ended above the elbow: long over-gowns, all these are characteristic of the sort of oriental dress of which a good

64

deal can be found in the frontispiece-paintings to the *Térence des ducs*. But so can more obvious forms of theatrical costume in the miniatures, worn by the masked *joculatores* who dance what would later be called a *moresca* – it may even have been called so at the time – to the accompaniment of a trumpet. These dancers, too, wear long pale loose under-sleeves and oriental-type head-dresses but short tunics instead of long gowns; their dress may have been taken from the costumes of players accompanying the emperors or, perhaps, from bands of travelling players from the Near East who came on their own; it corresponds in some details to the costume worn by Herod in some English works of art,[4] which cannot, from its design, have been a pure invention. Among the subsidiary characters standing round the dancers are some who look slightly oriental but others wear the normal north European fashions of their day. Although these might have been intended as members of the audience who had strayed on to the scene this is not necessarily the case, for in the fifteenth and sixteenth and even in the seventeenth centuries, actors who merely walked-on or who played very minor parts were seldom dressed in character.[5] They were unimportant, and among the leading actors who wore theatrical costume, their contemporary dress was too familiar to the audience to be disturbing.

Simple turbans composed of a narrow pale-coloured cloth tied round a close-fitting cap and large oriental-looking felt hats of the type to be found in the frontispiece of the *Térence des ducs* are also worn by the torturers in the Fouquet *Martyrdom of St Apollonia*. Presumably these men were intended as natives of Alexandria where St Apollonia was martyred[6] and were therefore dressed as orientals. But they would also be recognized by the audience as executioners, for coarse-faced characters, their heads bound with long strips of linen and a slightly Near Eastern flavour in their rough dress appear so frequently in works of art of the fifteenth century that it seems probable that non-Christians from North Africa were actually employed as executioners. The household livery worn by the torturers in the Fouquet miniature shows that they were meant as household servants of the potentate who condemned St Apollonia to death.

The illustrations to the Terence comedies in the Duc de Berry's copy follow the action in considerable detail and succeed in keeping the identity of each character by faithfully repeating each individual costume in every scene. Since several of the comedies by Terence depend on confusion of

6. French School. *Térence des ducs: The Eunuch*. Before 1416. The 'real' Eunuch wears a hat meant to be oriental with a tunic which belongs to the European fashion of about fifty years earlier. The two women are dressed in local working-class clothing of the early fifteenth century and the man on the left, the upper-class high-fashion of the same moment.

7. Another scene from *The Eunuch*. Before 1416. The hat and sleeves of the counterfeit Eunuch are lined with ermine but in other respects his dress resembles that of the 'real' Eunuch. The young man wears the youthful high-fashion of the early fifteenth century.

identity as a part of the plot this differentiation is very important. In the illustrations to all the plays identification of character takes precedence over the desire to show that the plays were written in ancient Rome though in *The Eunuch* this aspect is not entirely neglected. In this play most of the characters are shown wearing costumes in the fashion of the middle of the first decade of the fifteenth century but each is individualised according to age, occupation and social standing. The Eunuchs, both the true and the counterfeit, wear a dress that is very slightly orientalised, but not at all to the extent that some of the characters appearing on the frontispiece are. It also includes features of an earlier European fashion and, furthermore, one is a little more richly dressed than the other so that the audience —or the reader —

would, in spite of the intricacies of the plot, be able to distinguish between them [6 and 7].

The introduction of an earlier European fashion could have had the effect of throwing the whole play into a time which the audience would have recognised as the past. That is to say it is a fashion of about fifty years earlier and one, therefore, not totally obliterated from the memory but almost forgotten – the 'olden times' in fact – familiar only to the very old who would have been able to recall it to the young. In the dress of the Eunuchs this device is used in a very simple form but it is there. The strip of stuff which hangs from a band above the elbow was a part of the high-fashion of the 1360s [8] but had disappeared from fashionable dress during the next decade though, at an earlier moment in its development it had found its

8. Andrea da Bologna. Polyptych. *St Catherine:* detail. 1369. The saint wears the fashionable dress of Italy in the 1360s

way into academic and clerical dress, where traces of it remain to this day. Together with the very short close-fitting sleeve from which it hung, this long narrow strip probably actually originated in the East and, as a European fashion was borrowed from oriental dress. Later it played an important part in the ceremonial gowns of Grand Vizirs where it assumed a ritualistic signi-ficance but in fifteenth-century Italy it was evidently recognised as Eastern for in an *Adoration of the Magi* Mantegna used it as a part of the dress of an attendant manifestly intended as an oriental [9].

9. Andrea Mantegna. *Adoration of the Magi:* detail of orientals. The man in the pale tunic wears the Italian fashion of the second half of the fourteenth century together with a Near Eastern hat and quiver

Although by the time the miniatures in the *Térence des ducs* were done, at the beginning of the fifteenth century, fashionable sleeves had become im-mensely wide and so long that they often hung nearly to the ground, they were not the descendants of the narrow hanging-strip but derived from an earlier and different European fashion. In the Terence miniatures the largest and longest sleeves are worn by those characters who are clearly meant to be dressed in the height of the current fashion which included, too, a waistline set above its normal place. In contrast, a feature of the dress of the Eunuchs is a very low-set waistline, another ancient fashion which the artist incorporated in their dress and one which was current not in the 1360s when the hanging-strip was at the height of its popularity, but a couple of decades earlier. The effect of a long torso, produced by setting the skirt of the tunic on to the body-part at the line of the hips preceded and eventually led to the elegant close-fit of the male dress of the 1360s and 1370s. It made the body look smooth and elongated – rather like a vegetable marrow – an effect that would have been quite unacceptable in the later years of the fourteenth century. While the attempt to reconstruct fashions of the past may appear surprising, the slight confusion produced by the inclusion in one dress of features from two different periods is, of course, typical of stage design in any age.

The dress of the Eunuchs demonstrates, in a very elementary form, one of the main devices used by theatrical costumiers of the Renaissance. It is unlikely to have been an invention of the early fifteenth century but earlier manifestations of it, which must have existed, are difficult to distinguish in the present state of knowledge. The illustrations to the Terence plays with their miniature mansions, carefully differentiated dress and emphasis on character are good examples of the sort of staging and costumes in which plays of the time would very likely have been presented, whether these actually were or not.[7]

The illustrations to the *Térence des ducs* were executed in the north of Europe. To the Italians the problem of the dress of classical antiquity was less acute. The Pisano family had used it unselfconsciously in the thirteenth century when they carved their pulpits and fonts.[8] They worked in districts where sarcophagi and other fragments from the classical period lay about plentifully on overgrown sites of Roman temples or in the crypts of churches built over them. Later, in the early fifteenth century, Pisanello was making drawings from the antique and he was not alone in doing so.[9]

Whatever their attitude to the visual arts, Italians of the beginning of the fifteenth century were probably indifferent to the plays of Terence; classic rather than romantic in their temperament they were probably less likely to be amused by unfashionable trends. They too, however, were obliged on occasion to represent in their works of art characters both from the past and

69

from foreign countries, especially those from the East. Placed, geographi-
cally, rather nearer to the Orient than the inhabitants of the north of Europe
they were able to be more discriminating in regard to the customs of their
Near-Eastern neighbours and they seem not to have adopted in quite so
carefree a manner any dress or parts of dress worn between Constantinople
and Tunis as a suitable costume for characters meant to come from Greece,
Persia, Ethiopia or anywhere in between. In Italy no less than in the north
of Europe, religious dramas and street processions incorporating dramatic
interludes demanded costumes that would not only provide an arresting
spectacle – increasingly important as the fifteenth century advanced – but
would serve to identify the dramatis personae and in this respect the costu-
mier was in the same position as the painter who was required to produce
extensive narrative sequences on the walls of churches and cloisters or, on a
very much smaller scale, on the predella panels attached as the lowest
sections of altarpieces.

For the most sacred personages in these narratives, Christ, the Apostles
and, in the scenes following the Nativity, the Virgin, both painters and
stage-designers continued to use with only slight modifications, the style of
costume they had inherited from the Byzantine artists who had been responsible for establishing the types in the first place. At the beginning of the
fourteenth century Giotto, with great daring, had introduced considerable
changes into some of this traditional dress but his experiments were not
taken up by his successors.

Artists of the later middle ages thought of the New Testament as introducing the modern world – the present way of life – so that the saints, unless
they were Apostles, could reasonably be represented as wearing the kind of
dress that would be worn by those in the modern world who corresponded
to them in occupation or social position. Pilate and the High Priests of the
Synagogue on the other hand could not, since they represented the old point
of view, the world before the Redemption. They had, in addition, to be
distinguished from each other and, as pictorial subject-matter was enlarged
to include episodes from the Old Testament (the story of Esther for example),
there was evidently a feeling that these too must be shown by their dress as
events earlier than those related in the Gospels or by St Paul. The appearance of the Magi, who represented the first knowledge of the coming of
Christ to those outside the Jewish world (as well as outside the Roman

Empire) also had to be taken into consideration where costume was concerned. Oriental dress played, therefore, an important part in establishing these differences.

A singularly interesting contemporary account has survived which describes a representation of the journey and adoration of the Magi in the form of a procession with dramatic interludes which took place in Milan in 1336. Not only the details of the procession itself are related but the account ends by saying that the event was so successful that orders were given for it to be repeated annually. Milan may have borrowed the idea from elsewhere but the birth of a tradition in one city is important.

In the description of this Milanese procession of 1336 the Magi are called Kings and are referred to as mounted on great horses and crowned, surrounded by household servants variously dressed and preceded by a golden star which rode through the sky – *discurrens per aera*. They proceeded to the columns of St Lawrence where King Herod was represented surrounded by scholars and scribes whom he questioned as to the whereabouts of the birth of Christ. Turning over the pages of their tomes the sages replied that it was in Bethlehem near Jerusalem. On hearing this the three crowned Kings, holding in their hands vessels containing gold, frankincense and myrrh, preceded by the star in the air and accompanied by a crowd of followers with monkeys and baboons and various other animals – *animali variis* – proceeded to the Church of St Eustace to the sound of trumpets. There, beside the high altar, was a stable with an ox and an ass and the Virgin holding the little Christ in her arms. After saluting the Child the Kings retired to sleep whereupon an angel warned them not to return by way of the Church of St Lawrence but by the Roman Gate. This they did in the presence of a greater crowd of people, knights, scholars and clergy than had ever before been seen.[10]

References to processions that must have been very like this one are fairly numerous but in most of them the writer took it for granted that the reader was already familiar with their details and they are usually, therefore, brief. In 1439, when the Ecumenical Council met in Florence, however, the traditional procession which included the story of the coming of the Magi and which, in Florence, took place as a part of the festivities on St John's Eve, was recorded by a Greek visitor who says that the Greek contingent at the Council was kindly invited to attend. It is unlikely that this invitation

10. Gentile da Fabriano. *Adoration of the Magi*: detail. 1423. Here, too, the crowd includes orientals as well as men wearing the current fashion

did much to further cordial relations between the Eastern and the Western Churches for the Greeks were shocked by the mixture of the sacred and the secular in the procession and also harassed by anxiety as to whether they were witnessing idolatry. In the course of his description the anonymous Greek relates that on the 23rd June a grand procession and a festival in which the whole population took part was a prodigious and almost miraculous affair or, rather, one in which miracles were represented. It included the raising of the dead, the crucifixion of a man like Christ, the representation of the crucifixion of Christ, certain men dressed as Magi and, on the road, men representing the Nativity with the shepherds and the star and the animals, and the adoration of the Magi.[11] In this description, unlike that of a hundred years earlier, there was no question of including remarks such as, 'an angel warned them not to return by way of the Church of St Lawrence but by the Roman Gate' with its muddle of the actual and the historical. It is obvious, however, that like the procession in Milan, the Florentine spectacle included a great many members of the general public as well as those who were allotted special parts.

Since this study is concerned with the fifteenth and sixteenth centuries it is inappropriate to discuss fourteenth-century paintings of the procession of the Magi, of which Bartolo da Fredi's panel in the Uffizi is in many respects the nearest prototype to Gentile da Fabriano's enchanting altarpiece of 1423 in the same gallery. Like Bartolo di Fredi, Gentile used theatrical costume for the Magi themselves and included, among the members of the populace who followed them, some orientals. Monkeys, a camel, hunting-leopards and hawks as referred to in the description of the procession in Milan in 1336 are there too [10].

In Gentile's picture the youngest Magus, manifestly a very young man indeed, wears with his fanciful dress the same vestigial over-sleeves hanging from a band set just above the elbow that were used in the costumes of the Eunuchs in the *Térence des ducs*, a feature which, by 1423, had disappeared from the fashionable wardrobe nearly sixty years earlier. The rest of his dress has been designed with considerable ingenuity for although it suggests armour, on closer inspection it is plain that it is not armour at all [11].

Florentine painters knew very well what Roman armour looked like and often put it into their pictures but the Magi came not from Rome, of course, but from the East, thought of perhaps as quite specifically Persia or India.

11. Gentile da Fabriano. *Adoration of the Magi:* detail. 1423. The youngest Magus wears a hanging-sleeve; his dress resembles a mixture of Roman and Gothic armour, but is not armour at all

The costume of the youngest Magus is shown as being made partly of gold tissue, partly of brocade in a design inspired by Persian textiles and partly of embroidery. Round the neck, peacocks' feathers are suggested though not actually represented. From the low-set line of the knightly belt hang strips of embroidered textile edged with fringe which again refer obliquely to classical armour but which do not represent it. On his head the young man wears a padded roll covered with brocade and jewelled: it is surmounted by a gold crown. While in its general outline and in the length of what may be called his tunic the costume conforms to the current fashion, no single feature with the exception of his hose, shoes and tight-fitting under-sleeves, is fashionable.

Neither does the dress of the second Magus – in the centre of the group – conform to the current fashion any more closely. A long gown of brocade with very short rather tight sleeves would be unacceptable as the normal dress of the day. His head-dress is extraordinary and so is the length of his hair which belongs either to a fashion of the 1370s or, and this seems nearer the mark, to a Greek priest. The undignified pose of the old man – the third Magus – is ameliorated by a piece of drapery which conceals the lines of his back and limbs. His sleeves belong to the first half of the fifteenth century.

Some members of the crowd wear normal fashionable dress of 1423; for example the man who looks fixedly out from the panel between the youngest Magus and his white horse which is held by a squire wearing a baldrick embroidered with arabic letters. The dress of this squire is fairly up-to-date though not of the latest fashion – it may well have been out-of-date enough to have been adopted as livery but this is not certain. The red twisted hood which looks like a turban worn by the horseman far to the spectator's right is a part of the current fashion and so is his golden baldrick. The blue hat of the man just above him also belongs to the fashion of the time.

To claim that the dress of the Magi is theatrical because it fails to conform to the current fashion, and because one small feature of it belonging to an earlier period matches a similar feature in the dress illustrated in a book of comedies which may never have been produced, would of course be absurd if no further evidence could be produced. But it can. There are three other reasons apart from the anachronisms discussed above for regarding at least some of the dress in this painting as directly copied from costumes used in an actual procession which Gentile da Fabriano had seen.

In the first place, although very fanciful, the dress of the youngest Magus must have been the result of personal observation of a costume that had actually been made – a most important factor in the study of dress in works of art. The 'skirt' of his tunic, for instance, which looks superficially as though it were meant to be a decorative version of the leather strips that were a part of Roman military dress is, in fact, made of strips of embroidered textile each edged with fringe [12]. For a painter to invent a skirt composed of narrow strips of decorated stuff, especially with a vague idea of classical armour in mind, would not be difficult but to decide to edge each strip with fringe is the sort of invention that belongs to the designer of costumes and not to the painter. Furthermore, these little fringes were certainly painted from life: their behaviour as they are partly concealed by the next strip or emerge from it is not the sort of thing that a painter thinks out for himself. Clothes which are inventions of the painter and which have never been seen by him can always be recognised by the absence of purely unnecessary detail of this kind. When an artist of the Renaissance chose to embellish the clothes he invented with decoration, it was invariably applied to the surface of the garment and was not a part of the construction of the garment itself. Differences of this kind in pictorial rendering of dress, although they may not be

12. Gentile da Fabriano. *Adoration of the Magi*: detail, the skirt of the youngest Magus. 1423

distinguished by those who have no knowledge of the techniques involved in the construction of clothing, are easily seen by those who have. The most unconvincing part of the dress in Gentile's *Adoration of the Magi* is the mantle thrown over the back of the oldest Magus; this suggests a studio-arrangement but the same applies to little else in the painting.

The Magus in the centre of the painting is about to remove his crown from the curious head-dress of feathers he wears beneath it. He is not, apparently, going to take the whole thing off though the old man has removed his hat and laid it on the ground. The feather head-dress looks most improbable from the point of view of theatrical costume, oriental costume, or as pure

13. Gentile da Fabriano. *Adoration of the Magi*: detail, the second Magus wearing a feather head-dress. 1423

invention [13]. It is not, all the same, the only example of this actual arrange-ment of feathers in works of art – there are at least two more. It would be interesting to discover the source of the idea but so far this is not clear.[12] For the second example it is necessary to turn to the fresco of the *Procession of the Magi* in the Riccardi Palace in Florence by Benozzo Gozzoli.

Gentile da Fabriano's altarpiece of 1423 was painted for Palla Strozzi for the Sacristy of the Church of the Holy Trinity in Florence – Sta Trinità.[13] Gozzoli's frescoes were painted for Piero de' Medici and from documentary evidence seem to have been in the process of being executed in 1459.[14] They cover the walls of the tiny chapel in what was then the Medici Palace in the Via Larga but was later acquired by the Riccardi family. While they were being painted there is no doubt that Gentile da Fabriano's altarpiece was still to be seen in Sta Trinità.

A good many arguments have been put forward for and against the idea that not only do Gozzoli's frescoes portray members of the Medici family – the youngest Magus has been identified as the little Lorenzo who would then have been about twelve years old – but some art historians have thought that they also include people who were present at the Ecumenical Council of 1439. The Emperor, the Patriarch of Constantinople, Cosimo de' Medici and his son Piero, Lorenzo's father, are all thought of by some as being represented. If this is really a commemoration of a rather sad event which brought, perhaps, a little glory to the city of Florence it is curious that one of the leading actors, the Pope, was excluded. The argument is relevant here only because Medici devices in the form of badges occur more thickly in some parts of the painting than in others – cunningly tucked into the folds of the tunic of one of the servants on foot, for instance, in a manner that could only have been the result of direct observation of an actual garment.[15] They can also be found among the decorations on the trappings of some but not all the horses.

Like Gentile da Fabriano, Gozzoli used a variety of clothing for the crowd. There are orientals but there are also recognisable local fashions belonging to other parts of Europe and there is a good deal of straightforward Italian civilian dress as well as some which, while it looks like the dress of ordinary citizens, might be identified after further research as belonging to members of specific confraternities [14]. The artist distinguishes himself in the crowd by inscribing his name round his felt cap.

14. Benozzo Gozzoli. *Journey of the Magi*: detail of crowd. The man who wears three
feathers rising from a jewelled band is a German: the man in the fringed 'mushroom' hat is
French or Burgundian: the man with long curls is probably Bohemian

The young squires and pages who accompany the Magi, some of them on
horseback, wear the rich dress of young plutocrats of the various *potenze* –
Gozzoli shows them separated into groups each with its own uniform, as
members of several different *brigate*. An analysis of the clothes of the crowd
would be interesting but out of place here for it is the dress of the Magi
which is significant.

The youngest Magus is represented, as he was in Gentile's painting, as
being very young indeed, almost a child [15]. His dress, made in textile,
belongs to the same category as that of Gentile's boy-king and is remarkably
similar but not exactly like. It looks at first glance, that is to say, like a Gothic
version of Roman armour, but it is not. It has a similar hanging-sleeve but
one that has drawn a little nearer to the current fashion though it does not

15. Benozzo Gozzoli. *Journey of the Magi:* detail. The youngest Magus wearing a similar costume to that of his counterpart in Ill. 11

belong to it. The hanging-sleeve, recently become a part of the current fashion, was made with a slit from the armhole to below the elbow through which the arm could be passed. The sleeve of the youngest Magus is not like that, it still retains the tight-fitting upper-part, impossible as a part of the current fashion and a purely archaic feature. The strips of stuff which form the 'skirt' of the tunic are still each of them embroidered as a separate unit but they are no longer separately edged with fringe: the divisions between them are, in fact, vestigial – they have become a solid skirt. On his head the boy wears a padded roll, jewelled and surmounted by a gold crown. His dress, like that of Gentile's boy, looks authentic in spite of its strangeness. The profile view of the curious decorative treatment of the torso of the tunic, reminiscent of Gothic armour, is too convincing in its implied construction to have been an

79

invention by the artist but, on the other hand, if Gozzoli, admiring Gentile's treatment of the costume of his young king had decided to copy it, or if he should have been encouraged to do so by his patron, why should it be so like and yet so painstakingly different? The *palle* of the Medici arms[16] decorate the trappings of this young man's horse. His dress is even grander and more strikingly glamorous than that of his counterpart in Gentile's painting though its presentation is less poetic.

Gozzoli's second Magus, the man in the prime of life, wears a dress even closer to that of the corresponding Magus in Gentile's painting. Made of brocade woven in a slightly later though still oriental design and equally

16. Benozzo Gozzoli. *Journey of the Magi*: detail. The second Magus also closely resembles his counterpart in Gentile's painting

woven with gold thread on a background of dark silk or, more probably, velvet, the main difference between the two gowns is that while Gentile gave his Magus short sleeves bordered with a golden tissue in a small scale-like pattern, Gozzoli substituted sable. Gozzoli's Magus wears what is virtually a duplicate of Gentile's feather head-dress — even to the colours of the feathers, red alternating with white. Only the crown is different in shape [16].

Since this Magus, who is regarded by some as being based on the Emperor John Paleologus, is mounted his boots can be seen. They are not Italian but from the Near East and were certainly drawn from actual models. Rather similar boots can be found in a drawing by Pisanello usually considered to have been done at the Council of Florence.[17]

The eldest Magus in Gozzoli's fresco looks out towards the spectator and is sometimes thought of as being a portrait of the Patriarch of Constantinople who had accompanied the Emperor to Italy in 1437. The dress of this man is difficult to interpret for while it does not look like theatrical dress neither does it look altogether like a painter's invention. The short over-tunic appears to follow the current fashion in its length and the shape of the sleeves, but instead of being worn directly over long hose there appears beneath it a long-skirted gown – a device sometimes used for the dress of angels in fifteenth-century Italian painting [17].[18] It is remarkable, however, not for its composition but for the design of the textile of which the under-gown is made.

17. Benozzo Gozzoli. *Journey of the Magi*: detail. The third Magus wears an artificial-looking beard, a large oriental hat and a short tunic of the current fashion

This does not correspond to any Italian stuff of the period but it would hardly have been chosen by Gozzoli unless it could have conveyed a meaning to the contemporary spectator. The clothes of this man, like his counterpart in Gentile's painting, are a little unconvincing. Apart from their hats, which are the same shape, there is no similarity between the costumes of these two old men so far as can be seen.

The dress of the two mature Magi might have been equally enigmatic but for the chance survival, in the Cabinet des Dessins at the Louvre, of a drawing attributed to Pisanello or his studio. This drawing seems to be one of a series of drawings of large heads – some shown as far down as the bust – amongst them two musicians playing instruments.[19] The drawings in this group, originally in pencil which is very much rubbed, have all been gone over in indian ink but the ink lines appear to follow the pencil lines beneath faithfully.

18. Pisanello, or School of. Drawing of the head of a man wearing a wreath of feathers, held in an interwoven band, over a close-fitting 'coif'

The Pisanello-type drawing of a head which is relevant here shows a bearded man in profile – perhaps with a somewhat oriental look, wearing a head-dress which explains the extraordinary feather wreaths worn by the two mature kings in Gentile's and Gozzoli's paintings. The crown is absent so that the method by which the feathers are held firmly in their splayed-out positions can be seen [18]. This establishes the head-dress as something that was, for whatever purpose, actually constructed. The association of this drawing with others of a similar style representing musicians suggests that all may have been used for an event in which pageantry played a part.

Pisanello had on the occasion of the visit of the Emperor made not only a portrait-medal of John Paleologus himself wearing the hat with a high dome-like crown and a brim turned up at the back and down in front – which artists were quick to adopt as appropriate to visiting Eastern potentates, the Queen of Sheba for instance – but he had also done sketches mostly of men in Eastern costume who must certainly have been members of the Emperor's train [19, 20].[20] Here and there an inscription indicates the colour of some part of the dress. These little drawings are quite unlike the large heads referred to above which does not necessarily mean that they were done by a different hand: they may simply have been done for a different purpose, the little ones as notes, perhaps, for a later composition, the large heads as designs for a spectacle of some kind.

19. Pisanello. Study for medal of the Emperor John Paleologus

20. Pisanello. Drawings of heads of priests of the Greek Church

Although no single character in either the Gentile da Fabriano altarpiece or the Benozzo Gozzoli Riccardi Palace frescoes could be said with absolute certainty to be wearing a dress copied from one worn in a pageant, it is very difficult to explain the armour-like clothing of the two very young men and the feather head-dresses worn by the older men as being anything else, especially since what seems to be a working-drawing for a similar head-dress also exists. Contemporary documents describing processions in which the Magi appeared refer to them as being dressed as the wise kings – 'vestiti ai re Magi'[21] – so recognisable costumes must have become established for them in centres where such spectacles regularly took place and where, as in Milan and Forence, no actual king whose clothes could be taken as a model for royalty, sat on a throne. It is possible that painters and designers of theatrical costumes living in the same town had no contact with each other but it is unlikely. In the two works of art discussed above the fact that the costumes of the Magi are clearly shown to have a sound construction makes it clear that the clothes existed before the artists painted them and the fact that both painters lived in Florence, where a procession of the Magi was an annual event on the Eve of St John, further suggests that a tradition as to the kind of dress appropriate to each of the Magi had grown up there.

There are, of course, a great many Florentine paintings of the Magi in which this type of dress is not used. And Giovanni di Paolo, of Siena, though he used Gentile's composition and copied many of his details in one of his own paintings of the *Adoration of the Magi* did not borrow Gentile's dress which may have had special Florentine connotations that would be unfamiliar to the Sienese.[22] Fra Angelico who used a good many well-observed oriental details of dress in some of his paintings gave his Magi a Gothic rather than an oriental look.[23] Lorenzo Monaco chose on occasion to dress his Magi in very simple flowing white mantles which may have indicated that he was more familiar with representations of the coming of the Magi staged by monks and in church than with the public shows but, on the other hand, he may simply have preferred this effect.[24]

The question of the practicability of clothes represented in works of art is of great importance but is difficult for those who have no understanding of the construction of clothes to appreciate. Where dress of the current fashion was concerned painters had no need of models. Their experience of the clothing they put on and took off every day meant that they instinctively recorded it with such fidelity that details totally unnecessary to the aesthetic effect either of the whole work or of the dress itself were invariably included. The omission of – say – an eyelet-hole to correspond to a lace must have produced a sensation of discomfort although, naturally, spectators of later periods who could not be expected to know that laces were intended to be threaded through eyelet-holes would suffer no such inconvenience.

The armour of Donatello's St George, designed to stand in a niche on an exterior wall of Or San Michele in Florence is correct and functional in every respect except that it is not the armour of the period when the sculpture was executed.[25] It is fanciful and must have been copied from armour used in a parade or in the theatre for it would have been a most unlikely and gratuitous *tour de force* on the part of any sculptor to design, purely for representation in a work of art, a perfectly articulated suit of armour that had never before existed. St George wears armour which, though infused with the Gothic spirit, purports to be Roman.

Stage-designers with no knowledge of the basic techniques of tailoring find themselves today in the same predicament as artists of any period required to dress people in costumes which are familiar to them only through works of art or not at all. With a vague idea of how the finished costumes should look they are unable to make explanatory drawings for the guidance of the tailor. It is surprising to find that Giotto, usually so secure in his understanding of the structure of the clothes he chose for his characters, was extremely hesitant when it came to representing the armour of the soldiers who guard the Sepulchre.[26] Having decided, evidently, that the armour should be Roman, Giotto was unable to proceed from there. His 'Roman' armour consists, wherever it appears in the Arena Chapel frescoes, of a moulded sleeveless covering for the torso with neither fastening nor articulation, embellished with Gothic arabesques. To this he joins a little fabric skirt, shorter than the normal fashionable tunic of the time, which is shown as being worn beneath it. The outer-skirt hangs from the waist in deep folds but it is edged with a perfectly straight band which takes no account of them – a structural impossibility. Furthermore the skirt is painted not with the full rounded folds which Giotto normally expressed in *chiaroscuro* but in papery folds highlighted with the sharp lines of gold to be found in the work of artists of the Byzantine school, from which these folds must certainly have been derived but against which Giotto was normally in revolt [21]. But what

21. Giotto. *The Resurrection:* detail. The structure of the folds of the sleeping soldiers' tunics is quite misunderstood

is intended by this little skirt? Are the hard lines that divide the folds mis-interpretations of the edges of the leather strips that are a characteristic part of Roman armour? Giotto includes other misinterpretations of a similar nature in his rendering of this armour and, it seems, the artist was himself uncomfortable about it, as we can see by the fact that whereas in painting the sleeping soldiers guarding the Sepulchre he contented himself with a funny

22. Giotto. *The Resurrection:* detail. The pieces that fall from the soldiers' shoulders are also completely misunderstood

little frill which, emerging from a shoulder-cap composed of scales runs diagonally from a line drawn from elbow to armpit [22], when he was forced to depict a Roman soldier in action, casting lots for the garment of Christ, he made a fumbling attempt to explain the structure both of the frill and of the shoulder-cap above it [23].

23. Giotto. *The Crucifixion:* detail. An attempt has been made to design a sleeve that allowed for movement. The result is very strange

This sudden intrusion of areas of clothing treated purely decoratively comes as a surprise when it is discovered amongst the dress of other characters painted with so confident a sense of weight and volume. Giotto did not even attempt to give his soldiers a military aspect but, on the other hand, they cannot have been based on theatrical buffoons in spite of his feeble attempts at explaining their dress. Had he actually seen such clothes he would have painted their structure accurately; as it is the Roman 'sleeve' of the young man disputing the garment of Christ does not work and this is true of the dress of no other character in Giotto's painting. It happened only when he based his clothing not on life but on earlier works of art.

Gentile da Fabriano's and Gozzoli's mock-armour does work, although it is not armour at all and although it is even more elaborately ornamental than Giotto's. Whether Gentile's costume was originally made for a young member of one of the *potenze* – perhaps the son of a prominent citizen: whether Gozzoli's young Magus is a portrait of the little Lorenzo de' Medici is irrelevant here. Both are portraits of actual clothes if not of actual people.

It would be a mistake, however, to assume that because theatre-costume appears in some paintings of the fifteenth century all dress which cannot easily be identified as a part of the normal current fashion must therefore have been inspired by the theatre. Painters of the Renaissance showed, when they wished, considerable ingenuity in adapting pedestrian garments from the current wardrobe as suitable clothing for saints and angels, gods and nymphs. These selections and transformations may sometimes have borne some resemblance to contrivances produced by stage-costumiers but this was not always the case.

Garments that can be regarded as certainly based on dress used in the theatre include a further quality – the attempt of the dress itself to escape from the current fashion rather than the attempt on the part of the artist to transform current dress into an unrecognisable form. The feather head-dress of Gentile's and Gozzoli's second Magus is an example of this and so are the hanging-sleeves of the two younger men. The feather head-dress is exotic: it can be related to no contemporary counterpart and yet its construction is firm and logical. It was understood so well by both painters that Gentile actually showed the crown being removed to leave the feather head-dress still on the head, at which point it would have resembled exactly the Pisanello drawing. The mock-armour of the two young men, though strange, is less extraordinary than the feather head-dress but both suits include a detail from a fashion of between fifty and eighty years earlier and one which survived in that form, apparently, in no other type of fifteenth-century Western dress. The introduction of a structurally sound piece of archaism shows that, unlike the armour attempted by Giotto, the armour-like clothes of the Magi had already existed not in the form of two-dimensional images but as three-dimensional garments. Constructed of silk or velvet they may themselves have been embellished by paint after they were made.

Other and later painters than Giotto had difficulty with their Roman armour but although a good deal of what they produced looks more Gothic than Roman most of it looks three-dimensional. For his Or San Michele St George, Donatello was evidently unable to find a genuinely Roman proto-type; combined with a few generalised Roman details, St George's armour incorporates the tight waist and Gothic plaquet, both of which were con-temporary features of the kind that Giotto must have been determined to avoid.[27] Nor was Donatello any more historically accurate when he used Roman armour on his font in the Duomo in Siena to clothe the executioner who presents the head of St John to Salome. He had no such difficulties, naturally, over the dalmatic of St Stephen whom he represented as wearing vestments of his own day, already traditional enough to be acceptable as those of the time of St Stephen's martyrdom. By the time he came to design his Crucifixion for San Lorenzo in Florence, however, Donatello had learnt to understand the true character of Roman armour so well that he could represent its behaviour in movement − discoveries he had already made, in spite of some Gothic interpolations, in modelling the armour of Gattamelata.

The freedom from Gothic detail and the degree of authenticity in the design of Roman armour has nothing, of course, to do with its reconstruction as stage-armour − theatre-designers are as capable of historical inaccuracies as artists in any other field − but its behaviour in movement when it is portrayed in painting and sculpture must reveal whether it was actually observed and therefore derived from stage-designers' armour or not. Stage-armour must have existed in considerable quantity since it is constantly re-ferred to in inventories and other documents of the fifteenth century. Dramas on the Passion, if no others, could, indeed, hardly have been staged without it and however inaccurate its design in Italy it is improbable that it was, in any Italian production, as wildly mixed with Gothic elements as it must have been, from the evidence of works of art, in the north of Europe.

Apart from the unfamiliarity of Roman dress, artists of the north of Europe, no less than their Italian counterparts, included a wealth of structural detail when they painted clothes they knew from personal experience. To us this often comes as a surprise. In the altarpiece of the *Holy Lamb* in Ghent,

for instance, the van Eyck brothers provide information about current prac-
tices in tailoring which are fascinating to us but which must have been so
commonplace to their contemporaries as to have been virtually invisible.
There is a great deal of varied clothing in the Ghent altarpiece for it set out
deliberately to represent people of different ages and from different walks of
life. There is no need to regard any of these as being dressed in costumes
inspired by the theatre for practically every garment worn by an Apostle, a
Holy Virgin, a Warrior of Christ or a Just Judge could have been seen by
the van Eycks during the course of their everyday lives – in the street, the
church or the aristocratic court.[28] Among the Prophets in the altarpiece,
however, are some who wear turbans or large felt hats of a manifestly
oriental kind and these are presented as convincingly as the other details of
costume in the painting. Most of them are worn with gowns of Netherlandish cut and some correspond to similar hats in the *Térence des ducs* and
the Fouquet miniature but like the Near-Eastern hats in those paintings,
these too could just as well have been based on the head-wear of visiting
foreigners as on theatrical hats since there is nothing either fanciful or
archaistic about them. For the armour of St George among the Warriors of
Christ the van Eycks contented themselves with Gothic armour of the most
up-to-date pattern and made no attempt at all to give it a Roman or oriental
flavour.

If the structure of garments can be, and during the Renaissance almost
always was, indicated by the painter, the sculptor, if he was required to
represent a clothed figure had hardly any choice but to make the dress look
'real'. However historically inaccurate the armour of Donatello's St George
it looks as though it could have been worn. Like the van Eycks, Claus Sluter
was faced with the problem of finding an appropriate dress for the Prophets
in his sculptured group known as the *Puits de Moïse* near Dijon.[29] Zacharias,
Sluter presented as an oriental, he wears what was probably a Jewish hat
carved so convincingly in the soft heaviness of its apparently thick felt construction that the sculptor has explained not only what the particular hat he
used as a model looked like but also what it must have felt like to touch [24].
His model was probably the inspiration for the numerous similar hats to be
found in northern works of art, some of them rather feebly drawn by painters
who can have known them only at second hand through other works of
art.[30]

24. Claus Sluter. *Puits de Moïse*: detail. Before 1406. Over a thick cloth hood worn at the time throughout Northern Europe, the Prophet Zacharias wears a hat either Jewish or Near-Eastern in type

Claus Sluter's group of Prophets was probably originally associated with a well or water-cistern − a *puit* − in which case its situation alone might suggest a connection with dramatic performances for these were often done near or round holy wells.[31] The dress of at least some of the Prophets certainly looks in many respects like stage costume even though the hat of Zacharias may have been based on one worn by a travelling agent if not by a local Jew. The clothes of the Prophet David, however, do not resemble those of Zacharias, they are treated quite differently. As a king he wears a crown, a necessary part of his identity (to present him as an oriental was not necessary) and a long mantle, another symbol of royalty or at least nobility. Claus Sluter's King David wears a mantle edged with what must be meant to be a border composed of harps, a distinction of David the musician. This mantle with its border of embroidered harps can hardly have been based on a garment to be found outside the theatre and yet it has the appearance of having been seen somewhere. The border of harps, essential as a means of identifying the character both on the stage and in a work of art, looks too mechanical in its repetitive design to have been the invention of the sculptor responsible for the rich Gothic carving of the capitals and pedestals of the slim columns which divide the Prophets from each other. Nevertheless, David himself is not treated in the same mechanical way, his head is expressive but, it must be admitted, theatrical; his wig fits none too well round the forehead and, together with the beard of Zacharias looks suspiciously like the sort of *postiche* so often mentioned in inventories of the fifteenth and sixteenth centuries. David's hair could hardly have been inspired by that of a mature man of the period of the sculpture [25].

It is not surprising, therefore, to find that the scroll which each Prophet holds is inscribed with a quotation from the text of a religious drama and that the group of the *Puits de Moïse* must have been inspired by a specific play whose script has come down to us.[32] It would have been very difficult to explain the clothes of King David as having been based on something to be found in the wardrobe of a contemporary nobleman and although they are not, like the dress of the Magi in the Gentile da Fabriano and Gozzoli *Adorations*, imaginatively designed, they are no less theatrical.

Nothing unworthy is implied by the suggestion that Claus Sluter or any other artist may have used stage costume as a model for the dress in his work of art. The discovery that for the face of some Madonna of his a painter used

25. Claus Sluter. *Puits de Moïse*: detail. Before 1406. King David's mantle is archaistic in style. The stripes of his gown may indicate an oriental stuff, the gold stars represent the trimmings of *orfèvrerie*, highly fashionable in the 1350s

93

the likeness of the washer of his studio floor is as negligible as the discovery that the Madonna was painted on a panel of poplar-wood or that his bills for the week included purchases of terra cotta or lapis lazuli. The use of poplar-wood may throw light on the state of the forests in the locality in which the artist lived; the fact that he could afford a cleaner may be important to the sociologist. Aesthetically the figure of David is not the most successful of the Claus Sluter group but the likelihood that Sluter copied it from an actor wearing stage costume is important to the historian of the theatre for, supported by the evidence of the scrolls, the dress of David can reasonably take its place among the few more or less indisputable examples of stage costume to appear in works of art of the early fifteenth century.

CHAPTER 4

Stage Costume in Works of Art of the Later Fifteenth Century

Everybody knows that some kinds of dress or fragments of dress have the power of resisting the natural mutations engendered by fashion. In normal circumstances fashion presses gently but relentlessly on every part until what had seemed a stable composition is suddenly discovered to have dissolved and reformed itself into a completely new design. It is true that the tough exceptions to this rule do not remain as a part of the current fashion; they linger as the costume of officials or other minority groups, modifying a little as the years pass but much more slowly than fashion's normal pace. This kind of dress, since it changes little, is useful as a means of identification of those who wear it on whom, moreover, it can confer dignity. It should not be confused with the sort of clothing adopted by, for instance, the low comedian who may choose to wear a version of the dress of a particular social class of, perhaps, thirty years earlier, for in this case the disguise has been chosen by the comedian who wears it and not, as it were, by public acclaim.

'Public acclaim' is not too strong an expression, for fashions which linger must have caught the imagination in the first place; sometimes merely by their manifest utility, as in the case of the peaked-cap which was hardly thought of until the end of the eighteenth century but which, once it had appeared, was recognised as so useful that before long it had become the accepted head-wear for many categories of people, among them railway porters and Scandinavian students. The latter have come to regard the peaked-cap not as a useful eye-shade but as a mark of dignity; they wear it on the occasion of matriculation together with the most formal evening dress of the current style.

A more evocative fashion to be preserved beyond its natural lifetime was the gown of the International Gothic period worn, while it was still a part of normal dress, by both men and women. This gown can be divided into two kinds according to the pattern of its sleeves, one variety of which ended at the wrist as a wide-open mouth, in which case the sleeve was funnel-shaped, while the other variety was drawn into a close-fitting band at the wrist so that the sleeve hung as a large bag closed, more or less, at both ends. In Italy sleeves of the latter kind were likened to a bird's crop and named *a comeo* or *a gozzi*. The gowns to which these two kinds of sleeve belonged could be fairly short but were more often long and sometimes trailed on the ground. In cut they were ample and could certainly confer on men and women of good appearance considerable grandeur, a fact which seems soon to have been recognised.

It appears also to have been recognised that the gown with the open-ended sleeves, perhaps because they provided an opportunity for the display of a rich lining – often of fur – was more impressive than the gown with sleeves that were closed at the wrist even though these, too, could be large and bulky. Big wide-mouthed sleeves survived for a long time and can be found today in, for instance, official gowns of doctors of most faculties, judges and mayors. In the fifteenth century they were immediately adopted by nobles and senators and both wide-ended and bag-shaped sleeves soon became a significant feature of the official gowns worn by members of the complicated government of the Republic of Venice, and are described in the costume books published there in the sixteenth century. By this time the wide sleeves had been named *ducale*, or in its Venetian form *dogale*,[1] though as a matter of fact the Doge himself wore a robe descended from an even earlier fashion. Gowns with bag-shaped sleeves, worn by minor officials, retained the name *a comeo* (sometimes in the form of *a gomito*) or *a gozzi*.

Gowns of the International Gothic period (roughly the last decade of the fourteenth century and the first two decades of the fifteenth), often identified with the term *houppelande*, were usually, while they were in fashion, decorated at their edges with cuts or slashes, sometimes forming simple arrangements of scallops or rectangular tabs, sometimes more elaborate leaf-like shapes. This kind of 'dagged' decoration could be found especially at the edges of wide-mouthed sleeves but it was also used sometimes as an ornamental edge to the gown itself. It was also used on the edges of the rolled-hood called in Italy a *cappuccio* and in the north a *chaperon*.[2]

Corresponding, of course, to the mouchettes, fleurons, crockets and foliations of Gothic architecture, this sort of decoration which broke the massive amplitude of Gothic dress into a pleasing flutter of mobility was an essential part of the fashion on its first appearance. It was not, however, the aspect of Gothic dress that was likely to commend itself to later generations who were looking primarily for dignity. When, therefore, International Gothic styles of dress were perpetuated by later and more classically-minded generations, the impressive bulk of the gown was retained, but the dukes and senators, judges, mayors and doctors did not adopt the graceful serrated edgings. These did not, however, completely disappear, for by the curious paradox which ensures that the wise man and the fool shall not be separated by too wide a gap, International Gothic fashions loitered not only in legal and university circles but also in the theatre – especially in the dress of dancers and Fools.

In the theatre it was not only in the ponderous massive folds of heavy stuff that the appeal of the Gothic fashion lay but in the opportunity for contrast provided by a dress that could be at the same time dramatically large and unexpectedly mobile. Two hundred years after they had appeared as a part of the normal fashion with which we are familiar from the *Très Riches Heures* and the *Térence des ducs*, long open sleeves, their edges cut into scallops or dags, were still an almost necessary part of the dress of the masquerade and their counterparts, cut into long ribbon-like rectangles, survived much longer as an essential part of the dress of morris-dancers all over Europe.

Although there was probably a short pause during which the International Gothic fashion lost its glamour and seemed merely a tiresomely fussy manifestation of a spirit no longer admired, even during this pause it had probably begun to take on an amusing aspect – good for raising a laugh – while at the same time it was dragging its way through the gutters as the cast-off clothing of the rich worn with resignation by the poor. As we have seen it certainly could not have been regarded as suitably 'mature' to serve as 'old-time' dress for the Magi or other important characters in the paintings of the decades immediately following those during which International Gothic styles were high-fashion. Included among the predella panels of the Gentile da Fabriano *Adoration of the Magi*[3] of 1423 is one in which two ladies of fashion still wear long gowns with trailing open-ended sleeves cut into dags but this is a comparatively late appearance of the style which disappeared from the dress of fashion-conscious Italy after the middle of the 1420s. Nor had it assumed a sufficiently dignified aspect, from the point of view of the theatre, to be useful at the end of the 1450s to Gozzoli – or the pageant which inspired his paintings in the Riccardi Palace. Such a pause is perfectly normal: forty or fifty years passed before the long strip-like hanging-sleeves which appear in the *Térence des ducs* and the Gentile da Fabriano altarpiece had become theatrically viable.

Without attempting to assess the comparative aesthetic qualities in fashions of the past, it is still reasonable to see the clothes of the International Gothic period as far more daring and imaginative in their design than anything that had appeared in the early or middle years of the fourteenth century, when luxurious clothing had relied for its appeal not on its composition but on the decorative treatment of its surface. It is not surprising, therefore, that the striking and elegant silhouette of the dress of the beginning of the fifteenth century should have made the sort of lasting impression that very few periods in the history of dress have been able to achieve. Both the architecture and the painting of the time have struck many (though not all) later generations as having the same magical prettiness without banality that informed the clothing. As we can see from Elizabethan embroideries, sixteenth-century England certainly found its charm irresistible, but its appeal had begun to be appreciated much earlier.[4]

The tremendous decorative possibilities of the International Gothic period were felt even at the time. Descriptions of the liveries worn by the *potenze* of Florence show that aristocratic high-fashion was carried to extremes in the gala-dress of these young men. Embroidered on huge sleeves, open-mouthed or *a gozzi*, belonging in these instances to short tunics not to long gowns, they wore devices which were a part of the luxurious uniform of each *brigata*. A diarist writing in Florence in 1416 described the *Brigata della Spera*[5] as wearing turquoise blue with a sphere embroidered in pearls on the left sleeve and only a few years later the same writer referred to the *Brigata del Fiore* as dancing in the Mercato Nuovo wearing a livery of the colour of the flower of the peach, reaching to a little below the knee. On the left sleeve (they were *a gozzi*)[6] was embroidered an arm emerging from a little cloud scattering flowers over the whole surface of the sleeve so that it was entirely powdered with them. As a part of a livery worn by a *brigata* in 1421, although the shape of the sleeves was not mentioned, they were described as being embroidered all over with grass-hoppers; parti-coloured hose embroidered with pearls or beads were also a part of this livery.

But however charming the fantasies invented by the *potenze*, with the passing of time they inevitably reached the stage where instead of stimulating the imagination they merely bored. By the middle of the fifteenth century the sleeves of over-tunics, though they were still large, were no longer worn on the arm but, slit vertically along their length they hung from the shoulder, gradually shrank in size and eventually disappeared from fashionable dress. It is at this point that both open-mouthed and bag-shaped sleeves begin to be noticeable as a part of stage costume and before long they can be found in northern paintings of the *Adoration of the Magi*.

In the second half of the century it is easier in Italian works of art, to find, as might have been expected, examples of theatrical dress based on the armour and the clothing of classical antiquity than on lingering traces of the International Gothic fashion, but in the 1470s Botticelli, painting for an intellectual circle, chose to use a short open-mouthed sleeve with a serrated edge to add a flutter to the delicious dress of the Flora in his *Primavera* [26], a

26. Botticelli. *Primavera:* detail. Flora wears Gothic dagged edges, part of the high-fashion of seventy years earlier

figure which, in spite of slight indications of swelling belly and breasts, must surely have been drawn not from a girl model but from a young member of one of the *potenze*.[7] Botticelli is not quite alone among Florentine artists in mixing a Gothic element or two into his own particular brand of compromise between mock-classical dress and high-fashion, for a contemporary and fellow-student, Filippino Lippi did the same in a painting of the *Adoration of the Magi*[8] which must, from the fashionable dress it includes, date from the last years of the 1470s or the first year or two of the 1480s [27].

27. Filippino Lippi. *Adoration of the Magi*: detail. Both the young man on the spectator's right and the young Magus in the centre wear dagged edges

Filippino, less imaginative than Botticelli in the variety he imparted to the clothing of the very small crowd of spectators in this scene, used, nevertheless, very Botticellesque costumes for all of them. Most are wrapped in long rather nondescript gowns but wear on their heads hats and turban-like arrangements to give them an oriental look. Following Gentile da Fabriano and Gozzoli as well as Botticelli himself, the youngest Magus in this painting is romanticised and wears, attached to a gown meant, perhaps, to have a classical flavour, long trailing sleeves with edges cut deeply into leaf-like shapes. If details of costume from the International Gothic period were ever to reappear in paintings – and in the theatre – it is just about the time at which Botticelli was painting the *Primavera* and Filippino Lippi this *Adoration* that they might be expected to have been revived.

By this time, however, the majority of Italian painters were choosing not romantic clothing for their allegorical and historical scenes but classical dress with, as a rule, a good many oriental interpolations – especially oriental head-dresses. North European painters, on the other hand, had hardly discovered classical dress at all. Some northern artists seem to have found the clothes of the Magi a problem and many painted them in an elaborate type of dress which they probably thought of as oriental but which looks to us theatrical rather than anything we associate with the orient at that period.

There are, however, a few paintings from the north of Europe which include elements in the dress of the Magi that were evidently intended to represent not the orient but the 'old time' and some at least of these look back to the International Gothic period of the first years of the fifteenth century. In two of them, painted by Hieronymus Bosch at the end of the fifteenth or the beginning of the sixteenth century Bosch, like Gentile da Fabriano and Gozzoli, chose to take stage costumes as models for the dress of his youngest Magus; the youngest Magus was, by this time, usually represented as a negro.

Bosch is, of course, unique as a painter and full of a belated Gothic fantasy which informs the whole of his strangely archaistic vision, but in his painting of the *Adoration of the Magi* in Philadelphia his youngest Magus wears a dress deliberately and consciously based on International Gothic fashion [28]. As evidence of the kind of costume that must have been used in the theatre at the time this dress painted by Bosch is worth serious consideration because although it reflects the fashion of the second decade or so of the fifteenth century, that fashion has been misunderstood. Studied together with masquerade dress of about the same period from other sources it will be discovered that the same misunderstanding occurred elsewhere.

103

28. Hieronymus Bosch. *Adoration of the Magi*: detail.
The youngest Magus wears a sleeve *al ducale*

The huge hanging-sleeve – *al ducale* – in the Philadelphia *Adoration*, is embroidered with a device which shows the fall of manna from Heaven, designed in exactly the same spirit as the arm which scattered flowers on the sleeves of the young *potenze* of Florence three-quarters of a century earlier. Beneficent droppings from Gothic clouds formed a part of a great many devices on sleeves of liveries of the early fifteenth century [29]. In shape, the sleeves of his young Magus has nothing in common with any fashion current during the life-time of Hieronymus Bosch. Superficially the sleeve appears to belong to the International Gothic pattern but its dagged edge, instead of being cut into the mouth of the sleeve as it would have been at the beginning of the century, is simulated by a row of hanging ribbon-like tabs that have been attached (presumably by stitching) to make a decorative fringe falling from the length of the sleeve, a form of ornamentation that could never have

29. Franco-Flemish Ms. *Lovers in a Garden*: detail. The original version of the Gothic sleeve from which the sleeve of Bosch's Magus derives

been a part of the character of Gothic dress outside the theatre. This is a typical stage-designer's mistake. A second fall of ribbon-tabs, set in a cascade at the back of the sleeve, grows from nothing at all at the level of the shoulder. This feature plays no part either in the structure of the sleeve itself or of the shoulder to which it is attached.

Had Bosch, in painting this dress, referred to an actual work of art of the beginning of the fifteenth century he could not have made this mistake. The function of ornamental slashes and dagged borders of the Gothic period was to act as a 'hem' or 'finish' to the edges into which they were cut: they were never used as a decorative trimming sewn on to a fold or a seam. Since the same misunderstanding occurs in costumes which belong indubitably to the theatre Bosch must have been inspired in this instance not by an earlier work of art but by the costume of the contemporary stage.

And this is not the only occasion on which Bosch used a costume that can be matched by stage dress, for in another painting of the *Adoration of the Magi* – the St Gregory triptych in Madrid – he again chose an archaic type of sleeve for the dress of the youngest Magus (who is again represented as a negro) and here too the sleeve has Gothic connotations, though this time it is not *al ducale* but *a gozzi* [30]. Once again, from the point of view of historical accuracy, the sleeve is misunderstood, for from the lowest point of the hanging bag of the sleeve there appears a pendant tassel, made of strips of cloth-like ribbons, a piece of ornament which, however superficially Gothic in spirit, was never used during the International Gothic period when decorations were not attached in an arbitrary way. The sleeve of the Bosch painting in Madrid bears no relation to the fashion of his own day but it does, apart from the tassel, belong to Gothic dress; although the tassel, by weighing the sleeve down, alters its character so considerably that this in itself points to Bosch's personal experience of a sleeve of this kind. Like the fringes used by Gentile da Fabriano to edge the sections of the Roman-style skirt of his youngest Magus, this is not the kind of thing that the painter invents. Bosch was singularly precise in the dress he painted; he used it to intensify his narrative, usually by selecting details of actual clothing from the contemporary wardrobe and rearranging or reassembling them in strange and unexpected combinations. In spite of the extravagant fantasy of his work it is difficult to point to a single feature of dress in his paintings in which the structure is not completely explicit and the general style explicable as a part

30. Hieronymus Bosch. *Adoration of the Magi*: detail. The youngest Magus wears a sleeve
a gozzi

of current usage, though to be found only, perhaps, among minority groups
– foreigners, officials, servants in livery, or mummers. Only the rather wooden
St Bavon on the outer panel of the *Last Judgement* looks as though his dress
is something that the painter had attempted to invent rather than to record.[9]

There are other less interesting painters of the north of Europe who included features of Gothic dress for some of the characters in their pictures and there is plenty of evidence from a slightly later date that the theatre looked back to the beginning of the fifteenth century for its theatrical costume. Bosch himself used sleeves *a gozzi* for the dress of only one Magus, but several times for the dress of Fools, musicians and charlatans. Among the amorous couples seated on top of his *Hay Wain* is a young minstrel playing a lute and wearing a livery based on International Gothic dress with a dagged rolled-hood and sleeves *a gozzi*. In the same painting on the grass in the foreground a charlatan dentist has set up his scaffold. Quacks visiting fairgrounds habitually wore masquerade dress and Bosch's is no exception. He is dressed in a hood and gown very much like some of the costumes in the illustrations to the *Térence des ducs*: he examines a patient's tooth whilst his accomplice, dressed as a Fool, drowns the groans by blowing his bag-pipes. Both Quack and Fool wear sleeves *a gozzi*.

By the end of the fifteenth century the two types of International Gothic sleeve must have been generally adopted by musicians, dancers and Fools. The most interesting record in which both a minstrel and Fools appear is a painting by the Master of Frankfurt that has as its subject the meeting of four shooting-confraternities for, presumably, a gala shooting-contest. Sitting beneath a canopy in a fenced garden is the 'king' or 'prince' of the guild of St Sebastian. In the distance are four castles identified by heraldic banners which fly from their battlements as headquarters of the guild of St Sebastian and three others. The 'prince' is surrounded by liveried archers wearing a badge of St Sebastian on their chests or their left sleeves according to their station. Two Fools greet each other in the foreground [31], one, as a part of his motley, has a sleeve *a gozzi* weighed down in the same manner as the sleeve of Bosch's Magus, by a bell. The other Fool wears sleeves which extend to a sharp point at the elbow, a mere vestige of the old but no part of the new fashion. Approaching the Fools is a drummer, a young negro in parti-coloured livery of the kind that was beginning to be associated, about this time, with the *moresca*. The sleeves of his over-tunic are composed of ribbon streamers – they are the descendants of the wide-mouth sleeves of the International Gothic period with their cut-edges now so far extended that almost the whole sleeve is cut [32]. From this practice descended, later still, the ribbons which morris-dancers tie round their sleeves today. This

31. Master of Frankfurt. *Shooting Contest:* detail, two Fools

32. Master of Frankfurt. *Shooting Contest:* detail. A negro drummer wearing a sleeve rather like that worn by the mature Magus in Ill. 28

fascinating painting of a shooting-contest almost certainly dates from 1493.[10]

If International Gothic dress of the beginning of the fifteenth century can be thought of as surviving because it was among the most striking and perhaps the most attractive of any fashion that went before it, combining as it did aristocratic dignity with pretty gaiety, motley – or *mi-parti* – which made its way into high-fashion in the thirteenth century, is even more remarkable as an invention and it is not surprising that it, too, was prevented from disappearing. Like the dagging of sleeves and hoods in the Gothic period and like many other fashions before and after it, motley was fiercely attacked by moralists which did not preclude its survival as, rather surprisingly, the dress of lawyers and barristers in, for instance, Germany and England and as the gowns of municipal dignitaries in, for instance, Paris and Ghent.[11] The motley gown of the English lawyers disappeared only with the Commonwealth which disliked all traditional forms of dress and abolished most of them.[12]

109

It is perhaps the rather harsh design of motley that made it more popular in the north than in the south of Europe although of course motley hose were an almost indispensable part of Italian livery throughout the fifteenth century and beyond. But motley Fools themselves were more popular in the north of Europe than in the south. Borso d'Este's *buffone*, as one can see from his portrait among the courtiers in the Schifanoia Palace frescoes at Ferrara, wore a dress that differed only a little from his master's, though his bald or shaven head was probably thought of as funny.[13] Yokels replaced the Fools of the French theatre and the Netherlandish Chambers of Rhetoric in popular Italian drama, while in the princely courts of Italy dwarfs were particularly prized. Paintings of dwarfs form a part of the train of the Magi in some of Botticelli's paintings and wear motley dress but of a softened Gothic variety with dagged edges.[14] In Italy *mi-parti* never became a part of legal or municipal dress, nor did the idea of the Fool as it had emerged in the north from the 'Lord of Misrule' in the early Feasts of Fools ever become a part of the Italian theatre.

33. Albrecht Dürer. Wood-cut from the *Narrenschiff*. A Fool in typical dress with one sleeve cut like a hanging bag weighed down by a tassel

By the end of the fifteenth century the increasing popularity in the north of Europe of the Fool as a literary character began to be reflected in the outburst of Fools in works of art, especially, of course, in the illustrations to Sebastian Brandt's *Ship of Fools*, published in 1494 [33].[15] As Fools multiplied so their uniforms, varied but always recognisable, hardened and, moreover, Fools began to find their way into paintings of scenes in which they seem, at first glance, to play no proper part [34]. Unless the Fool was in disguise, in which case even though he might wear the gown of the doctor or the habit of the monk he could always be identified by his hood with ears or horns, his dress included motley, sleeves (or more often only one sleeve) *a gozzi*, ribbon-like dags or a combination of any or all of these.

34. Master of 1462. Wood-cut. *Procession with Hunter, Fools and Monkeys*. The Fools represent various characters – scholars, or lawyers and huntsmen. All wear either a sleeve weighed down with a tassel or serrated edges

A sense of the dress of the historic past is very noticeable in Netherlandish painting of the end, or even of the late middle, of the fifteenth century especially in a handful of paintings with unconventional subjects such as the painting of the shooting-confraternity discussed above which must have been linked with a Chamber of Rhetoric. In the enigmatic *Grimani*

35. North European School. *Grimani Breviary:* the month of April illustrated by a procession of young people

Breviary,[16] which is only a little later, is a miniature painting of a stately processional dance performed by young men and women wearing clothes which are varied in design and include not only fashions of the past but of other countries too [35]. This Breviary, richly illustrated with miniature scenes and with decorative borders, some of which quote directly from paintings of an earlier period, might be thought of as merely a pastiche but for the presence, in the painting of the dance, of a motley Fool who seems to give a further meaning to this particular scene [36]. The Fool belongs to the turn of the fifteenth–sixteenth centuries: to the time, that is to say, when the illustrations to the Breviary must have been done. He wears sleeves *a gozzi* trimmed with a line of ornamental dags sew along the underseam of the sleeve which corresponds exactly to the sewn-on row of dags worn by Bosch's young Magus in his Philadelphia painting. The Fool, furthermore, wears a curious hair-cut which will be discussed later in reference to the *Allegorical Love Feast* by Pourbus (see p. 242).

36. North European School. *Grimani Breviary:* detail of the Fool who accompanies the procession

Another strange Netherlandish painting of about the same date, and one which can be thought of as belonging to this unconventional group, is an altarpiece in which past members of the House of Burgundy are assembled in a landscape and pretend to be the crowd which witnessed the Miracle of the Loaves and Fishes.[17] Each wears the dress of his or her own lifetime often, as one would expect, misunderstood by the painter who must have relied on earlier works of art for his information. The same attempt to reach back into the past is apparent in several late fifteenth-century illustrated manuscripts of the *Roman de la Rose*. In one of these the hero – *l'Acteur* – is consistently shown in a dress that is intended to be mediaeval though the result is quite unconvincing. *L'Acteur* wears long pointed shoes, no longer fashionable at the time that the manuscript was illustrated, a tunic meant to belong to the fashion current between 1420 and 1430, and a curious cap [37]; the artist was unable, or unwilling, to extend his attempts at historical dress to most, though not all of the other characters in the Romance.

Paintings of this kind seem to be linked by the fact that no corresponding group can be found in any other part of Europe. They are not necessarily inspired by the theatre but they show an awareness of fashion in dress of at least one period of the past, of which the contemporary theatre would be unlikely to be unaware, especially since, as has already been pointed out, the presence of actual stage dress must be suspected when fashions of the past appearing in paintings show dress which is structurally valid though historically inaccurate.

'Structurally valid', that is to say from the point of view not of the painter but of the tailor – a distinction not always clear to those whose knowledge of the techniques of tailoring is limited. Once it has become apparent in works of art, sound tailoring is easily recognised. The seams in the heavy woollen cloth gowns of the Patriarchs in the Ghent altarpiece; the contrast of soft-padded areas and those which were unpadded and the faint indentations in the hat of Sluter's Zacharias in Dijon; the stitches which thick pleats of stuff drag apart in the Schifanoia Palace frescoes in Ferrara[18] – these are details unconsciously recorded by the painter of the clothing that was familiar to him in the course of his everyday life. When such details, painted with such intimate understanding, can be found in paintings of clothes that are manifestly not of the artist's own day they can only be accounted for by the supposition that some form of unconventional dress such as livery or stage costume had been available as a model.

37. Flemish School. *Roman de la Rose: Bel-Acueil shows l'Acteur the Rose. L'Acteur* wears a
tunic of the 1430s, a very theatrical belt, and long pointed shoes

In Italy it was not necessary to wait for the first productions of plays on classical themes to find people dressed in the clothes of classical antiquity either in paintings or in dramatic spectacles. It is clear from frequent references in contemporary documents both to heroic characters from the ancient world and to actors dressed in appropriate antique clothing that although grandiose dramas based on Biblical stories or incidents in the lives of the saints continued to be popular after the middle of the fifteenth century, street processions, especially those held in Florence in connection with the Feast of the Baptist which depended solely on religious subjects, were becoming wearisome. The result was that soon after the middle of the century subtle means began to be found to excuse a reduction in the number of traditional sacred 'edifices'[19] carried through the streets and the introduction, in their place, of *trionfi* on which what appear to be strangely inappropriate classical personages began to be mounted. Attached to these triumphs people wearing imitation classical armour must have been a familiar sight and it is interesting to observe the forms it took in contemporary painting and sculpture.

The fact that it was becoming a commonplace may have been responsible for the Roman armour to be found in a good deal of Italian painting of the middle of the fifteenth century; usually it was represented by a kind of shorthand formula in which the construction of the armour itself was suggested only in the most half-hearted way. On the other hand, although the Roman armour in works of art was almost always wildly incorrect from a historical point of view, there were some painters who recorded with considerable accuracy the behaviour of its various parts in movement, and it is through the eyes of these that the theatrical armour of the day can best be observed. The fact that in most paintings the breast-plate, or covering of the torso, was far more Gothic than Roman is unimportant; the same was probably true of theatrical armour. It is not unlikely, indeed, that actual contemporary armour was, on occasion, adapted for stage use by the simple addition of a 'skirt' made of strips of leather – regarded as an essential part of the armour of the ancient world. Shorter versions of similar leather strips were substituted, in works of art, for Gothic arm-pieces. This is the kind of compromise usually to be found in painting and sculpture of the period but very occasionally artists reproduced more faithfully the torso-covering thought of as Roman. Since antique sculpture, in relief or in the round, survived in most parts of Italy it would have been surprising if none of it had served as a model for armed men in static or classical poses; it is when Roman armour is shown in movement that it can reveal its theatrical origin.

Although it might be assumed that the more romantic the painter the greater his interest in portraying romantic dress this is not necessarily so. Cosimo Tura, for example, appears at first glance to use exotic dress in his paintings and frescoes but this is true only up to a point. Tura was, in fact, interested in neither the construction nor the behaviour of the clothes he painted but only in the pattern of folds that wander over their surfaces. These folds do not, as a rule, bear any relation to folds that would have been produced by real textiles in the situations in which he shows them. The *mouvementés* effects he liked were not the result either of the behaviour of the people he painted or of the draperies in which he clothed them but purely of his love of surface pattern.[20] In this he is totally unlike Bosch, all of whose effects rose from what would have been the logical behaviour of the clothes he represented could those clothes have been found in the fragmentary or composite form in which he chose to arrange them.

Cosimo Tura, in his lack of interest in the construction of clothing is untypical of painters of the Italian Renaissance. Piero della Francesca, Botticelli and Mantegna, although very different from each other in their attitude to dress were, nevertheless, all typical of their time in their refusal to ignore either current fashion or the structure of the clothes they painted, not only in general terms but in their insistence on recording the exact behaviour of textiles that had been under the tailor's hand – their seams, their gathers and even the eyelet-holes that were essential to their fastenings. When, therefore, it was necessary to include dress that was unfamiliar the means by which each of them approached the problem is revealing. Mantegna, for instance, was required to face a variety of demands in his sequences of narrative frescoes, his altarpieces and his ambitious *Triumphs of Caesar*, now at Hampton Court.[21] In these paintings, which were reported by Vasari as having been commissioned by Lodovico Gonzaga but still unfinished at the time of his death, the attitude of the late fifteenth century to antique dress as well as the extent to which the dress that appears in the paintings was related to that in the popular *trionfi* of the streets can be seen clearly.

The extraordinary introduction by Lorenzo de' Medici of four triumphal cars furnished as incidents from classical antiquity, into what had been the purely religious procession in honour of St John the Baptist, is one of the

117

earliest recorded occasions on which a specific attempt was made to reconstruct a triumphal entry on the military pattern of ancient Rome. Cars — *carrozze* — flat heavy drays used to bring in the harvest must have been a part of European life ever since they had first come into being in an untraceable past. During the middle ages, carrying the standard, they were the rallying-point in battle and for this reason the capture of an enemy's *carrozza*, the symbol of his strength, was a matter for great rejoicing.[22] The *carrozza* was used as a peripatetic platform to carry the throne of the conqueror when he returned triumphant to his native place or entered the city he had conquered: it could equally be used as a part of a religious procession to mount a set-piece, as in Florence where an actor representing the Baptist was precariously posed, as though a statue, on the top of a column: it could become a temporary stage on which, drawn aside from the highway, a complete scene from a religious drama could be performed: it could be dressed-up as one of the 'Triumphs' of Petrarch. Today the *carrozza* of Siena brings in the *Palio*, a revival of the mediaeval custom of displaying the prize as a prelude to a sporting event — often, during the Renaissance, a length of expensive silk sometimes lined with fur.[23]

Each of the four new triumphal cars introduced into the procession on St John's Eve in Florence in 1491 was surmounted by a throne on which sat an actor representing a hero of ancient Rome attended by appropriate followers on foot, some bearing trophies, others representing troops. Julius Caesar appeared as the virtue of Mercy since he had been generous in pardoning his enemies: Pompey appeared as Liberty combined with Generosity: Augustus, Peace and Trajan, Justice. Each hero was accompanied not only by attendants on foot but also by a calvalcade. This is only one of the numerous triumphs of the fifteenth century but its context makes it remarkable and adds considerably to our understanding of the taste of the Medici and their fellow Florentines.[24]

Heroes mounted on triumphal cars were popular subjects for paintings that decorated the marriage-chests — *cassoni* — of the Italian fifteenth century. A great many of these were almost certainly based, even if not very closely, on theatrical spectacles which had been seen by the artist, just as the famous '*Adimari*' *cassone* was undoubtedly based on an actual wedding procession witnessed by the painter. The *Adimari* painting, which includes the official trumpeters of Florence wearing the civic badge on their sleeves,[25] and the heaven – *cielo* – of stretched cloths, which extend along the street and protect the heads of the *magnifici* from the rays of the sun and the droppings of birds, is recorded in careful detail. Since a *trionfo*, bearing an appropriate hero of antiquity was often introduced as an *intermezzo* into an ambitious theatrical production, such a scene would be only a little less familiar than an important wedding. It is also clear that the *Triumphs* of Petrarch, which are the subject of several small paintings and which found their way into engravings too, were presented as theatrical performances.

Mantegna's *Triumphs* at Hampton Court are more ambitious and easier to study than the cramped little paintings on *cassoni* panels. They include, as might have been anticipated, considerable scholarly research into the trophies and the general trappings of corresponding processions that appear in antique works of art but they also include more than one *carrozza* which rolls along on wheels which, although decorative, are quite unfunctional, wheels which are manifestly covered by scenic superstructure of a kind that does not appear on Roman reliefs [38]. Mantegna's interest in the social history of

38. Andrea Mantegna. *Triumphs of Caesar*: detail. The wheel of the car on which Caesar is seated has spokes painted onto a decorative disk

classical Rome and his use of works of antique art is conspicuous both in the Hampton Court paintings and in his other *Triumphs*. Had more authentic material been available to him at this period of his life he might have used it, but he might, on the other hand, have considered it too pedantic to confine himself exclusively to scholarly reconstructions. In the event he made use of some classical features side by side with what can only have been theatrical dress and stage properties designed, in the first place, perhaps, by himself for an actual production and used later in the representation of one.

The *Triumphs* at Hampton Court have suffered considerably and what we now look at is certainly very different from the work that Mantegna completed at the end of the fifteenth century. But what remains, however rubbed or even destroyed, reveals so much that is present also in other paintings by him and his contemporaries that it can be examined honestly from the point of view of dress – a subject with which he must have been greatly concerned. For those characters in the *Triumphs* meant to be wearing the civilian dress of classical Rome, Mantegna used basically the male shirt of his own day which, to judge from contemporary documentary references to theatrical costume, was the usual practice. In these sources the term for the garment used to represent the *tunica* of ancient Rome was *camicia*.[26] In Mantegna's day the white linen male shirt was handy and fairly suitable as a substitute for the *tunica* but it was scarcely glamorous as fancy-dress and in records of actual performances *camicie* which were used to represent the antique soon began to be covered, at least partially, by draperies of brocade and cloth of gold since stage costume had to hold its own against the splendour of the normal upper-class dress of the time. Mantegna rejected the mantles of cloth of gold but he conceded a good deal – long curly hair dressed in the fashions of the 1480s and 1490s for example – which he could never have reconciled with the images on vases and sarcophagi that he studied.[27] He allowed, too, long full sleeves to the more eye-catching of his foreground characters who, as might have been expected, are of exactly the right age to have belonged to the play-producing *brigate* [39]. And the long sleeves – considered impossibly decadent in Julius Caesar's day – do not, in most cases, flow uncouthly from the shoulder but are held by bands set at intervals, to bring them nearer to the outline of the current fashion to which the eye of Mantegna's day was accustomed [40]. The word 'current' is a reminder that the work on these paintings extended over a long period and, although it is not relevant here, it

39. Andrea Mantegna. *Triumphs of Caesar:* detail. Wearing the everyday *camicia* but longer than would be usual, this young man is meant to be dressed as a Roman. His hair is dressed in the fashion of the late fifteenth century

40. Andrea Mantegna. *Triumphs of Caesar:* detail. The sleeve is held in by two points on the arm, a fashionable device of the end of the fifteenth century, also the date of his hair-dressing

is possible to find several mutations in the fashion of the dress and some alterations to the original design on Mantegna's part.

The shirts of the graceful glamorous youths in the foreground of the *Triumphs* must have been painted from life. Their behaviour in movement – movement produced both by the action of the wearer and by the currents of air created by that action – can only have been the result of observation of a model. But however convincing, Mantegna's shirts cannot be said to resemble those to be found in works of art of classical Rome at all closely. Historical inaccuracy is not, of course, in itself an indication that the sources for these shirts were to be found in stage-costume but references to *camicie* as the costume appropriate for spectacles demanding antique dress suggest that Mantegna's young men, painted in carefully-observed shirts rather but not exactly like those they wore everyday, were based on actors wearing theatrical costume. Other aspects of the costume in the *Triumphs* – particularly the armours – are more conclusive.

121

The long 'musculated' cuirass of the Romans, made either simply of leather or else of leather reinforced by metal scales, studs or bosses, was the only form of cuirass which could reasonably extend from armhole to thigh without a break at the waist. The alternative Roman pattern, a cuirass composed of over-lapping horizontal strips of metal – *lames* – though it lacked the flexibility of leather, was sufficiently articulated to allow some freedom of movement. Once, however, plate armour had been adopted as a complete covering for the body, the cuirass necessarily ended at the waist, where it was met by a skirt of *lames* (which varied with the fashion) so that the torso could bend, to some extent, at the waist. Gothic armours, the first to be made in this way, often included some contrivance above the waist too, to allow for a little contraction and expansion of the ribs.

In endeavouring to copy long Roman musculated cuirasses which covered the belly and extended at the sides well below the waist, stage-designers of the Renaissance encountered difficulties since they apparently envisaged them as being made, as Gothic armour was, of metal. Attempts to solve the difficulty can be seen quite plainly in armour which Mantegna included in his *Triumphs of Caesar*. Two cuirasses, not worn but carried on poles, although they are designed to look like Roman musculated armour, are split horizontally at the waist where they are loosely fastened together by ties set at intervals. Here the device is quite unnecessary since the cuirasses are not shown as being worn [41]. The method of fastening them with laces follows, of course, the invariable practice in the civilian dress of Mantegna's day when long hose were tied at the waist to close-fitting jackets by means of threading ties through corresponding eyelet-holes in the two garments. The application of this technique to armour – which occurs in other works of art not all by Mantegna – must mean that stage-armour, made on that principle, was used as a model. Mantegna's own attempts at Roman armour in the Hampton Court *Triumphs* are extremely varied. If the difficulty of wearing copies in metal of the Roman musculated leather armour, with its long torso, had not been encountered by actors, cuirasses split horizontally at the waist could hardly have occurred to him or to his contemporaries who chose the same painfully unfunctional design which would expose the body's most vital parts to a sword or spear thrust. Naturally no such vulnerable armour had ever been worn either by the Romans themselves or by their Renaissance counterparts as a defence in battle or the tournament.

41. Andrea Mantegna. *Triumphs of Caesar:* detail. Roman-style armour carried as trophies on poles

123

In the Mantegna *Triumphs* some armours intended to be antique, both carried as trophies and actually worn, are more closely based on classical models. Other cuirasses, though their decorated surfaces are reminiscent of Roman design, end quite frankly at the waistline. Even more suggestive of the theatre is one armour, worn by a man tucked into a corner of one of the paintings, which consists of an actual Gothic cuirass which is detached from its skirt of *lames* so that the wearer's shirt is exposed from the waist downwards. A row of strips, hanging from the armhole, lends a faintly Roman air but this is destroyed by the presence, beneath the strips, of Gothic upper and lower arm-pieces. Between these the sleeve of the shirt oozes out at the elbow since the Gothic elbow-piece has been omitted, perhaps because to include it would have been too incongruous to be acceptable even in this overtly theatrical make-do. Although it naturally changed with changing fashions in dress, armour of the late fifteenth century still retained a Gothic character. The term 'Gothic' in this connection does not, therefore, imply that the contemporary armour which appears in the *Triumphs* was archaic in design.

Standing beside the youth who wears the ill-concealed Gothic breastplate described above are two characters who are the most vivid reminders of the theatrical ambiance of the paintings – a Fool and a dwarf. The Fool, or *buffone*, for he does not wear Fool's dress, grimaces straight at the spectator and makes a gesture of salute with his right hand. Round his wrist he, like the dwarf in front of him, wears a ring of small bells attached to a wristband. His cap is Mr Punch's: his boots are of the current fashion and his sleeve is, like that of Bosch's Magus, weighed down with tassels, but three instead of one [42]. Although, because of his gesture, this sleeve can be seen only in violent movement, its shape is explained by the similar sleeve worn by a negro musician in Mantegna's *Triumph of Scipio* in the National Gallery in London.[28] In this painting the boy fifer-and-drummer wears a sleeve *a comeo* with one tassel only, associated, by this time only with the dress of Fools and musicians.

In his *Parnassus* in the Louvre, Mantegna painted Mars, represented as a pretty long-haired youth, wearing a musculated armour of the same pattern

42. Andrea Andreani, after Andrea Mantegna. Sixteenth-century engraving of the *Triumphs of Caesar*: detail of a buffoon, dwarf, and young man wearing an ill-concealed Gothic breastplate

as those carried on poles as trophies in the *Triumphs of Caesar*, split at the waist and joined by ties. Here, since the armour is not carried but worn, the wearer's shirt shows through the opening at the waist [43, 44]. This is not the only work of art in which this uncomfortable effect can be found, others include a little Italian painting of the end of the third quarter of the fifteenth century, which shows a charming but most improbable ship, overcrowded

43. Andrea Mantegna. *Parnassus:* detail, Mars and Venus. Mars wears Roman-style armour; his hair-dressing is late fifteenth century (cf. Ills. 39 and 40)

44. Andrea Mantegna. *Parnassus:* detail, Pegasus. On the spectator's right in the picture
Pegasus is wearing not only jewellery but also make-up

45. Italian School. *Argonauts:* detail. The young men wear very unconvincing versions of
Roman armour; one wears an oriental (and therefore Greek) turban

with young men and women proportionately too big for the space they fill, three of whom are youths of the *potenze* type in armour; all three wear fantastic versions of classical armour, one of them an armour which is split horizontally at the waist to show a good deal of shirt [45]. Whether or not these boys and girls were meant as Argonauts or some other characters from classical antiquity, they certainly seem to be mounted on the kind of theatrical ship which often appeared, on concealed wheels, either as an *entremet* at a banquet or as a part of a street procession [46].[29] The Argonaut painting,

46. Italian School. *Argonauts.* This is the kind of ship which was often used in pageants or theatrical shows

which is probably Ferrarese or Paduan, is certainly not by Mantegna who, by the way, never used classical armour of a debased theatrical kind in his earlier paintings. The armoured figures in his lost *Eremitani* frescoes[30] almost all stand rigidly upright and the armour they wear is manifestly copied from works of art of the classical period; since the armed men are not shown in action Mantegna had no need to explain the articulation or flexibility of the armour they wear. Once in Mantua, however, he must have been drawn into the general enthusiasm of the court for theatrical productions to which his Louvre paintings, *Minerva Expelling the Vices* and *Parnassus* are certainly related.

Related does not, of course, mean that these paintings are records of a specific moment in a specific play but rather that both the clothes and the settings are based on the type of theatrical *mise en scène* of the period when the 'locations' – mansions – of the mediaeval mystery plays were still in use. Paradise, the Mount of Calvary, Hell's Mouth, appearing together, each in its appointed place on the stage, was still the underlying plan of every production whether of a religious or a secular play.

The costumes in Mantegna's Louvre paintings are, as has been shown elsewhere, scrupulously functional in their structure and it is reasonable, therefore, to suppose that in these paintings we are able to look at rather simple versions of the costumes of the nymphs and goddesses and the general scenic presentation of the Italian court theatre as it was at the end of the fifteenth century. A convenient formula for a feminine dress of ancient Greece or Rome was the female equivalent of the male shirt – the chemise – bound round the waist (or above or below it) with a girdle over which the stuff of the chemise was pouched. So many versions of this simple form of dress can be found in Italian painting of the later fifteenth century that its importance can be overlooked. If these chemises are compared with the gowns that are to be found in portraits of the period, or in other works of art in which upper-class women appear, it will be seen that they are entirely different in character from the dress of the current fashion. Chemises, which as underwear were an essential part of the wardrobe, when they were used as classical dress have nothing in common with the stiff gowns of heavy silk-damask which fitted the body closely and were usually laced decoratively up the front of the bodice. Although this was the typical upper-class fashion of the time it must, however, be pointed out that a secondary fashion seems to have existed though one which was worn only, perhaps, by members of the intellectual or artistic set.[31] This dress was a sort of compromise between classic softness and Renaissance stiffness and consisted of a filmy loose chemise-like over-dress in a pale colour and semi-transparent, mounted over a rigid darker under-dress. It is interesting but not strange that a subsidiary fashion of this kind should have existed at a moment of such enthusiasm for works of art of classical antiquity. It has, moreover, been pointed out that it is rare, if not impossible, to produce acceptable theatrical costumes based on a specific period of the past unless some traces of a similar kind of dress are also to be found in the current wardrobe, even though it may be a style that is worn only by a minority group.

The evidence of theatrical dress to be found in surviving works of art of the fifteenth century, discussed in this and the previous chapter may have seemed slender but, it is to be hoped, valid. From documentary sources, to be discussed next, it is clear that dress which could only be called theatrical did exist and that it could be recognised by contemporary audiences. In the sixteenth century both pictorial and documentary evidence of its existence is profuse.

The previous chapter, in which theatrical dress in some works of art of the fifteenth century was discussed began with an examination of some of the illustrations to the *Térence des ducs*. There are at least two distinguished writers on the history of the theatre who have claimed other pictorial records of a similar kind: those, that is to say, which record actual theatrical productions. Both argue that when painted or carved illustrations to the life of Christ or of the Virgin include incidents which, whilst they cannot be found in the Bible, appear in surviving texts of religious dramas, these works of art must have been directly inspired by the theatre. Among examples of this kind are the roof-bosses in Norwich Cathedral transept and a set of miniature illustrations to the manuscript of the Passion play by Eustache Marcadé known as the *Passion d'Arras*: there are others.

Although both M. D. Anderson's examination of the Norwich roof-bosses[32] and Gustave Cohen's researches on the *Passion d'Arras*[33] are convincing and extremely illuminating, they are not quite relevant here because in none of the examples they give is it possible to distinguish with absolute certainty what can be nothing but theatrical costume reported by the artist from personal observation. In the *Passion d'Arras*, for instance, the illustrations are manifestly by more than one hand with the result that *Jaspar*, the Magus from Arabia, is shown alone in one painting, catching his first glimpse of the Star in the East, but in the later illustration of the *Adoration of the Magi*, none of the three Kings resembles him facially or in costume or hair-dressing. But, at the same time, many of the costumes both in the Norwich roof-bosses and the Arras *Passion* are quite unrelated to the current fashion and it is difficult to see how they could have come into being except through the medium of the theatre. Their presence in these two cycles, which must themselves reflect theatrical productions, means that when similar dress is found in works of art less plainly related to the theatre it, too, is probably theatrical in origin. If this inadequate comment on two important pieces of evidence on the penetration of the visual arts by religious dramas is not further expanded here, it is because the present study is concerned not with the production of plays during the Renaissance but with the recording of stage costume, both in works of art and in literature, with a verisimilitude that could only have been the result of direct contact between the writer or the artist and the actual costume mentioned or portrayed. And, in fact, if a discussion on stage costume in England had been included here it would have been impossible to ignore the Norwich bosses in which the construction of at least some of the dress looks very much like the result of direct observation.

Documentary Evidence on the Subject of Theatrical Dress in the Fifteenth Century

Only the most imaginative writers and the most pedestrian trouble to record the normal happenings of everyday life. The majority, being neither, confine themselves to noticing what is new. It is almost impossible, therefore, to gather from contemporary literature what the great traditional productions of the fifteenth century looked like. Conservative presentations of religious plays are unlikely to have included much that was original in the way of costumes, and even innovations, when they did occur, would not have been easy for members of an audience unused to discussing the arts to describe. Hence, no doubt, the tiresome repetition, in accounts of what must have been outstandingly elaborate productions, that the costumes were 'strange' or 'very strange'.

When costumes were based on foreign fashions the difficulty of describing them did not occur because Europeans of the fifteenth century were evidently familiar with each other's clothing and a reference to characters dressed as Germans or Italians seems to have been enough to call their fashions to the mind of the contemporary reader. Exotic clothes and those from remote parts are occasionally mentioned in letters and memoires and sometimes an effort was made to describe them. A gentle conversation in the *Cortegiano*, for instance, drew out the opinion that it would be foolish to laugh at those who seemed to wear strange clothes since this might simply mean that they obeyed different customs. If a dress that was tied together with numerous lacings and trimmed-up with fringes seemed ridiculous, go to Lombardy where you would see that it was as common there as the wearing of hanging bag-like sleeves – *a comeo* – in Venice or rolled-hoods in Florence.[1] This intellectual group had already discussed the fashions of Darius and Alexander but, when they spoke of Italians, they could not agree on any dress that could really be termed Italian. Since Lombardy, rather than Milan, was mentioned in connection with ties and fringes it may be that the little community in Urbino, worldly as they were, while they were certainly familiar with the dress of Venice and of Florence, knew less about local Lombardic fashions.

In his day-to-day account of the doings in Venice, Marin Sanudo[2] must have felt that it was a part of his official duty to describe not only the exact dress worn by every Venetian aristocrat on each Feast day but also anything of interest worn by foreigners visiting the Republic; naturally he also recorded the dress worn in stage productions or dramatic pageants when these were of an official nature. But the numerous Feast days in which the members of the Venetian government walked in procession almost amounted to public spectacles and the dress chosen by individual members of the various councils depended on a very complicated combination of circumstances and even foreign visitors did not, apparently, always wear what might have been expected of them. When, for example, Mathias Lang, Bishop of Gurk and the Emperor Maximilian's representative, arrived in Rome in 1512 Sanudo, in Venice, made a note that he had appeared in a French cap and a German coat – in fact in secular dress.[3] When it made news, then, dress either in the theatre or outside it was usually described by official secretaries and diarists such as Sanudo and the author of the *Diario Ferrarese*.

One of the most complete accounts of the dress of foreigners in Italy was not, however, a report by a diarist but contained in letters home from the Ferrarese ambassador to Milan who was a guest at the festivities there arranged for the wedding of the young duke, Gian Galeazzo Sforza, and Isabella of Aragon in 1489. This event, in which many foreigners took part, is memorable mainly because Leonardo da Vinci designed a *paradiso*[4] as a part of the entertainments provided. The ambassador, Paolo Trotti, wrote not only of the *paradiso* itself but of the proceedings at the party before it was revealed. The whole occasion would have been of great interest to his Este employers who were soon to be connected by marriage with the Milanese house themselves.[5] Although the *paradiso* was the climax of the festivities the earlier ceremonies must have seemed equally important to those who were present since they consisted of flowery tributes from most of the leading royal courts of Europe.

Trotti reported that at the beginning of the evening Gian Galeazzo's uncle, Lodovico il Moro, Duke of Bari, had assembled his attendants in Spanish dress as a compliment to the bride's Aragonese connections and he described their liveries in detail. Once in the great hall and mounted on the platform specially built for them, the young couple received the first felicitations which were presented by the ambassador of the 'King of Spain'. Each ambassador, as he approached the dais, was followed by a small troop of dancers wearing luxurious versions of their national dress who performed a traditional dance of their country, accompanied by their own musicians. Spaniards were followed by Poles, Poles by Hungarians, Hungarians by Turks. The Turks – Turkey was fast becoming the most important power in

Europe – arrived at the foot of the dais on horseback and were too arrogant to present a dance. They were followed by a knight and several nobles who led a group of dancers from the Emperor of the West and finally there appeared a contingent sent by the King and Queen of France.[6] To speak of national dress in this context means, of course, the dress of high society, not of peasants, for unlike the fashions of the beginning of the fifteenth century which, so far as Europe was concerned, had been more or less uniform in design, by the century's end national differences were very marked.

Since Trotti took pains to describe the dress of both the male and the female dancers with great precision he must have known that Ercole d'Este and his wife and daughters cared to hear about it and it is, surely, interest of this kind that led to the outburst of books on the costumes of 'all nations' which appeared all over Europe in the sixteenth century.

Although no doubt increased, the interest in foreign dress was not altogether new; foreigners had been included in the crowds that streamed down the roads in comparatively early Italian paintings, especially those of the *Adoration of the Magi* in the earlier versions of which, although the fashions of the European communities cannot be separated from each other, oriental dress is always distinguishable. By the time Gozzoli painted his *Adoration of the Magi*, at the beginning of the second half of the fifteenth century, he was able to include recognisable Frenchmen, Netherlanders, Germans, Hungarians and Turks as well as people from other parts of the Near East which, while it may suggest that people of various nationalities always took part in the annual procession in Florence that included a journey of the Magi, certainly shows that Gozzoli's patron, Piero de' Medici, found them interesting.

Interest in the dress of foreigners was not confined to Italy in the fifteenth century, it is also described by officials attached to the princely courts of the north of Europe. When the newly-elected Emperor of the West, Frederick III, appeared at the joust arranged in his honour by the Duke of Burgundy in 1443, his clothing was noted. Germans always attracted attention by their archaistic dress and their blond hair, worn long whatever the fashion, and especially amused the fashion-conscious Italians. At the joust at the *Arbre de Charlemagne* near Dijon in 1443 they were evidently equally conspicuous for Frederick's long blond hair and his dress, described as being in the Bohemian style, was carefully recorded. It consisted, apparently, of a

137

dull-blue doublet and, at his neck, a rolled-hood with a long end cut into deep serrations which hung down to the saddle of his horse. On his head Frederick wore a little grey hat made of felt with a short pile, encircled by the small upright crown, the first of the Imperial crowns and the one used at his recent coronation in Aachen.[7] The reference to the dagged edges of the hanging end of his rolled-hood means that the Bohemian fashion worn by the Emperor still included the typical decorative edges of the International Gothic fashion which no well-dressed European would have worn as late as 1443. Here is, in fact, a relatively early example of the preservation of the striking Gothic fashion by a manifestly conservative community; the reference to Frederick's dress as being Bohemian shows that it was not merely an example of his personal taste.

The joust at the *Arbre de Charlemagne*, romantically named for the occasion, was a part of a political event, a meeting between Philip, Duke of Burgundy and Frederick III to discuss a recent appeal for help against the Turk issued by John Paleologus, Emperor of the East. Germans were not the only foreign visitors, Philip had called on all his vassal-nobility to attend. They came with their retinues and so did the various foreign knights who had answered the challenge to the joust, among them a knight who was accompanied by six pages wearing green in the 'Italian style'.[8] The German pages with their abundant blond hair, curled and fluffed out, aroused the suspicions of the chronicler who thought that it was not their own but artificial.[9]

The same writer, Olivier de la Marche, page to Philip of Burgundy, later Chamberlain to his son and heir, Charles the Rash, and throughout his life a faithful servant of the House of Burgundy,[10] recorded the dress of distinguished foreigners on many later occasions, among them those who were present at the wedding of Charles to Margaret of York in 1468. Described as the representatives of 'the nations' they rode together with their attendants in the bridal procession. First the Venetians, then the Florentines who were followed by the Spaniards, the Genoese and the Germans.

The care with which La Marche recorded the dress of each group is a further example of the interest aroused by the dress of foreigners which, although it had no connection with the dress of the theatre, certainly played a part in the design of stage-dress as will be seen later. It is worth noticing here that foreign dress was not worn only by foreigners but was sufficiently recognisable to be employed also as 'fancy' dress. At the *Paradise* Ball in Milan in 1489, for example, Lodovico il Moro, an Italian, had dressed both himself and his suite as Spaniards as a compliment to the bride, Isabella of Aragon – it is most unlikely that the compliment was recognised by Isabella alone. (See p. 136 above.)

In the north of Europe important weddings were accompanied by jousts, jousts by banquets. Both had a marked theatrical side and, like the joyous entries with their *tableaux vivants* mounted on triumphal arches built across main streets, included actual theatrical performances. Such courtly festivals were naturally described not only by ambassadors writing home but also by the chamberlains of the households involved. Although some of the shows they wrote of were more or less private affairs, even banquets were always watched by some members of the public; jousts must have had a much larger uninvolved audience and joyous entries were designed as much for the amusement of the populace as for the celebrities in whose honour they were arranged. Anything that went on in any of these entertainments, whether it was written about or not, would rapidly have become known and discussed.

The joust which followed the marriage of Charles the Rash – *le Téméraire* – and Margaret of York in 1468, the *Pas de l'Arbre d'Or*, was even grander than the earlier *Pas de l'Arbre de Charlemagne* and most of the champions who presented themselves at the lists appeared surrounded by considerable fantasy. Exotic liveries sprinkled with the letter 'y' (for York) were a commonplace. John de Chassa, Lord of Monnet, went much further and took part in the parade before the joust preceded by four gentlemen dressed as Moors and accompanied by four more dressed as Turks. In addition to a Fool who played 'divers musical instruments', was a young girl wearing green striped silk in the Turkish fashion and it was she who led in the knight who was, himself, dressed as a Turk. After the parade each knight retired to his own tent to change into armour for the day.[11]

Striped textiles used in the dress of the Near East are often referred to and can be discovered in a good many fifteenth-century paintings worn, as a rule, by those who wore also turbans or large felt hats of a Jewish character. Cottons and woollens woven in stripes of different colours were made in North Africa and were certainly used by painters to identify Jews, Turks and, in scenes of the Crucifixion, St Mary of Egypt.

Stripes are described as being worn by a *Sarracen* who appeared in an *entremet* at one of the extraordinary banquets, held in the evenings after the jousts, that formed a part of the event known as the Feast of the Pheasant at Lille in 1454 – the occasion of a further attempt on the part of Philip of Burgundy to whip up enthusiasm for a Crusade in the year following the fall of Constantinople. Olivier de la Marche, in his description of these banquets, divides the *entremets* which were set-pieces placed on the dining tables (a pie filled with musicians and a church which emitted sounds of an organ, for instance), from *entremets vifs* which were either short dramatic scenes played in front of the tables or huge moving property beasts, or a combination of the two. At the Feast of the Pheasant an *entremet vif* involved a giant bigger, without any artifice, than any the writer had seen, clothed in a long gown of green striped 'in many parts' with, on his head, a *tresse*[12] in the fashion of the *Sarracens* of Granada.[13] The giant, who carried in one hand a great old-fashioned axe with a double edge led, with the other, an elephant with a castle on its back in which sat a lady dressed as a nun – though in white satin, covered by a black mantle.

In a long series of plaintive verses addressed to the assembled knights of the Order of the *Toison d'Or* the lady, who represented Holy Church in distress, appealed for help. When, with a final plea the verses came to an end, the herald of the Order replied pledging all possible aid, at which point a door in the great hall opened to admit a joyous crowd of musicians and torch-bearers who presented to the company a second lady, also dressed as a nun but this time in white satin unshrouded by black. A scroll arranged over her left shoulder bore her name in golden letters, *Grâce Dieu*. She was followed by a troup of young knights wearing garlands on their heads who were accompanied by as many ladies whose head-dresses were designed in the Portuguese style, in the form of roses, a compliment, presumably, to the Duchess of Burgundy, Isabella of Portugal.[14]

Grâce Dieu which, the author of the script explained, signified Faith, then recited further verses expressing gratitude to the Order for its promises of help and, these ended, the rose-crowned ladies, each identified by a scroll on her shoulder as Charity, Justice, Reason, Prudence, Temperance, Might, Truth, Generosity, Diligence, Hope or Valour spoke a verse in turn after which, the serious business of the entertainment completed, pious sentiments were laid aside, identifying scrolls removed and the whole company gave themselves over to a dance which 'took the form of a mummery'.

The survival of a long account of these performances at the Feast of the Pheasant (from which the above description is a mere outline) is no accident. It is due to the fact that not only the record itself, written in affectionate detail, but also the verses which formed the script were the work of Olivier de la Marche who, in addition to acting as producer of the whole affair, appeared himself in the part of the nun, *Sainte Eglise*, which immediately suggests that all the other women's parts were played by men as they would have been in Italy at the same period. On this occasion, however, such was not the case, for later in his account Olivier de la Marche lists each of the ladies who played the Virtues by name and they turn out to be not young men at all but aristocratic females of the court circle, many of them wives of the nobles inscribed in the Order of the *Toison d'Or* who were present at the Feast.[15]

The allocation of speaking parts to women at this early date, though admittedly at a more or less private function, is interesting but so is everything else about this curious and presumably not altogether unique occasion. The entertainments formed, for instance, what was virtually a microcosm of the contemporary theatre in all its aspects. In the first place, mounted on banqueting tables, were ambitiously designed and constructed set-pieces, some of them mechanised, many of which appear to have been miniature versions of the kind of edifices that were usually built at focal points in the cities and towns to celebrate victories, joyous entries or other happy occasions: secondly a miniature morality play was performed, allied to a peripatetic procession: there was a *moresca* and, finally, in a proscenium area, revealed by the drawing aside of front-curtains, a series of short scenes amounting to a historical drama were performed.[16]

Since the chronicler laid no particular stress on the presentation of these dramatic scenes within a confined space at the end of a great hall, it must be assumed that this was no innovation though even if it had been it would still be a very early example of the concept of the proscenium stage. In 1489, at the Sforza wedding in Milan, dramatic dialogues and mime accompanied by music were similarly performed against an arrangement of scenic effects set up at the end of a long rectangular hall and revealed by the drawing back of curtains. On this occasion the scenery consisted of the famous *paradiso* designed by Leonardo which was built against the wall that faced the temporary row of raised seats and during the preceding speeches and dances was concealed by a curtain.

At Lille, the dramatic scenes consisted of episodes from the life of Jason and were performed between the courses of the banquet, divided from each other by processional interludes such as the pleas of *Sainte Eglise*, during which the curtains which concealed the acting area in which the Jason plays were performed were closed. It is difficult, in this instance, to arrive at any conclusion as to the relative importance of the dramatic scenes and the processional interludes with their *moresche*. It is regrettable that no mention was made of the costumes worn in the Jason scenes, which were designed, of course, to remind the audience of the hero's prowess and its relevance to the Order of the Golden Fleece; some attempt was probably made to construct costumes that would suggest to the Burgundian audience the dress of classical antiquity.

At the period of the production of the Jason episodes audiences in the north of Europe were not ignorant of at least the main themes of classical literature. Soon after 1450 Jacques Milet had written a drama on the history and destruction of Great Troy[17] and, on the occasion of Philip the Good's victorious entry into Ghent in 1458, among the scenes staged to build up an atmosphere of victorious grandeur at this emotional event was a dramatisation of Cicero's speech before Caesar in defence of Ligarius and another of Pompey's mercy to Tigranus.[18]

No less important in the history of the Renaissance theatre is Olivier de la Marche's description of the identification of allegorical characters by inscribed scrolls. This is by no means the only reference to the practice but in its application to a secular not a religious drama it is an early one. Since scrolls had long been used to identify certain characters in paintings and sculpture, documentary references to their use in the theatre may be illuminating.

Apart from a small group of German artists who scattered inscribed scrolls freely over their little painted panels (the most important of this minor company being known as the Master of the Banderoles, some of whose figures are placed in landscapes which look suspiciously theatrical), inscribed scrolls in works of art were most frequently reserved for Prophets and Sybils. As a rule these important characters were painted in rich clothes though this is not invariably the case. Since, unlike the saints, few of the Prophets could be identified by personal attributes, when several of them were required to appear together both painters and theatrical designers were faced with the problem of making them individually recognisable. In Claus Sluter's *Puits de Moïse*, for instance, Moses can be identified by his horns and David by his crown and the border of harps round his mantle, but how could Isaiah, Daniel, Jeremiah and Zacharias, however differently dressed, be distinguished from each other? Sluter dressed Isaiah as a sober and prosperous citizen of contemporary Dijon, gave Zacharias an oriental hat and, as has been seen, he gave all of them inscribed scrolls to carry as well as books. Since the texts on the scrolls carried by Sluter's Prophets have been identified as quotations from a religious play, it is interesting to notice that in writing of Sluter's work as long ago as the beginning of the present century, André Humbert described the beard of Moses as 'ridicule en elle même comme un postiche de théâtre'.[19]

In works of art, the practice of using identifying scrolls is very old and may have inspired their use in the theatre where, as an alternative, characters were sometimes identified by inscriptions embroidered on their sleeves and round the hems of their garments. Inscribed scrolls were called, in Italy, *brevi* and are fairly often referred to in fifteenth-century documents. In a Passion play produced in Pistoia, in which Prophets appeared, for instance, a character was identified by means of a scroll as *Vainglory* and in Revello, in the south, the Sybils in a religious play are recorded as having long *brevi* on which were inscribed not only their names but descriptions of their achievements as well; they are said to have worn various colours.[20]

The fanciful clothes usually worn by Prophets and Sybils in works of art and, apparently, in the theatre, though decorative were obviously difficult and tedious to describe in words and, from such descriptions as do survive, are not easy to visualise. When they are mentioned in letters or inventories that refer to stage costume, Prophets in Italy are usually referred to as wearing a rich brocaded long gown called a *turca* and hats in the Greek style – *grechesca*. This is not very enlightening since the term *turca* was not confined to the stage nor to the Orient for, by the end of the fifteenth century, it had come to mean a long dignified gown of expensive material suitable to gentlemen of ripe years and high social position.[21] As for the hats, when they appear in paintings of the fifteenth century, contemporary Greeks and Armenians, unless they are priests, usually wear high hats rather like the tall hats of the early nineteenth century but with wider, flatter brims; these are very rarely used to identify Old Testament Prophets.

The hats referred to as *a la grechesca* were probably not the tall hats of the early Victorian type to be found in paintings by, for instance, Carpaccio, but variations of the kind of hat made famous by Pisanello in his medal of the Emperor John Paleologus who wore it, presumably, at the Council of Florence in 1439.[22] This hat became popular among artists of the time as suitable to identify sympathetic characters from the East – the Queen of Sheba for example – though seldom for the Magi. In Finiguerra's Florentine *Picture Chronicle* both Prophets and Sybils wear hats of the Paleologus kind. A third type of hat that could have been called 'Greek' was tall and brimless and widened as it rose. This, too, was drawn by Pisanello among his studies of members of the Florentine Council and it often appears in Piero della Francesco's Arezzo frescoes; it is an early version of the present-day hats of priests of the Greek Church. A tantalising item in the sixteenth-century section of the inventories of the *Compagnia della Purita* of Pistoia runs: 'uno cappeletto alla greca, nero, di cartoni, impastiti per fare philosophi',[23] which shows that Greek philosophers, thought of as Greeks but looking like Old Testament Prophets, appeared in religious dramas long after both painters and the secular drama had adopted a form of dress based on antique sculpture for their classical themes.

Prophets, usually bearded and wearing long gowns with either large felt hats of curious shape or turbans, or a combination of the two, abound in works of art of the fifteenth century. It would be unwise, therefore, to consider that the dress of any of them was specifically connected with the theatre unless it shows in its construction the kind of detail that suggests that the artist had actually seen such a garment. Naturalistically painted fringes and borders sewn with over-large jewels do suggest the stage, especially as the use of fringe as an edging did not appear in the current fashion of either the West or the Near East [47].

Although from references in documents, where they do occur, it seems likely that costumes in religious dramas echoed those in paintings (unless it was the other way round), productions of religious plays, however ambitious, are seldom described in detail unless some new and exciting piece of mechanism that seemed really worth reporting, had been introduced. Apart from annual spectacles, such as the processions of the Magi which were to be found in most cities and which were probably kept up-to-date, it is unlikely that, although their opulence seems to have increased as

47. Flemish School. *A Prophet:* detail. Careful observation of an actual garment with braid and fringe trimming round its hem is evident here

the century advanced, the traditional forms of the costumes changed very much. In 1492, for the wedding of Alessandro Bentivoglio in Bologna, there were festivities lasting for several days, one of which was the Feast of Corpus Christi. On this day, to translate the account of an eye-witness, a remarkable production by the *Compagnia del Baroccino* started with Adam and everything in the Old and New Testaments, with most beautiful costumes of gold, silver and silk and with an infinity of jewels and pearls which was an affair to cause the spectators to marvel greatly. Since the Bentivoglio liveries were also described and appear to have been, as usual, immensely rich, any theatrical production would have to have been sumptuously presented to hold its own against them.[24]

This account of the drama produced in Bologna on the Feast of Corpus Christi is typical and in spite of the frequent references in inventories to individual garments, none suggests that any serious attempt was made to reconstruct the actual dress of biblical times. In the list of payments to people who carried costumes and stage-properties from one place to another for the annual productions of religious dramas by the *Confraternita del Gonfalone* which played in the Colosseum, various garments for the Virgin Mary appear over and over again. Sometimes the reference is simply to a dress – *veste* – sometimes to a silk veil 'to cover her face', but at others to a blue dress sprinkled with stars. In these the reference is, rather surprisingly, to *vestis* and not *manto*. In the same list, undated but before 1488, is an entry for a black mantle for the blessed Virgin. This is not the only time that black clothes are mentioned in this connection, for between 1490 and 1493 both a black dress and a black mantle are listed and both appear again in 1494. In 1498 a mantle of blue cloth with stars in beaten gold-work appears and also, in the same year: *Item* another widow's mantle of black cloth for Our Lady – 'uno altro manto di panno negro vedovile per la Nostra Donna' – as well as a widow's gown of black cloth.[25]

The blue dress sprinkled with gold stars immediately recalls the paintings of Fra Angelico who added a sparkle of stars to the clothes of those who achieved heavenly bliss, including the black habits of Dominican monks once they had reached paradise. Ornaments in goldsmiths' work, sewn over entire garments, had been a high-fashion of the fourteenth century – quantities of these pretty metal ornaments (usually silver-gilt) have survived, some of them in the form of stars. The fashion had been long forgotten in all but the remotest places in Italy by Fra Angelico's time but it may never have died out in the theatre. The appearance in the *Confraternita del Gonfalone* inventories of the end of the fifteenth century of 'uno manto de panno cilestro per la Nostra Donna con fresco di orpello et stelluze di battita'[26] means that while in their shape the clothes of the Virgin followed an early pattern, their added trimming of stars in beaten metal maintained a tradition derived, not as the form of the gown and mantle was, from Byzantine proto- types, but from a fashion that was current about a hundred years before the production took place. Romanesque painting, following the Byzantine tradi- tion, often shows the Virgin in a dark-blue mantle with a single star on one shoulder but the sprinkled surface, evenly covered with stars, was a Gothic device. In fifteenth-century paintings the Virgin is very rarely shown as a widow dressed entirely in black: the mark of her widowhood is usually a wimple under her chin and very occasionally a black mantle.

Among the miscellaneous costumes listed as belonging to productions mounted in the Colosseum are four *tonicelli* of silk of various colours for Pharisees. These are probably the short tunics worn over long gowns which often appear in paintings of orientals of high rank, especially Jews. In style they may have been derived from the actual vestments worn by Jewish high priests. Other entries in the long lists refer to *multi et divirsi* wigs, curled beards and angels' wings; a gown for Christ of new damask in pink lined with fur; gowns and hose for thieves; clothes for the dead and for devils and, among the dozens of entries for wood for raising Christ at the Resurrec- tion, numerous odd lengths of taffetas – some new, some old. Crowns of silver with lilies and small jewels are mentioned (recalling the crown of the Madonna in the Ghent altarpiece); flesh-coloured hose simulating the nude; Pilate's sceptre. Of all the entries, however, the references to the stars on the Madonna's mantle are the most interesting.

Although it had disappeared from the high-fashion of Italy by the begin- ning of the fifteenth century, in the north of Europe goldsmiths' work in the form of little ornaments stamped out of beaten silver or silver-gilt remained not only in the theatre but also as an embellishment for ceremonial and parade dress. Few knights appeared at fifteenth-century jousts unaccom- panied by spare horses, loaded with *orfèvrerie*, in addition to their own mounts. Horse-cloths, made of rich materials, jingled with the noise of little bells, some of them described as 'pear-shaped', or were thickly sewn with metal letters of the alphabet, metal heraldic beasts or other little devices, which must have caught the light and, reflecting the sunshine, sent out brilliant darts with every movement.

Olivier de la Marche was not the only court official to record details of the entertainments at the Feast of the Pheasant, in which a lot of goldsmiths' work was used. A contemporary living in Peronne, Mathieu d'Escouchy also described the Feast, omitting a detail here and adding one there, although the two accounts are very close. The knights who escorted *Grâce Dieu* and her ladies, says d'Escouchy, were very decoratively dressed in *palletots* embroidered with gold leaves and richly charged with *orfèvrerie*, with, in addition, gold masks over their faces. The ladies, referred to by La Marche as wearing Portuguese head-dresses wore, according to d'Escouchy, no masks but their faces were completely covered by veils that floated in the air behind them – veils so thin that they were able to see through them perfectly.[27] With these added details the scene suddenly comes to life and when we remember that the knights had worn not only gold masks but garlands on their heads, we realise that at last we have descriptions of costumes that can really be called theatrical.

The effect of this kind of goldsmiths' work, scattered over the surfaces of ceremonial and theatrical clothing, cannot be appreciated from contemporary paintings in which, apart from the work of Fra Angelico, it seldom appears. It is, however, referred to fairly frequently in accounts of dramatic entertainments and constantly in descriptions of clothing worn at jousts. The letter 'y' freely used to embellish the gala-clothes worn at the wedding of Charles the Rash and Margaret of York in 1468 must have been *orfèvrerie* used in the same way as it had been at the Feast of the Pheasant fourteen years earlier and for the mantles of the Madonna in the Colosseum productions of forty years later. In 1468 the letter 'y' had been used as a symbol for 'York' but other liveries worn on the same occasion were sprinkled with all the letters of the alphabet purely as decoration.[28] As a means of decoration metal studs sewn over the entire surface of garments was of very ancient origin but in the middle of the fourteenth century it seems to have greatly increased in popularity while at the same time the design of the little pieces appears to have become not only more varied but also more fantastic. It is, presumably, from this high-fashion that the goldsmiths' work used in fifteenth-century

48. French School. *Heures de Marguerite d'Orléans:* detail. In this late manuscript the
border is decorated in a sophisticated and amusing way

stage costume was derived; it was retained as a decoration for both masquerade and theatre costumes until well into the sixteenth century.

By the end of the fifteenth century small letters of the alphabet, stamped
out in gold or silver, were apparently considered attractive and quaint
enough to be used as motifs in the ornamental border in illuminated manuscripts [48].[29] It is from these painstakingly executed miniature paintings that

we can really see what the *orfevrerie* used as decoration for masquerade dress and jousting equipment must have looked like. Cut out, not as letters of the alphabet but as small geometrical shapes moulded in relief and further elaborated by little metal pendants swinging from their centres, these gold and silver studs were often sewn all over a ground of velvet or brocade which was itself bordered by bands of metallic embroidery and edged with metallic fringe. It was effects such as this, illuminated by the flickering light of torches mounted on long poles and carried by the liveried torchbearers who were an inevitable part of all theatrical entertainments, that earned the inadequate comment of *riche* or *moult riche*.

Scanty as most records of theatrical costumes are, however, there are a great many of them, some from surprising places. Together with the more detailed descriptions such as those of La Marche and d'Escouchy, the picture that can be built from documents of the fifteenth century is certainly one of richness and fantasy and, to some degree, of characterisation. When, for instance, the Duchess of Calabria visited Siena in 1465, the apparatus set-up in the Piazza della Signoria to welcome her included a huge gilded wolf from the belly of which emerged *una moresca* of twelve persons very 'finely and richly' dressed with, in addition, one more dressed in a religious habit who sang a song which ran, 'I no longer wish to be a nun', a reference to the Duchess's intended marriage.[30] The use of the religious habit to represent, apart from its overt significance, the Church, Faith (as in the case of *Grâce Dieu*) or simply virginity, as applied to the Duchess of Calabria, is probably typical of the kind of loose symbolism that must have been perfectly comprehensible to the contemporary audience.

The gilded wolf of Siena is one of the many examples of the love of gold in stage costume and decoration. In documents references to gold – *oro* – wigs and beards are frequent and must have signified metallic gold, otherwise the word *biondo* would have been used. In Italy wigs are often referred to as *zazzare*, a term used for the bouffant and bushy hair-dressing affected by fashionable young men in the 1480s which, in connection with theatre costume, appears much earlier in reference to long curly wigs. Not only wigs but beards too are often called *postiche*, and, like make-up and masks appear frequently in documents. Among several instructions inserted in the script of the *Passion* performed at Mons in 1501 is, 'NOTA: here Jesus enters the mountain to dress himself in a white robe, the whitest that can possibly be found and a face and hands of burnished gold'.[31] In this case the face must have been covered by a gold mask and the hands by gold gloves.

This was, however, not the only way of presenting the *Transfiguration*, for in a *Passion* of 1490 the text for which, including stage directions has been preserved, the directions show that it was contrived in a far more imaginative way than at Mons. This may have been traditional in the area to which the play belonged, Revello in the principality of Saluzzo. Here the script directs that 'when Jesus shall be on the mountain there is to be a polished basin which assures that when the light of the sun falls on it, it shall be thrown up on to Jesus and his disciples. And also he shall let fall his vermilion gown and remain in his white one. And if the sun should not shine, have a lighted brand or some other light ready.'[32] This was a device which was a normal way of increasing the light in dark interiors of the houses of the well-to-do in Renaissance Italy. In most paintings of sixteenth-century banquets – Herod's, Levi's, the Pharisee's, the Marriage at Cana, even the Last Supper – a dresser banked high with silver vessels which would catch and throw back with a dancing brilliance the flickering light of the torches, candles and huge log-fires, is an essential part of the furnishing.

If the Revello *Passion* was typical of the religious productions of the fifteenth century, the degree of realism attempted was remarkable. In the scene of the *Agony in the Garden* the script directs that 'Jesus shall extend himself on his face on the stage, while below him shall be one who shall paint his face and hands a reddish-colour, like sweat. And then when he shall have been there a little time he shall rise. . . .'

Although, to us, a flushed face is inappropriate as a representation of the sweat of mental agony, the fact that it was considered important to use make-up to emphasise the emotional aspect of the situation is fascinating. It is, however, at the same time puzzling when it is recalled that in a famous stage-direction in the text of the *Passion* at Mons a painter is ordered to stand-by to paint the face of the Archangel Raphael red. The painter here was required to go to 'paradise' to carry out the instruction as a preparation for the appearance of Raphael as the angel who was seen by the holy women sitting on the empty tomb after the Resurrection: '. . . et devera Raphael aoir la face toute rouge de painture que ung paintre luy fera'.[33]

The changing of the character of the face by the use of make-up as an alternative to a mask appears to have been normal in stage productions of the fifteenth century. In an Italian spectacle of 1473, in which all the Virtues were represented, they were dressed as women with their faces disguised by painting – *contrafatti et depincti*. Later, in Venice, a mummery was performed in honour of the visit of Beatrice d'Este in 1498; the actors were men dressed as sea-horses, their faces silvered all over.[34] Artificial effects were not confined, however, to faces and hands; in Pistoia, for instance, Death is described as represented by a nude man painted to represent a corpse – *come morto*.[35] In general in scenes of martyrdom, actors were replaced by dummies wearing replicas of the costumes which the actors had worn for the earlier scenes before the martyrdom.[36] Scenes involving torture and the putting to death of a protagonist were performed realistically and it is not impossible that even in the Fouquet miniature the torture and eventual burning of St Apollonia may have been performed with a dummy rather than an actor trussed-up as the saint.

While documents from the north of Europe emphasise the Gothic fantasy of this belated age of chivalry (expressed above all in tournaments), in Italy contemporary historians busied themselves with reporting a different interest – the representation of the antique in the sense of classical Rome and, in a more tentative way, classical Greece. Italian documents from centres quite far apart begin, after the middle of the fifteenth century, to record the excitement aroused by the new kind of *trionfi*. These, it appears, no longer looked like the *cassoni* panels of the century's middle years on which stiff little Gothic heroes, Hector or Achilles, rode seated on their thrones wearing Pisanello hats shaded by fantastic little umbrellas. The Trojan wars had receded from the limelight and, instead, the *Triumphs* of Petrarch had come into fashion and were evidentally considered worth reporting. Triumphal cars, rolling in procession round the city squares, along main streets or, alternatively, when the performance was held indoors, forming a parade round the great hall, were no innovation but the characters who rode on them were news.

When Lorenzo de' Medici, reducing the sacred edifices and increasing the secular *trionfi* in the procession of St John's Eve, introduced Caesar and Pompey into the traditional spectacle he also included four *spiritelli*. One of these, according to the contemporary account, was Fame, 'her whole person covered with peacocks' feathers and human faces', and another was Midas, 'wearing armour such as at one time used to be made, beautiful to see, face and hands and all in gold'.[37] These costumes must have been still more than half Gothic; the armour of Midas, 'armato come altre volte s'e fatto'[38] may have included classical features but in his reference to it the author of the account had not yet made use of the expression all'antica which had, by this time, begun to appear. A few years earlier, in 1475, when Roberto Malatesta and his bride Elizabetta of Urbino had made their joyous entry into Rimini, they were greeted with the usual set-pieces erected in the streets and, at one point, by eight men – the usual curious mixture – including Hercules, Caesar, Themistocles, all of whom recited verses and were described as being dressed all'antica.[39] When, a few days later, the Malatestas went on to Pesaro, verses were recited by thirteen boys, dressed as nymphs and accompanied by their leader who represented Diana. They were followed by a 'triumph of Chastity' and, among other characters, the Muse Erato wearing a 'light dress sprinkled with stars, her hair loose under a crown of ivy'.[40]

At the unfortunate wedding of the very civilised King of Hungary, Mathias Corvinus, to Beatrice of Aragon in Naples, in 1476, the six Triumphs of Petrarch were presented by members of the Florentine community resident there. Since this is not the only time they are mentioned as organising dramatic spectacles on important Neopolitan occasions it seems probable that the fashion for mounting Petrarch's Triumphs on processional cars had spread from Tuscany. A few small paintings of the Triumphs of Petrarch have survived, among them a series ascribed to Pesellino in which each of the Triumphs is mounted on a car [49, 50].[41] Although Petrarch himself referred to only one carrozza, the car of Love, his text does suggest that his vast crowd moved as a procession and it would certainly have been in the form of a procession of carrozze that his Triumphs would have been staged as a drama. In Pesellino's paintings each car is surrounded by a little group of people on foot, greatly reduced in number from Petrarch's majestic vision. These little bands of citizens, most of them young men and women, are in general dressed in the fashion of Pesellino's own day with an added fanciful detail or an oriental hat here and there, though a few wear costumes that are stage-versions of the antique. With the exception of Eros, who is shown completely nude (an impossibility in the Renaissance theatre), the allegorical figures mounted on the cars do look as though their appearance was inspired by actors who took part in an actual procession of the Triumphs.

Although in their rather feeble efforts at classical dress these Pesellino

49. Pesellino. *Triumphs of Petrarch: Triumphs of Love, Chastity and Death*

Triumphs cross into the realm of the secular theatre, they include a totally mediaeval set-piece to represent the *Triumph of Eternity*, which is presented not on a car but as a static *Paradise* from a religious drama, awkwardly placed

50. Pesellino. *Triumphs of Petrarch: Triumphs of Fame, Time and Eternity*

at the end of the road along which the procession moves (though *Time*'s chariot faces the wrong way). The *Triumph of Eternity*, though anachronistic, is completely theatrical.

Pesellino's *Time* is shown as an old man, bearded and wearing a toga in the traditional manner; his wings are dark, his car is drawn by stags. *Death – La Morte* – is more surprising. She is represented not as the usual cadaver of the macabre paintings of the Dance of Death so popular in the north of Europe, but as a blanched, emaciated woman – *come morto*. She is not

51. Pesellino. *Triumphs of Petrarch*: detail, Triumph of Chastity. Apart from a few pseudo-oriental head-dresses, the girls surrounding the car wear the fashionable dress of the 1450s

presented as old but as a corpse recently dead, although she stands upright on her car, her black dress, like her sleeves, hacked off short in a faintly shocking way. Riding through the bleak landscape that forms the background to her car, her hair flies out behind her as though blown by a cold wind. This is certainly Petrarch's *Death* and it is the *Death* of the Campo Santo frescoes in Pisa but it is also a plausible theatrical presentation of the character. *Death*'s car, a catafalque covered by a very ecclesiastical pall, is drawn by four black buffaloes.

Like *Death*'s ragged garment, the dress worn by Pesellino's *Chastity* could equally have belonged to the theatre [51]. It is a compromise of the kind often found in Italian paintings of the second half of the fifteenth century, a simple contrivance which could achieve an approximation to the *stola* of ancient Rome by looping up, over a girdle tied round the hips, the normal chemise worn by every woman of the Renaissance. One of the girls in the group that surrounds *Chastity*'s car wears a similarly looped-up chemise but it is only in the dress of the characters grouped round the car of *Fame* that Pesellino made a serious attempt to suggest those heroes whom Petrarch had considered worthy to form *Fame*'s entourage [52]. The costumes worn by members of this small crowd include the elementary version of the toga regarded by the fifteenth century as no more than a straight piece of cloth passed over one shoulder and under the opposite arm; the laurel-wreaths of victors (worn by men with suitably 'Roman' cropped hair); the flat caps of the learned doctors (recognisable to the contemporary spectator); the turbans of the Orient and the tall hat of a Greek priest probably considered appropriate to identify Plato or Ptolemy. One man wears rather meagre 'Roman' armour, his arms intended to be bare below the usual short arm-piece essential in representing armour of the classical periods. His helmet too is derived, though it is very feebly drawn, from an antique head-piece.

Whether Pesellino was quoting from an actual procession representing Petrarch's *Triumphs* or not, this is what they had looked like in their early days as dramatic spectacles, long before the more authoritative versions of

52. Pesellino. *Triumphs of Petrarch*: detail, Triumph of Fame

stage-classical dress painted by Mantegna in the *Triumphs of Caesar*. Pesellino presented *Love* as a nude boy but it is doubtful whether even small children ever appeared naked for they are referred to as *vestiti a ignudo*, with super-imposed draperies. Not surprisingly, their veils were commented on with admiration for in contrast to the rigid tailoring of the fifteenth century they must have appeared pleasingly ethereal. At a tournament in Bologna in 1490 four children *vestiti a ignudo* were described as wearing round their heads and arms the softest veils which fluttered in the wind;[42] they were accompanied by four men, Plato, Cato, Quintus and Scipio (the usual abbreviation of a Petrarch cast) dressed *all'antica* and wearing togas. There appeared on the same occasion four mechanised beasts, a Minotaur, a Griffon, and an Eagle and with them a gentleman – *signore* – mounted on a ferocious horse disguised as a lion.[43]

This last is not quite so startling as might at first appear – the dressing-up of horses was not uncommon; it was, indeed, necessary in the realistic presentation of most *Triumphs*. Horses camouflaged as unicorns or stags are referred to and once this fact has been appreciated it can be seen that in some paintings this is exactly what must have been done to the horses the artist had used as models [53]. To make them appear less like horses, those dressed as unicorns were given not only a horn but a thick mane like a mat which covered their necks; used of these theatrical beasts the Italian word *camuffati*, meaning both disguised and muffled-up, is very appropriate. Occasionally 'light' horses are referred to, light, that is to say, of build, and these must have been chosen when it was necessary to represent stags.

One of the results of the appearance of the *Triumphs* of Petrarch as drama-tic presentations was that allegorical personages – Fame, Chastity, Fortune – began to dissociate themselves from the grandiose remains of religious dramas and to take to the streets in the company of the heroes of antiquity. They could play no part in the new-style moralities based on the life of the Magdalen or the Prodigal Son, with their interpolated hunting or banqueting scenes and their generally extended emphasis on the pleasures of the worldly life. Although they were still to be found embedded in the *intermezzi* of plays on the Passion, the look of the Virtues and their sister and brother Qualities was ceasing to be mediaeval – the garments 'covered with pea-cocks' feathers and human faces' were vanishing – to be replaced, whether as

53. Jacopo Bellini. Drawing of a man riding a horse which is disguised as a dragon

part of a Petrarch *Triumph* or in some other similar context, by their appearance as Vestal Virgins or Muses. The warrior maidens of the *Psychomachia* of Prudentius, fully armed, might perhaps claim as descendants the lightly-armed Virtues by Botticelli and Pollaiuolo, but these young women are really nearer in their dress to Minerva than to Judith and by this time Judith, too, appears in paintings in open Roman sandals and a filmy white chemise girded at the hips like any Proserpine.[44]

At this moment when mediaeval Virtues, Roman generals, Greek philosophers and the Gods of Olympus could appear together in the same cast, and when side by side with Sybils, Prophets and Kings of the Old Testament, heroes from classical mythology were treated as historical characters and allocated specific dates, it is not surprising to find Hermes Trismegisthus taking his place among Prophets and Sybils in the procession on St John's

159

Eve in the year 1454.[45] His costume can only be guessed at but once the range of dramatis personae had been so greatly enlarged the necessity for devising something less cumbersome than inscribed scrolls as a means of identification must have been pressing. Pesellino still relied mainly on hats to separate Greeks from Romans, but at the Milanese wedding at which Leonardo da Vinci's *Paradiso* was only a part of the entertainment, a more ambitious attempt may have been made to devise a dress that was Greek as distinct from Roman.

The wedding festivities included a state banquet which was, like the rest of the programme, described in detail. During the meal itself there were *intermezzi* which, from the point of view of elaboration (though not, apart from the appearance of Jason, of theme) were reminiscent of the *entremets* at the Feast of the Pheasant. Apollo, Diana – accompanied by Actaeon in the form of a stag – Orpheus, Atalanta, the rivers Po, Adda, Ticino as well as various shepherds and naiads sang and recited to the diners. After the dishes had been cleared some sort of drama was performed by Orpheus, described as being dressed *alla greca*,[46] with Helen of Troy, Medea, Conjugal Fidelity, Mercury, Fame, Virgil and Livy as part of the cast. This was a pattern common to all similar occasions although, no doubt, each succeeding event was designed to outdo in grandeur everything that had gone before it.

It may be that at this Sforza banquet of 1489 we can find at last the term *alla greca* used in a new sense. Not, that is to say, to indicate a philosopher wearing long stiff robes and a curious hat based on the fashions of the Greeks at the Council of Florence but to mean, rather, *all'antica* in the sense in which it was beginning to be applied to costumes of the gods and nymphs of classical antiquity. By the end of the fifteenth century a good many references to entertainments in which soldiers armed *all'antica* had appeared can be found in documents from various parts of Italy but not many attempt descriptions of antique dress. Writers on the whole contented themselves with mentioning that floating veils and all-over tights were worn; the majority, indeed, simply called the costumes *habiti vaghi*, an adjective which may have meant either luxurious or loose. Looseness and width, as applied to clothing were, in fact, in themselves theatrical and, furthermore, a dress that was romantically asymmetrical was beginning, paradoxically, to be associated with the dress of the classical periods – 'uno et decci uomini fincte nudi cum veli a traverso' was considered worth recording.[47]

But some informative and interesting descriptions have survived; two of the most important date from the early 1470s by which time a theatrical version of antique dress had been so satisfactorily worked out in the sophisticated courts of Italy that later generations were to elaborate but not seriously alter it. In 1474, during a festival at the court of Urbino, a masque was arranged in honour of Frederick of Aragon who was paying a state visit to the city. The principal characters in the masque were Penelope and twelve queens of antiquity (some virtuous, some rather less so), Modesty, and twelve supporting nymphs. On her entrance Penelope appeared crowned and wearing cloth of gold, her hair spread over her shoulders. She was followed by Modesty wearing a chemise of finest, thinnest lawn and over it an ermine mantle, she led in, on a chain, a unicorn. Modesty's twelve nymphs also wore chemises of fine lawn edged with gold fringe, three fingers wide; their skirts reached only to mid-calf. Over these chemises the nymphs wore waist-length garments of flowered silk and round their necks necklaces of silver-gilt set with pearls. They were shod with golden boots, painted with pearls and jewels, which extended half way up their legs. Each carried in her hand a dart and wore on her head a lovely little cap.[48]

The lawn *camicie* of these nymphs is actually described as being *tela di Ren*, the famous fine linen of Rheims which had a reputation all over Europe as being, together with that of Cambrai, the finest on the market. These early references to particularly fine white *camicie* – shirts – are valuable as evidence of the use in the theatre of thin white garments, plain in cut, to represent the kind of classical dress that was to be developed later by Mantegna.

In the year following the festival at Urbino an even more decorative entertainment was held in Pesaro for the wedding of Costanzo Sforza and Cammilla of Aragon in 1475. The Planets appeared, represented by youths dressed according to 'descriptions by the poets and astrologers';[49] two ravishing boys, playing Castor and Pollux, were dressed in white garments sprinkled with gold stars, on their heads were golden wigs and on their feet golden boots. Classical boots had become important: they had been worn by the nymphs at Urbino and at Pesaro by not only Castor and Pollux but also by the Muse Erato, by Fortune and by Iris. Iris, *una vergine* with a beautiful face and beautiful hair wore, like the Urbino nymphs, a dress that ended midway between the knee and the ankle made in red and blue and edged with cotton-wool of various colours to look like clouds, penetrated by golden rays. Her boots, also of gold, were ornamented with peacocks' feathers. Hebe, an equally lovely young girl, wore a green dress *all'antica* edged with flowers and lifted at one side to show her chemise and one leg.[50]

Among the more curious costumes that appeared on this interesting occasion were those of Orpheus, Triton and Romulus. Orpheus was presented as a venerable elderly man with a grizzled beard, a Greek hat on his head with a laurel wreath (presumably surrounding the crown) and a yellow tunic to the calf over which a mantle was knotted on the shoulder *all'antica*. Triton, his face greenish-blue, wore on his head a crown of branching coral, whilst Romulus wore armour and a remarkable helmet *all'antica* in gold and silver. On the helmet's crest was a little bird of gold and many colours, its wings spread wide and, according to the report, rams' horns curled over the ears. These are only a few among the numbers of costumes that are spoken of in the account of the entertainments at Pesaro; the detail in which they are described suggests, surely, that only a stage-designer or a court tailor could have written about them so lovingly.

Although, however, festivals in Italy could include actors wearing costumes that could be described in such terms as, '*lascivamente vestito,*[51] with a lute in his hand, very suitable to Pleasure', or, '*abito leggiadrissimo* and plain, very suitable to Virtue', the idea that clothes worn by the Greeks and the Romans of the classical periods must have been light in weight did not, apparently, occur to stage-designers in the north of Europe until considerably later. When for instance, Louis XII and his Queen made their ceremonial entry into Rouen in 1508, they encountered, among the entertainments in the streets, a *théâtre*, called Mount Olympus on which stood Apollo, God of Wisdom, with his bow and his *trousse*, dressed in white damask. Round a nearby laurel-bush, were nine beautiful girls representing the Muses and wearing damask in various colours, each differing from the other in the style of her dress; one was clothed as a Sybil, another in the fashion of Italy and 'others in other ways but all gorgeous'.[52] It seems, therefore, that even at this comparatively late date, chemises in simple shapes, diagonal draperies and floating veils were not yet associated with characters from Greek mythology.

This apparent ignorance of works of art of classical antiquity does not mean, however, that no sense of the historic past was to be found in descriptions of costumes in the north of Europe for in accounts of ceremonial, if not

162

of theatrical dress, it was recognised that certain elements from past fashions had been preserved. In 1459, for example, Mathieu d'Escouchy, describing the funeral procession of Charles VII of France in as much detail as he could, wrote that the cortège included, as was customary, as well as the late king's body in its coffin, an effigy of him mounted on a bier – 'la semblance du Roy trepassé' – which lay on a coverlet of cloth of gold, wearing a crown over a coif which covered the ears. Its dress consisted of a *pourpoint* of violet damask with sleeves made in the antique fashion, very wide – 'a l'ancienne fachon bien larges'. Over the *pourpoint* the effigy wore a long close-fitting gown of blue velvet powdered with fleurs-de-lis and over that the great royal mantle also powdered with fleurs-de-lis and lined with ermine. On the hands were new gloves; the right held the royal sceptre.[53]

The ermine-lined French royal mantle, open down the right side, is familiar, especially from portraits in manuscripts. In cut it was derived from the knightly mantle of the Romans and was the most ancient in shape of all the garments retained in secular European ceremonial dress. The same pattern was worn by the ambassadors of the proud Republic of Venice. The wide sleeves of the violet velvet *pourpoint* were, in 1459, recognised by Mathieu d'Escouchy as the *ancienne fachon*; in fact they were a survival of the International Gothic fashion of fifty years earlier. These sleeves – *al ducale* – had by this time become royal and ducal features; Charles the Rash was noticed by Olivier de la Marche to be wearing a gown with wide sleeves, 'very princely' at his wedding in 1468.[54] The coif worn on the head of the effigy of Charles VII had appeared as a part of the fashionable masculine wardrobe in the thirteenth century and had been popular enough to have remained in fashion for more than a hundred years. By the end of the fifteenth century, however, apart from conservative peasants here and there and some German soldiers of the rank and file, it was worn only as a part of official dress – legal, academic, governmental and royal – and in the theatre.

For the sleeve of the monarch touched the sleeve of the Fool. In Dijon *La Mère Folle*, calling to herself the Fools from all countries ordered them to,

Vestez de velours hardiment
De satin pourpoins a grans manches
Et hocquetons pareillement . . .[55]

to appear, in fact, as princes.

163

It is clear, therefore, that in Italy there had appeared, simultaneously in paintings and in written accounts of stage productions of the fifteenth century, a dress that was recognisably classical in character. In the early days there were hardly words to describe it but in 1474 the nymphs who danced at Urbino, their jewelled and gilded classical boots meeting their short skirts at the calf, had already achieved the dress that was to see their choreographic descendants through the masques, the operas and the court ballets of Europe for the next two hundred years.

In the north of Europe no such dress had emerged in paintings of the fifteenth century nor, apparently, in the theatre. In the north, on the other hand, the presence of a 'Gothic revival', almost unknown in Italy, can be discovered in the dress recorded in both paintings and documents. Not only Bosch but other and less imaginative painters made use of it; it can be found in the descriptions of the theatrical chivalry of the courts of Philip the Good and Charles the Rash; it can be deduced from expressions such as, 'their housings *bien decoppé*'[56] applied to horses ridden by children dressed as angels and a *pourpoint decoppé* worn by a Fool.[57] In Italy, apart from the Flora by the romantic Botticelli, and the youngest Magus by his fellow-student Filippino Lippi, it would be difficult to find a trace of the survival or the revival of the International Gothic fashion, with its serrated edges, *bien decoupée*, in a dress recorded in a painting or a document of the second half of the fifteenth century.

Both the classical dress of the Italian theatre and the Gothic dress of the north European theatre were to play an important part in the design of stage costumes in the sixteenth century.

CHAPTER 6

Entertainments at the Court of Maximilian 1

The splendours of the House of Burgundy came to an abrupt end in 1477 with the death of Charles the Rash on the battlefield at Grandson. Its dukes had claimed descent from Hercules, their Order of Chivalry was named after the exploits of Jason with a pious side glance at Gideon and the mysterious rites that linked a pheasant with the Holy Trinity at Lille must have been meant to establish a connection with Alexander the Great.[1]

Since the immense success of the first production of Poliziano's *Orfeo* at the court of Mantua coincided, very roughly, with the death of Charles of Burgundy, once Burgundy had fallen it would seem reasonable to look to Italy rather than farther north for pictorial evidence of theatrical presentations. As it happens, however, the first vivid pictorial records of what are indisputably theatrical costumes of the beginning of the sixteenth century emanate, as a direct result of the Burgundian tradition, from the court of the Emperor Maximilian. In marrying Charles's only heir, Mary, Maximilian clearly felt that he was, himself, cultural heir to the Burgundian house and he certainly considered that destiny was to direct him to follow in the footsteps of Philip the Good and indeed to outdo him. In this he was only developing the inborn sense of grandeur for which he became famous.

In 1487 Maximilian's father, the Emperor Frederick III had crowned Conrad Celtes as Imperial poet with the poets' laurels.[2] Following this event Celtes proceeded both to study further and to travel. Ten years later he was appointed by Maximilian, who by that time had succeeded to the Imperial throne, to the Chair of Poetry and Rhetoric at the University of Vienna. For the occasion of Maximilian's second marriage to the daughter of the Duke of Milan in 1501, Celtes wrote the first of his little plays about Apollo, Diana and the Muses in the approved classical manner; they were very much like the kind of thing that unambitious Italian poets were doing at the same time. The *Ludus Dianae* was produced before Maximilian, his new Italian Empress and members of the court circle and Celtes himself played a part in it. The wood engravings that illustrate this and some of his later plays have, from their earliest publication, been ascribed by some to Dürer but in fact most of them are by Hans von Kulmbach, a greatly inferior artist which is not, by any means, to say that they are without interest. From the point of view of stage costume their only importance lies in the fact that the characters are shown clothed in vaguely classical garments.[3]

The publication, in the heart of the Empire, of Celtes's classical verse-plays must have meant that Maximilian was aware of the fashion for this kind of thing. As patron of the University of Vienna he was closely involved in its conduct and founded, under the direction of Celtes, an institute for the study of the Humanities on the Italian model. But in spite of this progressive gesture, Maximilian's tastes seem, from the curious collection of books which he either wrote or caused to be written under exacting supervision, to have been far more sympathetic to old-fashioned Burgundian-type chivalry than to new intellectual movements of Italian origin.

The first decade of the sixteenth century which, in Italy, saw numerous performances of the sort of run-of-the-mill playlets that Celtes was writing, was used by Maximilian (and probably most other patrons of drama in the north of Europe) to perpetuate and perfect the kind of spectacle that had been familiar at the court banquets in Burgundy in the middle of the fifteenth century. Side by side with these the traditional religious dramas and moralities certainly continued to be performed, but artists in Maximilian's circle do not seem to have recorded them.

Court mummeries (*moresche*), on the other hand, like the jousts with his peers and hunts involving deeds of valour against savage beasts, were recorded as a part of the Maximilian epic, for in his later years the Emperor was determined that posterity should be aware, not only of his political and cultural achievements but should savour his whole personality and appreciate the rich variety of his tastes.[4] To ensure this end Maximilian devised a series of illustrated studies, designed for publication, which would present him to future generations in the light in which he desired his memory to be preserved.

The best known of these works is the *Triumphzug*, for which most of the wood-cuts are by Dürer and Hans Burgkmair.[5] The exuberance of the great spaced-out procession of pageant wagons, each magnificently robust in design, is produced as much by the attendants on foot as by the lumbering state-cars themselves. The heavy tramp of bearded men-at-arms dressed, mainly, in *landsknecht* costume, is broken here and there by the sudden sprint of a single youth or of two or three together or, at one point, by five masked torch-bearers walking abreast elegantly, with toes turned out. These are Maximilian's *moresca* linkmen [54]. From their shoulders stream down long ribbons, the decorative vestiges of dagged-edged, wide International Gothic

54. Hans Burgkmair. *Triumphzug:* detail, *moresca* linkmen

sleeves preserved, in this form, a hundred years after their disappearance from high-fashion as a part of the dress of *moresca* dancers and their attendant torch-bearers. By this time the dress had become a livery; it can be found in a Flemish miniature of about the same date, illustrating the month of February, carnival time. In this painting mummers wearing a dress very similar to that of the torch-bearers in the *Triumphzug* perform a dance by torch-light in a great hall [55].[6] Another group of mummers wearing the same kind of livery can be found in the calendar of the *Grimani Breviary*.

Maximilian was notoriously fond of mummery so it is natural that it should have been represented in the *Triumphzug* among his other favourite pursuits, mounted on cars as a part of the triumphal procession. The torch-bearers on foot wear masks of black netting which cover their faces like the masks of modern fencers and which were normally worn by *moresca* dancers at the time; of the enormous number of dancers who appear in pictorial representations of festivities at the court of Maximilian, only a very few are unmasked. From the engravings in the *Triumphzug* devoted to showing music and the theatre it is clear that music was considered the more serious and important, for while four cars are filled with musicians only two carry actors. In one of these Fools cavort; in the other, players of rustic farces. Religious drama is, quite naturally, unrepresented since productions of religious plays are unlikely to have been arranged under Maximilian's direct patronage.

But neither is the polite theatre to be found in the *Triumphzug*. The omission suggests that while entertainments corresponding to the French *sotties*, played by Fools, as well as something very like the Italian bucolic farces in which the Rozzi of Siena specialised, were both very popular, when more refined entertainments were required they did not follow the Italian courtly drama. In their place it seems likely that elegant dances were performed, represented in the *Triumphzug* by the graceful liveried linkmen, but it is clear from other illustrations of entertainments inspired by Maximilian that his particular love was for grotesque or fantastic mummery of the kind to be found in the *Freydal* drawings.

---

55. Flemish School. *Calendar: February; Dance in a Great Hall*. Ribbon-like sleeves are part of the dress of the leading male dancer. A Fool, in white, peeps out behind the female dancer who is dressed in the current fashion

The Fools on the cars in the *Triumphzug* are worth careful scrutiny [56]. Although they differ from each other in type they seem, in fact, to inhabit both wagons. The rear portion of the car which belongs more specifically to Fools rises as a niche-like canopy in the form of a Fool's hood cut into florid edges, even to the ears themselves, from the tips of which hang bells. Enthroned within this niche is a frenetic, gesturing, mouthing creature who wears his hood so twisted round his head that any ears which may belong to it are concealed – it has become rolled into the twisted hood of the 1430s. In the wagon's prow is poised a far more sophisticated though equally theatrical character, whose clothing suggests the type of court Fool privileged to hang about the person of his master. From the square toe of his shoe, made in the prevailing style, grows the long point of the shoe of the Fool's own archaistic Gothic fashion. A border, cut into leaf-shapes, edges his tunic and another lies round the deep armhole of his sleeve which is *a comeo*. The torso of his tunic is striped vertically with the wide fashionable stripes in alternate colours so often worn by Maximilian himself. Between these two characters – one crazy, one wisely sane – are three of a low roistering type who indulge in horse-play. A dramatic scene seems to be in progress

56. Hans Burgkmair. *Triumphzug:* Car of Fools

57. Hans Burgkmair. *Triumphzug:* Car of bucolic mummers

(vividly caught by the artist's snap-shot vision) to which the elegant Fool, apparently acting as philosopher-compère pays, as he addresses the spectator, no attention.

In the second wagon, too, a scene is being played. The car itself is designed as a hay-wain [57]. Framed, as though by scenery composed of leafy branches set up fore and aft, are four actors accompanied by a fifth who plays a jew's harp. He wears the dress of a Fool but the hood has been thrown back to look like a collar and on his head is a rakish feathered hat. Three of the other four have also pushed back their eared-hoods. One of them wears a wreath and what may well be an attempt at classical dress; his clothing is

173

certainly abnormally soft for the period and, since he appears to declaim with hand uplifted, he may represent a comic version of a poet or an author of classical antiquity. He is listened to by a stolid man wearing a hat covered with pigs' ears and another who plays a cornet. The fifth actor in this car wears an expensive-looking gown of brocade and a hat of fashionable style but stuck with leafy twigs, a feather, and too elaborately trimmed with little bows. Although none of these players wears a costume that is really bizarre, neither does any one of them wear normal contemporary dress but, rather, comic clothes whose strange details have certainly been recorded – or invented – with meticulous care.

While, however, compared with his knights on horseback and his *landsknechts* on foot, Maximilian's actors are restrained in their dress, these two little groups arranged on their pageant-wagons provide what is probably the most faithful surviving record of a stage production of the Renaissance. It is strange that such a fascinating source should, apparently, have been overlooked.

The popularity of Fools in the theatre of the north of Europe during the second half of the fifteenth century was reflected in the literature and the art of the early sixteenth. The Fools with which Dürer illustrated Brandt's *Narrenschiff* are, unlike Maximilian's, of the standard kind that appeared in, for instance, the shooting-contest painting already referred to.[7] They wear, for example, one sleeve only *a comeo* weighed down with a tassel which must have been the acknowledged convention for the costume of the *Fous* and *Sots* to be found playing *sotties* and scraps of drama on temporary stages – *puys* – set up in towns and villages, or, at country fairs, paid to cheer up the patients suffering under the hands of quack dentists. Like Lear's, the favourite Fools and buffoons of the powerful were of a different order. Their importance can be judged from the fact that we know the names of a considerable number of them.[8]

If, from the point of view of theatrical history, the behaviour of the Fools in the *Triumphzug* is important, their costumes, though interesting are not sensational. But another work inspired by Maximilian and devoted to his pursuits contains one of the two surviving sets of pictorial records of the sixteenth-century theatre which demonstrate without a shadow of doubt an awareness of the fashions of the past. It is impossible to believe that the dress of the mummers in the *Freydal Codex* was the first of its kind but it is not unlikely that, with the arrival of the sixteenth century, a sense of the past was becoming more highly developed.

Like the *Weisskunig*[9] and the *Theuerdank*,[10] in which Maximilian was constantly present under a pseudonym that underlined the beneficent aspect of his personality, *Freydal* again represented the Emperor as hero. And here he brings other people, his contemporaries, into the picture with him under their own names. But unlike the *Weisskunig* and the *Theuerdank*, the *Freydal* was never published nor were its numerous coloured drawings ever used as designs for engravings on wood, which means that they are less widely known than any of Maximilian's sets of wood-cuts. The text of the *Freydal* is confined to captions to the drawings and does little more than give the names of the protagonists – and not all of these. On some pages corrections have been made in a hand that has been recognised as Maximilian's own. The drawings, which show Maximilian's prowess in the tilt-yard and in single combat on foot as well as his interest as a producer of mummeries, are arranged in a monotonously regular pattern: three pages of combat – *rennen, stechen* and *kämpfen*[11] – are followed by one in which the subject is a mummery that takes place in the presence of at least one spectator but usually more. Since Maximilian does not seem to appear among the members of the audience he can, perhaps, be identified as the lone figure wearing grand but not masquerade dress, who carries a lighted torch and directs or watches the performance at close-quarters. This man wears a netted mask.

Unlike the *Triumphzug* and the *Theuerdank* the name of no distinguished artist can be associated with the *Freydal*, though one or two loose leaves of rather similar subjects which might conceivably have escaped from the whole work have been ascribed by some (very implausibly) to Dürer. This does not mean that no name has been put forward as author of at least some of the drawings in the *Freydal* itself, for a Master Martin was apparently involved in its production and there is some justification for assuming that this refers to Martin Trummer, court-tailor to Maximilian and mentioned in various manuscripts in connection with costumes for mummeries from 1498 onwards.[12] The *Freydal Codex*, which was in progress in 1512, was deposited in the Schloss Ambras and is now in Vienna. A 'facsimile' – its drawings in black and white – was published in 1882 with a long introduction including notes on the colours of the costumes in the original water-colour drawings

175

as well as biographies of many of the protagonists but this publication is, itself, very rare.[13]

The drawings of jousts and contests on foot in the *Freydal* have attracted some attention from those interested in heraldry and armour, but the pages that show performances of *moresche* have been almost entirely overlooked in spite of their unique importance in the history of the theatre and especially of stage costume. The mummeries occupy more than sixty pages and although they are, with some outstanding exceptions, rather similar to each other as far as the behaviour of the performers is concerned, most of the costumes are interesting and some are astonishing.

They can be roughly divided into three groups. In the first place there are those which belong basically to the current German fashion but which have been given a theatrical flavour by the addition of special ornaments, decorations or arrangements of colour. Secondly, there are those which belong to clowns or buffoons and a third large group includes costumes which are oriental, fantastic in design, or, and these are the most interesting, those which are deliberate attempts at the recreation of a fashion of the past. In some of the mummeries only men appear, in others women take part but, apart from a few which are exceptionally interesting, the dress of the women is less theatrical than that of the men and many give the impression that women guests may have taken the floor to dance with the male masquers.

From the point of view of stage costume the first of the groups referred to above is naturally the least important. The normal German fashion of the first decade of the sixteenth century consisted of a skirted tunic, either open or closed down the front and reaching to the knee; its upper part fitted closely as far down as the waist, its skirt fell from the waist in large pleats. Hose, often striped vertically, were worn with this tunic, and a largish hat, sometimes trimmed with feathers. The hair, which was usually cut into a fringe across the forehead, either reached the nape of the neck or the shoulder. Sleeves were fairly full and were usually gathered into a band at the wrist; a revival, in fact, for sleeves both *al ducale* and *a comeo* were a part of the current fashion, as might have been expected in view of the interval of time that had elapsed since they had first appeared as a part of the current wardrobe.

Those mummers in the *Freydal moresche* who wear this German dress are distinguished from the guests by some uniform decoration which gives them

the air of wearing livery. The tunics of one set of dancers are divided vertically into two equal halves of differing colours: another set of dancers wear
tunics decorated with small flames, scattered evenly over the hose and the
upper part of the tunic but not the skirt. About half a dozen mummeries are
dressed in costumes of this character – they need not be discussed further.

In the second group are two mummeries performed by buffoons, in
whose acrobatic dance no women take part. They wear 'all-over' tights or
'liotards' striped vertically in red and yellow. Another tumbling company is
made up of Punchinello-like creatures with padded bodies, conical caps,
short staring wigs and masks with chubby round cheeks [58]. Another group,

58. German School. *Freydal.* Dancers wearing bells round their ankles, moulded masks
and wigs

177

in contrast, though it also wears vertical stripes is slim and lithe with streamers which flow out from the armholes and from bands round the heads. The clothes of all the mummers in this group are lively and important in establishing the existence of a type of theatrical dress which owed nothing at all to the prevailing fashion. Others in this category, who behave in a less violent manner but wear similarly close-fitting combination-like garments from throat to ankle and to wrist, most of them striped, wear over the top some small cloak or short garment of the kind.[14] Among the latter is a set of dancers described by the nineteenth-century editor as wearing 'mountaineering dress' whose short hooded tunics are, indeed a stage-version of the clothing of the workers in the salt mines in Maximilian's day. In all these costumes the normal Renaissance method of bracing the hose to the doublet by tying them with laces at the waist is absent so that, if they existed as one-piece body and leg coverings they must, like nineteenth-century combinations, have been knitted. It seems unlikely that this was an invention on the part of Maximilian's tailor, techniques of the kind are usually traditional, but earlier prototypes cannot easily be found either in documents or in works of art.[15]

Of the costumes in the third group, which can be subdivided into fantastic, exotic or oriental and historical, the last named are naturally the most interesting. Among the fantastic masquers are two sets of male mummers, who appeared, evidently, on different occasions, marching in military order. The first masquers are dressed in what would be thought of today as 'Hungarian' uniform, the second as Turkish Janissaries but all have the faces of birds: masks modelled naturalistically as roosters [59]. Since the only *moresca* represented in the book of Maximilian's life as the *Weisskunig* shows mummers dressed in somewhat similar uniforms and also masked as birds, they must have appeared sensational enough at the time to have been repeated in this later collection of pictures of the Emperor's day-to-day pursuits.[16]

Others among the fantastic costumes are those worn in two *moresche* in which giants and dwarfs take part. The giants, wearing long robes which cover their feet evidently walked on stilts. They carry poles with which they support themselves and wear over their faces not masks of netting, as is most usual, but masks modelled as bearded faces large enough to harmonise with the height of their figures on stilts. The lady companions of these giants may have been dwarfs but seem more likely, from their uniform size, to have

59. German School. *Freydal.* Dancers wearing 'Hungarian' costumes and masks of birds

179

60. German School. *Freydal:* dance of giants wearing striped gowns, probably meant to be oriental, and sleeves *al ducale*

been children; they wear the normal court fashion of south Germany or Bohemia [60]. An all-male *moresca* of hatted and cloaked pilgrims is masked with the usual semi-opaque netting but to it is attached, in this case, a long beard; another mummery, in which the protagonists are labelled by a caption as nobles of the Gale, Frethworest, Glasser and Drechsel families, the court Fools are also mentioned as being among the maskers. All the Fools wear bells round their ankles as well as round their calves just below the knee. Apart from the principal Fool who is traditionally dressed with sleeves *a comeo*, they all wear streamers which serve as skirts to their tunics.

Among the second subdivision, the *moresche* in which the dancers appear in oriental dress, some wear long coats, calf-length boots, curved scimitars, turbans and masks of swarthy complexion with black false beards. If these, the Turkish Janissaries and two or three other mummeries in oriental costume are compared with earlier descriptions of stage Saracens it will be noticed that the concept of the typical inhabitant of the Near East had changed. The barbaric Saracen in striped silk robes who wielded a club was now superseded by a member of a well-drilled company wearing military uniform. The Turk was no longer, in other words, seen as a being from a remote and almost legendary world who could suitably appear as a member of Herod's retinue but as a unit in a well-organised military power which threatened the heart of the Empire itself. When Turks appeared as a part of the entertainments at the Emperor's court, not dancing but marching in military formation, they must have represented a dream in which, subdued by Maximilian's superior strength, they had become a docile part of the rank and file of his own armies.

An exception among the mummeries in oriental costume is one danced by – presumably – men representing women [61]. Since little was known of the appearance of women in the Near East their costumes seem to have been based on a type of dress thought of as both feminine and oriental in miniatures of a hundred years earlier, for while they look unlike anything that could have been found in works of art of the early sixteenth century, they do resemble some oriental dress to be found in a manuscript painting of a *moresca* which must have been executed in the first decade of the fifteenth century. This manuscript has as its subject the wonders of the world; known as the *Livre des Merveilles*, it is a collection of travellers' tales including Marco Polo's and the long-believed fabrications of William de Mandeville. Like so many other recondite objects of the period this manuscript found its way into the collection of Jean de Berry.[17]

In the *Livre des Merveilles* several mummeries are represented, amongst them one danced before a funeral pyre to the accompaniment of harp and trumpet in, according to Marco Polo, 'la grant province de Tangat' [62]. The

61. German School. *Freydal*. The Fool wears one sleeve *a comeo* weighed down by a tassel (see Ills. 33 and 34) and a dagged edge. The masked 'women' wear oriental dress

artist, probably a Netherlander, had evidently had difficulty in depicting the funeral pyre itself since it was outside his experience, but both the postures of the dance and the clothes (which his patrons would have regarded as authentically oriental) were well within his powers. Although it is unlikely that he had any ideas as to the geographical origin of his costumes there is no doubt that at least some of them were drawn either from life or from careful drawings by somebody who had actually seen dress of this kind. The *Livre des Merveilles* is among the manuscripts which Paul Durrieu regarded as owing

182

62. French School. *Livre des Merveilles*. An illustration to the travels of Marco Polo showing a dance before a funeral pyre. The dress of the woman in profile may have resembled the prototype for the clothes in Ill. 61

the authenticity of their costumes to the visits to Paris in 1399 and 1400 of the two Paleologus emperors. (See p. 65 above.)

It is not necessary to assume that Martin Trummer – or whoever designed Maximilian's mummeries or recorded them in the *Freydal* – was familiar with the *Livre des Merveilles* for it is not by any means the only surviving manuscript that includes oriental clothing of this apparently early fifteenth-century pattern and at the beginning of the sixteenth century there were, presumably, many more. It is worth referring to this particular manuscript, however, not only for the dress but also for the three or four miniatures which illustrate a type of dance far more likely to have been performed in the great halls of the courts of France and Burgundy than in the strange lands visited by the authors of the texts. The main difference between them and the dances in the *Freydal* is that whereas in the *Freydal* in almost every case each *moresca* is performed by dancers wearing costumes that are uniform in design, in the *Livre des Merveilles* the dancers display no such uniformity in their dress.[18] Only one costume is relevant here, the dress of a woman who is

183

seen in profile among the dancers before the pyre. Except by chance a source for her dress would be difficult to discover, it may even have been worn by a man, but it seems to have been among the types that were still perpetuated at the court of Maximilian worn, in this instance, by the set of dancers which included Oswald Windischgertzer and Sigmun von Liechtenstein. In shape the costumes worn by these theatrically oriental 'women' with their wide over-sleeves and tight under-sleeves; their marked waistlines but low-set belts and their rolled turban-like head-dresses have nothing in common with any fashion current in Maximilian's own day. They have, however, many features in common with the dress worn by the woman seen in profile before the funeral pyre in the Marco Polo story.

If it is correct to assume that this particular kind of pseudo-oriental feminine costume was based on a tradition which, although at least a hundred years old, was still interesting enough to have found a place among the theatrical costumes used at Maximilian's court, it would be reasonable to suppose that this was not a revival, but that the same type of design had been used throughout the fifteenth century at festivities held in the princely courts of the north of Europe.

Far more interesting than the rather academic problem discussed above are the *Freydal* mummeries which were deliberately dressed in earlier fashions not of the Orient but of the north of Europe. There are several of these, all of them fascinating and one or two important. Among them is the only mummery in which a dramatic scene is evidently being acted. This interlude is presented to a few spectators on the floor of the usual great hall in which has been set up a bell tent inhabited by monkeys, one of them certainly and both apparently chained to the tent-pole [63]. A dialogue seems to be in progress involving two women wearing the steeple head-dresses and V-shaped necklines of the Burgundian fashion of the 1470s, and two men dressed in the European fashion of the 1450s. A third man, wearing similar dress, holds a torch whilst a fourth, perhaps Maximilian himself dressed in the current fashion of the first decade of the sixteenth century, intervenes. It is unlikely that the anachronistic mixture of the fashion of the 1470s, worn by the women, and that of the 1450s, worn by the men, was more disturbing at the court of Maximilian than it would be in the theatre or the cinema today. Monkeys had already performed at the Burgundian court at the time of the wedding of Charles the Rash and Margaret of York. On

184

63. German School. *Freydal.* A dramatic scene appears to be in progress

that occasion they seem to have been counterfeit monkeys,[19] but as live animals they had long been prized as pets. The costumes in this little scene are not, of course, completely accurate reconstructions of the fashions they attempt but they are remarkably good and could only have been the result of careful study of works of art of the middle and early second half of the fifteenth century. Since Maximilian's first wife Mary was the daughter of the marriage of Charles and Margaret, there would be those still alive, and perhaps at Maximilian's court, who could have remembered the Burgundian fashions of the 1470s if not those of the 1450s.

The clothes of the men masquers in the monkey-mummery are not exclusively Burgundian. They belong to the Italian-dominated high-fashion of the 1440s, which was still more or less internationally acceptable and which continued to be worn even in Italy, though with, naturally, some modifications through the first years of the 1450s by which time, in Burgundy, men's clothes had developed a much harsher character. In an early sixteenth-century illuminated manuscript of the *Roman de la Rose*,[20] the hero – *l'Acteur*, the Lover – wears a tunic of this archaic fashion throughout, though in doing so he is almost alone for very few of the other characters in the romance wear clothes that are meant to represent an earlier fashion. The Lover wears not only a tunic in a style current fifty years before the illustrations were painted, but also long pointed Gothic shoes which had quite disappeared from high-fashion by the beginning of the sixteenth century. In dressing the hero in a costume intended to convey the period at which the book was written but leaving the minor characters in modern dress the artist was following a practice used in the theatre throughout the sixteenth and seventeenth centuries.[21]

Remarkable, however, as the appearance of dress belonging to styles which had been worn fifty years previously, even more astonishing is a *moresca* in the *Freydal* presented by Franciscus Prager, in which both men and women take part in a round dance wearing costumes of the International Gothic fashion [64]. The men's sleeves are, in shape, *a comeo* trimmed along their length by a serrated fringe in the same manner as the similar ornamentation that Bosch used to decorate the seams of the sleeve of the negro Magus in his Philadelphia *Adoration of the Magi*. On their heads the men in the *Freydal* dance wear rolled hoods – *chaperons* – in the simple form in which they could be found at the beginning of the fifteenth century. The costumes of the women dancers in this mummery are as striking as those of the men. As their long gowns lie on the ground in long trailing trains they fall into soft heavy folds, reminiscent of paintings by Campin or the van Eycks but quite unlike the gowns of the beginning of the sixteenth century which depended for their effect on stiff folds. Round their waists the *Freydal* women wear

64. German School. *Freydal.* Dancers performing a round dance wearing costumes based on those of the early fifteenth century

belts with immensely long ends which hang down behind, a feature of the high-fashion of the first decade of the fifteenth century. Although one of the women is crowned so that her hair is to some extent concealed, the other two are bareheaded and, most surprisingly of all, wear their hair dressed in a fashion that would have been reasonable at the beginning of the fifteenth century but quite unacceptable at the beginning of the sixteenth.

As almost always happens when actresses on the stage or the screen wear fashions of an earlier period their stance is wrong for the date of the dress they wear. The *Freydal* women, too, affect a wrong posture for they stand erect whereas, had their gowns been reconstructed accurately from the International Gothic model, the waistline would have been set higher and the wearer, in consequence, could have carried the weight of her train only by thrusting her hip-bones and, to balance them, her neck and her head forward. Worn in this way the International Gothic character of the dress would have been instantly recognisable but this would have been a great deal to ask of any period.

The *Freydal* mummers described above are dressed in costumes that are different from each other in date; they are not the only dancers to wear fashions of the past. A third, a *moresca* presented by members of the Thurm family, explored another decade – the male dress of the Burgundian 1460s [65]. This, with its small balloon-like projections at the top of the arm and its conical cap was distinctive and national. Its reconstruction is, more-over, the most accurate of the three, involving as it does a tunic whose construction, though rather elaborate, was entirely obsolete at the *Freydal* period. An inserted segment of a circle at the back of the tunic, its rigid folds held firmly in place by means of an internal mechanism, was an idea so fully exploited in the second half of the fifteenth century that it had worn itself out and disappeared by the beginning of the sixteenth.[22] In addition, the dancers wear not only pointed shoes – still fashionable in the 1460s – but over them the fifteenth-century *pattens* which survived as functional protec-tions from the weather but which were, briefly, a part of high-fashion and worn at the courts of Philip the Good and his son Charles.[23]

The reproduction of past fashions not merely in works of figurative art – images in paint or pen on a flat surface – but as articulated structures, must have been the result of a combination of scholarly research with skilled tailoring (the two may have been carried out by the same person). This must finally remove any doubt as to the ability of stage-designers of the Renaissance to use the source-material available to them with a sympathetic understanding both of the homogeneity of each fashion and, to a remarkable extent, of the system on which each was made.

65. German School. *Freydal*. The male dancers wear French or Burgundian dress of the late 1450s to early 1460s

From the theatrical costumes represented in the *Triumphzug* and the *Freydal* it may be concluded that such Italian engravings of classical themes as must have penetrated Maximilian's court had no great appeal as sources for the more popular forms of entertainment. But experimental productions,

66. German School. *Freydal.* An enthroned king and queen bestow gifts on masked figures, probably women

staged, perhaps, in universities, probably did venture away from the theme of the past glories of the ancestry of Maximilian's first wife, Mary of Burgundy (who had died long before the *Freydal* was composed), and explore the kind of thing that was being performed in the contemporary Italian theatre.

Not all the references implied in the *Freydal* can be understood today. Some masquers certainly represent huntsmen and some others may wear rural or even romantically pastoral dress. There is a *moresca* in which men, wearing short soft tunics with hanging-sleeves *al ducale*, wear an ornament on the left sleeve reminiscent of another aspect of the fashion of the beginning of the fifteenth century. There is also one in which the dancers wear south German masculine dress of the early 1490s, which is nearer to the *Freydal* in period but still 'antique'. Different from any of the other mummeries is a remarkable scene performed either by women or by actors dressed as women who distribute and receive prizes of wreaths and little money-bags [66]. All wear elegant striped gowns, red, white and green, which reach the ground and extend upwards, fitting the torso closely, to form tightly fitted hoods that cover their heads; over their hoods they wear crowns. The mummery, which is not performed as a dance, appears to have been set in the open air among trees and tents and it seems likely that the masquers are meant to belong to a period much earlier than the fifteenth century. The scene has a legendary air and might, perhaps, look back to the Crusades or represent some romantic episode of the court of King Arthur. What is astonishing is that the costumes are entirely free from the influence of the fashion that prevailed at the time.

The *Freydal* drawings show that, though courtly, these entertainments were simple, unsophisticated and a little lumpish. They were seen, of course, through the eyes of an artist of very minor talent and if they lack the swagger of the masquers in the *Triumphzug* they also lacked a Dürer or a Burgkmair to report them. But their importance as evidence of stage costume of their period cannot be over-estimated. Not only do they demonstrate a highly developed historical sense of fashions of the past which could only have been the result of considerable research, but they support the discovery of similar past fashions in works of pictorial art, some of them important paintings, inspired, in all probability by theatrical performances. Bosch's careful selection of certain characters, such as the minstrel who sits on the hay-wain (see p. 108), to wear the dress of the past, is an obvious example, but there are other paintings of the north of Europe executed in the fifteenth and sixteenth centuries which deserve to be looked at with a fresh eye once the dress recorded in the *Freydal* mummeries has been studied.

The *Freydal* shows that in the interval which had elapsed since the beginning of the fifteenth century a new appreciation of the effect that could be produced by the grouping together of costumes of uniform design had emerged. This had been accepted in Italy considerably earlier – the dress of the nymphs that danced at Urbino in 1474 had already achieved the unity of costume design of a modern *corps de ballet* that is planned to provide a background against which the dress of the prima ballerina, of unique design, stands out. The effectiveness of this repeating pattern which produced a unity of both colour and composition was realised partly, no doubt, as a result of the fifteenth century's growing taste for ornamental household liveries of uniform design, based themselves, very probably, on the liveries of the *potenze* of the early years of the century. It was a dramatic effect well understood, from its very early days, by the Church, and it was to lead, in the seventeenth century, to the creation of a uniform dress for military wear. The costumes in the *moresche* depicted in the *Livre des Merveilles*, which include various costumes of oriental design, have no aesthetic unity. Compared with these the Maximilian entertainments look very modern or, rather, very much a part of recent taste.

CHAPTER 7

Costume in the Italian Theatre of the Sixteenth Century

If it is true that some fashions in dress excite the imagination to such a degree that before being allowed to disappear they are retained as official or theatrical costume for a long period of time then, having discovered that one such fashion was motley, or *mi-parti* and another the sweeping sleeves with serrated edges of International Gothic dress, it should be possible to find others. It would, at the same time, be unreasonable to expect ideas as strikingly original as *mi-parti*[1] or as romantically appealing as International Gothic compositions to appear very often or at short intervals.

Leaving aside small details of dress that were bound to survive as vestiges, the next important additions to the static official and theatrical wardrobes were two types of male dress which emerged in the last decade of the fifteenth century. The first of these consisted of long tight-fitted hose which extended to the waist where they were met by a close-fitted jacket or waistcoat; the second was a fairly voluminous knee-length tunic. Both, retained beyond their natural span as livery, eventually found their way into the theatre but not, of course, immediately.

Throughout the fifteenth century all masculine dress had included long hose, joined at the crutch and covering the buttocks, attached, by means of ties passed through a horizontal row of eyelet-holes to a firmly constructed, tight, waist-length jacket which can probably be identified with the English *doublet* (a lined or *double* garment), the French *pourpoint* and the Italian *farsetto* or *farsettino*. The upper part of the hose was lined with leather or some stiff textile so that it fitted smoothly round the hips. Normally hose were braced so tightly to the jacket that in order to perform actions demanding freedom of movement it was usually necessary to loosen the ties at the waist, a practice that was recorded by a number of Renaissance painters portraying scenes of violence.[2] Over these two under-garments was worn a tunic, a gown or a sleeveless tabard: beneath them, the shirt. Tunics and tabards varied in length and design according to the current fashion, and gowns according to the standing of the wearer for they usually represented either some form of official dress or were worn by gentlemen of exceptional dignity. It became apparent towards the end of the fifteenth century, however, that an over-garment of any kind could sometimes be dispensed with by young men of fashion – at first this was exceptional but by the century's end it had become almost the rule. A loose coat or mantle, often slung carelessly across the body, was sometimes added as an affectation or to provide extra warmth but it was no longer a social necessity.

As a result, the effect of a naked body was produced, coloured variously according to trifling changes of fashion or to the taste of the wearer. A further slight elaboration could be etched, as it were, on the surface of this outer skin by cutting small slits in its fabric (usually to reveal a lining of a different colour), which were terminated, sometimes by little hanging ties. The effect of decorated nudity was enhanced by a separate covering to fit over the genital organs to which attention was called by additional ties or ribbons. It was, needless to say, hardly a fashion to recommend itself to the middle-aged – less still to the aged – a point which the theatre eventually took up. (See pp. 261–5 below.)

The coincidence of a costume of this kind with the discovery of the aesthetic possibilities of the nude and its consequent acceptance in works of art was not, of course, accidental. Young men who had stripped themselves of their outer garments began to appear in works of art of the 1470s, but as subsidiary characters; the fashion for imitation nudity in dress reached its height at about the time that Michelangelo was painting the Sistine Chapel ceiling.

The second fashion from the same period which was to be retained beyond its normal span was one that belonged essentially to the north of Europe and which was often associated with the Emperor Maximilian I. It is the kind of dress in which he most frequently appeared in works of art associated with him, especially, if Quirin von Leitner was correct in identifying him as the lone figure in most of the *moresche*, in the *Freydal.* Although this type of dress is familiar to us mainly through south German works of art – by Dürer and Hans Burgkmair especially – as a fashion it was international, for it certainly spread from the north of Europe to Italy in due course. It provided a comfortable alternative to the exacting fashion for mock-nudity and even as high-fashion it survived for a comparatively long time; Henry VIII is shown as wearing it in most of his portraits by or after Holbein.

The characteristic features of this garment were a fairly close-fitting upper part, that followed the lines of the torso down to the waist, moderately ample sleeves drawn to a narrow opening at the wrist and a skirt that hung in heavy pleats to about the knee or a little below. It could be either open or closed down the front, but the closed variety was the more typical. The neckline of this tunic (for which it would be unwise to attempt to find a contemporary name) was often cut to a fairly low square or oval shape in front to show an expanse of shirt rising to a tight neck-band, but as slight changes in fashion occurred necklines of both tunic and shirt varied a little. In view of the fact that at the beginning of the sixteenth century both the forms of dress discussed above were a part of the current fashion, when they appeared in the theatre of the time it was as normal modern dress not as stage costume. Neither could play a useful part as historical costume until towards the end of the sixteenth century although the jacket and hose combination was soon appreciated for the sprightliness of its design and when it began to retreat, as popular contemporary dress, in the middle of the second decade of the sixteenth century, it passed almost immediately into both civil and military livery. It was as livery that it appeared, with the addition of streamers attached to the shoulders and bells round the knees, as the uniform of the masked torch-bearers in the *Triumphzug*.

Apart from this special use as livery, like the Maximilian-type skirted tunic, the jacket and hose disappeared from the fashionable wardrobe for a long time before it could emerge, as antique dress in the northern sense, towards the end of the sixteenth century. Once they had made their reappearance, however, these two fashions were found to be extremely useful, both to painters and in the theatre and, like International Gothic sleeves, they remained for a considerable period of time, during which they served all sorts of romantic purposes.[3] Having more or less worn out this second usefulness by the end of the seventeenth century, they sank into oblivion once more, to be given yet another revival as a part of the Romanticism of the end of the eighteenth century. The earlier eighteenth century had, itself, adopted its own type of romantic dress, based mainly on paintings by van Dyck, but that is of no concern here.

In the Italian theatre, meanwhile, few productions seem to have looked back to anything but classical antiquity for their themes, with the result that there was no necessity to discover types of dress appropriate to the presentation of historical dramas of any other kind. Gods, demi-gods and nymphs appeared in garments of increasing richness and, since no male equivalents of nymphs could be found (apart from satyrs, too uncouth to be suitable partners for the boudoir nymphs of Renaissance drama) shepherds were promoted to a higher station in life in order to play opposite them; the idea was borrowed, of course, from Ovid and Virgil who were responsible for the whole of the pastoral revival. In the sixteenth-century theatre shepherds usually appeared not singly but in troups.[4]

Social changes, as is natural, seldom coincide with the change from one century to the next; the various types of theatrical entertainment which had been developing in Italy throughout the fifteenth century remained in being during most of the sixteenth. Drama itself ranged from elaborate productions of religious plays, through the classical pieces given in the princely courts, to the rustic low-comedy offerings of the Rozzi of Siena and their brethren assembled under similar rough names. Translations of the plays of Terence and Plautus were performed more and more frequently in the princely circles and, as their names became over-familiar and especially after the encouraging success of Bibbiena's *Calandra*,[5] new plays, not unlike them in character, setting and plot, but more topical in detail, were written and produced in increasing numbers. As for other forms of entertainment, bands of young men such as the *Compagnie della Calza* of Venice and their counterparts in other cities still provided the spectacles required for joyous entries and other noble or elegant occasions (they performed at weddings and banquets), and undoubtedly, though unrecorded, street-shows and fragments of drama performed in markets and fair-grounds remained unchanged except for details of dialogue which must, of course, have been kept up to date.

Important developments in the Italian theatre of the sixteenth century were not so much in the kind of entertainments provided as in the increasing luxury with which they were presented. Mechanical effects, designed with ever greater ingenuity, although staged in the intervals between the acts of dramas, seem often to have been the main attraction of the evening. The most popular of them were transformation scenes which frequently included the use of artificial fire and it was *apparati* of this kind which, used as *intermezzi*, could replace the simple mummeries of the fifteenth century, although these, too, still survived and, embedded in complicated stage sets, were presented in a new form in which little mimed narratives were acted out to the accompaniment of music.[6]

All this meant that such greatly elaborated entertainments could no longer be staged on triumphal cars in streets and city squares since they needed skilled preparation in suitable conditions. Even if they were intended to be presented out of doors they probably included water-shows, designed to take place in shallow water round small artificial islands from which were launched little boats that did battle with huge mechanical sea-monsters. They needed conditions, that is to say, only to be found in private parks or, if they were to depend wholly on specially constructed settings, enclosed courtyards, free from daily traffic.[7] Those entertainments which were planned to be produced indoors required, to an increasing degree, large halls, appropriately equipped — halls which began to be, in fact, private theatres. There were exceptions; joyous entries by their very nature had to be conducted in the public life of the city and productions involving a good deal of careful preparation were still, now and then, presented in public, but they were growing less and less frequent.

With the growth of the private theatre grew the importance of the engineer and, side by side with him, the stage-designer whose presence, although he is seldom mentioned, can often be deduced from descriptions of the results of his work. Stage costumes such as those worn by the nymphs at Urbino or by members of the *Freydal* mummeries could only have come into being through the offices of a designer who, in the earlier days, may very well have been the master tailor too. The apparent progression from a collection of costumes, individually designed, to the sort of uniformity of the groups of costumes worn at Urbino and in the *Freydal moresche* was already a move towards greater theatricality in the modern sense and as the sixteenth century advanced, it can be seen that massed effects of this kind, as well as subtle mutations within them, were increased in size and significance.

Meanwhile a vocabulary of terms which could be applied to stage costumes began to appear which meant that descriptions of them ran more smoothly and, probably because details of costumes could be more precisely named, they began to be seen more clearly. As early as 1513 the newly-elected Pope, Leo X, ordered a grandiose banquet accompanied by a production of the *Penulo* of Plautus in Latin as a part of the welcome to members of his family.[8] This was supported by an eclogue and other delightful inventions of the *letterati*, all of which were minutely recorded. It was ordered that no actor taking part should be a foreigner or a person of low descent; in the event almost all were sons of the first families of Rome, charming youths, the majority still unbearded, who spoke the purest Latin and wore, for the occasion, the ultimate refinements in antique dress.[9]

All wore flesh-coloured hose which, by appearing as bare legs, would resemble the antique, and over them boots of classical design which, the writer (an eye-witness) reported, were called *socci*. The *socci* were, it appears, sky-blue tied with knots of ribbon and ornamented with various precious stones of immense value. The first character to appear on the stage was the poet himself who, having outlined the action of the play, gave way to the reciter of the Prologue. Apart from his classical shirt of finest white material and exceedingly ample cut, the latter wore *socci*, and a white damask mantle lined with gold and knotted on the shoulder in the antique manner. He called upon the audience to give their attention to the play about to be performed whereupon the first actor in the drama, Agorastocles, made his entrance, a shining garland of gold on his head. He wore a rich *camicia* of transparent silk with touches of black, its sleeves elegantly wide and trimmed with tassels of black silk, and over this a tunic of cloth of gold covered with white damask slashed here and there so that the gold showed through. Over his shirt and tunic, Agorastocles wore a mantle of turquoise blue lined with gold, knotted on the shoulder and thrown back so that more of the lining than of the right side could be seen and almost the whole of his tunic was revealed. His bare-headed servant, Milfiones, was dressed in an ample tunic of black silk and an over-tunic knotted on the shoulders. The two sisters, Adelphasio and Anterastile, were clothed not as prostitutes but with the grandeur and dignity of two queens. They wore chemises with immensely wide sleeves which trailed on the ground and over them gowns which were thickly embroidered on the breast with jewels. Beneath their gowns they wore farthingales the better to show off the splendour of their dress. They, like the male characters, wore magnificent mantles knotted on the shoulder.

The description of the clothes, which by no means ends there, shows that apart from *socci* and wide, loose shirts or chemises, one of the characteristics of classical dress in the Renaissance theatre was a mantle knotted on the shoulder. This, in the costume of Artamenides who appeared in classical armour, was thrown back to show his epaulettes that had been contrived from silver scales and the masks of lions. Old Annones, who wore a white beard and a fur cap, sent the audience into fits of laughter by speaking in an accent and using words meant to be Carthaginian. The whole thing, which included dances and music carefully chosen to correspond with the instrumentation that would have been used in the days of Plautus and Terence, was an immense success. The spectacles had been directed by two 'producers' working in collaboration with contemporary poets including the poet laureate.[10]

Although Leo X may have set a new standard of taste where the settings and costumes were concerned (as well as a new degree of licentiousness to judge by later performances in 1518), his predecessor, Julius II, had by no means ignored the artistic side of the theatre. He had employed, for instance, distinguished designers such as Baldassare Peruzzi, who was working in Rome not only for the Papacy but also for members of the wealthy Chigi family at the time of Leo's succession. The description, of which very much abbreviated extracts were quoted above, of the costumes worn by the actors in the *Penulo*, whilst it emphasises both the magnificence of the individual costumes and the attempts to recreate classical dress with a new accuracy, does not suggest that a planned colour scheme had been aimed at or, if it had, it had passed unnoticed. What did not pass unnoticed were arresting details of costume, such as the sleeves worn by the two sisters which swept the ground. Wide sleeves had returned to fashion in Italy during the first decade of the sixteenth century, but not wide to that extent. Farthingales, too, were enjoying a short fashion, borrowed from a curious type of dress worn in fifteenth-century Spain, but in Italy they had been fiercely banned by sumptuary laws which would not, of course, have touched the Papal theatre. Sleeves which swept the ground suggest, suddenly, a hint of Gothic romanticism to enhance even further the luxurious dressing of the play.

The importance of the account of these costumes, contained in letters of an eye-witness writing to a friend in Bologna, is that for virtually the first time it is not the dress of mummers and dancers that makes news but the costumes of actors appearing in a comedy. Since in the account itself this fact is not emphasised it seems reasonable to assume that even if this production was more than ordinarily splendid, the use of a form of classical dress in productions of plays by Terence and Plautus could, by 1513, be regarded as a matter of course.

Throughout the remainder of the sixteenth century innumerable grand spectacles were mounted all over Italy and of many of them detailed descriptions have survived, often transcribed and printed in the little booklets designed as wedding-presents in which Italian scholars of the nineteenth century specialised. Accounts of endless *intermezzi*, a necessary accompaniment, apparently, of any wedding between members of noble houses, soon become wearisome for while it is clear that each successive engineer was required to produce effects that would surpass those at any previous festival, there can have been very little difference between one set of grand entertainments and the next.

During the carnival in Ferrara in 1562 the usual theme of gods, nymphs and shepherds was replaced by rather ponderous allegorical dramas of chivalry involving beleaguered castles, African princesses, corsairs and Mameluks which provided opportunities for the appearance of dragons breathing fire and elephants (property elephants) ridden by knights. The costumes are not described, though the jousts disguised as attacks on the castles are: orientals of whatever kind were no innovation in the Renaissance theatre; the knights wore, in all probability, the highly decorative tournament armour of the day.[11]

The clothes of nymphs, on the other hand, continued to be described in great detail and in spite of the tradition that the characteristic of classical dress was a loose lawn chemise very little of this was allowed to remain exposed [67]. At the marriage of Eleanor of Toledo and Cosimo de' Medici in Florence in 1539 the sumptuous wedding banquet was followed by the appearance of Apollo and the Nine Muses.[12] Here there is no doubt that the designer of their costumes had planned each one, as it appeared, to startle and enchant the audience by its contrast to the last. Not only the detail in which each is described, but the detail in the costumes themselves is staggering. The first Muse, for instance, in draperies of palest colour scattered with branches of olive wore on her head a helmet in the discarded antique style – *disusata foggia antica* – ornamented with crystals and beryls and, as a crest, a chameleon. Her flowing wavy hair was sprinkled with flowers of wild thyme among which could be seen bees. A Panther-skin was flung across her breast and her little classical boots were covered with cat-skin.

The hair of the second Muse was scented with the flowers of marjoram with which it was sprinkled:[13] her dress of greenish-yellow was partly hidden by a hyena-skin: a parrot was mounted on her helmet which, enriched with agates and topazes, was garlanded with pimpernels. Her boots, covered with the skins of monkeys, were ornamented with their heads, placed behind the knee. A Muse in gold and crimson wore with it the skin

202

67. B. Buontalenti. (Formerly attributed to Vasari.) Designs for costumes of the kind described as *habiti vaghi*, of two female performers in the Florentine *intermezzi* of 1589

of a lion-cub. Another wore boots of white lambskin, their gilded faces decorating her calves and, to match her dress, over which was the skin of a doe, her lemon-yellow helmet was topped with an eagle. One was entirely in blue, another in black-and-gold and another in white with touches of silver that looked like crystal. The Muse in blue had blue hair as well; on her helmet sat a cupid, his face, apart from the eyes, covered by his hands.

The Muses were necessarily more resplendent in their dress than mere nymphs but they wore, in common with them, short skirts and boots which reached at least as high as mid-calf and the tops of which were evidently clearly visible. As features of the dress of females of classical antiquity these short skirts could not have been altogether easy to justify from the evidence of history and works of art, but there is no doubt that they provided one of the greatest attractions of dress *all'antica*. Together with the little boots, which never failed to be included in descriptions of antique dress they provided, in a period when women's legs were never revealed, the counterparts of the tight black laced-up boots and frothy short skirts of the can-can girls, a delectable sight in another period when women's legs were, normally, completely concealed.

To understand fully the impression made on male members of sixteenth-century audiences by these floating skirts, edged with flashing gold fringe above classical boots cut-open and held together with ribbon ties, one must read not the careful accounts sent home by members of the diplomatic corps in the courts of Italy (though their accounts would, no doubt, have been well interpreted by their readers), but the *Mémoires* of Pierre de Bourdeille, seigneur de Brantôme, whose retrospective descriptions of the girls who took part in the festivals of his youth betray an emotion that seems to make his words positively tremble on the page.[14]

Perfectly well aware that his theme did not really allow for the time he spent discussing the legs and feet of the dancers at the court and apologising time and time again for the deviation from the argument he was supposed to be pursuing, Brantôme kept returning, nevertheless, to his delightful topic.

The festivities arranged in the name of Diane de Poitiers for Philip II at Lyons in 1548 may, in view of the ecstasies into which Brantôme allowed himself to fall, have been the first at which the Italian fashion for nymphs dressed *all'antica* appeared at the French court.[15] 'We have seen,' he relates, 'the most charming ballets; we cast our eyes upon the feet and the legs of the ladies who performed them and felt the greatest pleasure in watching them use their legs so delightfully and place their feet so adroitly. Their skirts being very much shorter than usual, though not so much so as those in the *nimphale* style nor raised so high as one could have desired. Nevertheless we especially lowered our eyes when they danced the *volta* which made their skirts fly up — always an agreeable thing to happen.'

And again he noticed that the lords, the gentlemen and the knights of the court circle, 'amused themselves by contemplating the beautiful calves and lovely little feet of the ladies for, being dressed *à la nimphale* and therefore in short skirts, they provided the most beautiful exhibition of them, better far than their beautiful faces which one can see everyday – but not their beautiful legs. Many, therefore, fell in love with these lovely legs who had not fallen victim to their lovely faces. After all, above beautiful columns one discovers fine cornices, friezes and architraves, rich capitals excellently carved and polished.' And yet again, 'for, splendid as it is to see their faces how much more so to look at their beautiful legs and calves, so well displayed in boots invariably so charmingly well-fitted and laced together; for they know very well that they should wear their gowns short, *à la nimphale*, in order to step more lightly. The fashion for dressing oneself *à la nimphale* was never in vain for it drew appreciative glances and, moreover, besides being short, skirts could be slit up the sides as we can see still in the beautiful works of art of classical antiquity that can be found in Rome.'

After praising the girls of the island of Scios who still wore short skirts in his day, Brantôme went on to censure the fashionable practice of wearing high-built soles to the shoe – *patins* – (in the Venetian manner) for these simply ruined the appearance of the foot. Two ladies of the French court, however, lingering to admire some tapestries portraying the hunts of Diana, agreed that it was a good thing that nobody wore such clothes nowadays, otherwise their *patins* would be exposed and they would be discovered to be less elegantly tall than they appeared.[16]

In Florence, for Cosimo de' Medici's wedding in 1539, the short-skirted Muses were not the only characters to appear in costumes which approximated, however distantly, to classical dress; bacchantes and satyrs were also included in the cast and in dressing the satyrs some scholarly research had evidentially been permitted to play a part for they are described as being naked – *ignudi* – with hairy chests and flanks and goats' feet [68].[17]

From about this time, nearing the middle of the sixteenth century, there have survived a considerable number of drawings, many of them by respectable artists, done specifically as designs for costumes to be worn on the stage. Although, therefore, dress that must have owed its inspiration to the theatre can still be found in Italian paintings, especially those of allegorical and mythological subjects, it is no longer necessary, as it was in the fifteenth

68. Andrea Mantegna. *Bacchanale:* detail. Engraving. The satyr on the spectator's right
wears *moresca* dancers' bells round his elbows and ankles

century, for the student of stage costume to depend solely on them for evidence of the theatrical dress of the time. The art of theatrical design was becoming accepted as a part of the new enclosed theatre and from the care with which some of the costumes designed by, for example, Primaticchio and Vasari, are drawn and coloured it seems probable that they were submitted for the approval of an employer before being used.

It is impossible to discover one single direction from which the first impulse towards this theatre came. The increasing importance of the princely courts which were replacing, or had replaced, the mediaeval communes all over Italy: the fear that politics, especially religious politics, might flourish dangerously in theatres free from control: the growth of academies in which the cultural life of communities began to be concentrated, must all have played their part. The courts, first of Ferrara and soon after of Mantua, have always been regarded as pioneers of theatrical experiment but it was in 1513 in Rome that a building was actually designed and erected to serve only as a theatre; it housed the production of the *Penulo* discussed above.

This theatre, built by order of Leo X, was put up on the Capitol and involved the removal of several mounds of earth and pieces of ancient wall. It is described in considerable detail by two eye-witnesses, one of whom wrote, as has been related, of the costumes and another who described the entertainment rather more briefly. The two accounts of the theatre itself do not absolutely agree as far as its dimensions are concerned but it is clear that although it was designed as a temporary building, and made in wood, it was extremely elaborate. A colonnade, between the columns of which were situated large paintings showing the history of Rome and badges of the House of Medici, ran along the outside. Inside, where, according to those who wrote of them, the decorations were no less beautiful and grandiose, was a raised stage. The concept of a building that was intended to be used only as a theatre was, therefore, already in being early in the sixteenth century. The *Confrèrie de la Passion* had settled into its own building in Paris very soon afterwards.[18] Inevitably the drama of the sixteenth century was required to find not only buildings but permanent staffs to serve in them.

To the performance of the *Penulo* in 1513 a very large section of the public was admitted. It was, in fact, no longer a question of recording those who were present but, instead, of those who were kept out. A huge multitude, hoping to see the play, assembled before the performance outside the doors of the theatre, which were guarded by custodians armed with maces and instructions to let in only those who seemed worthy to be admitted by virtue of their dignified appearance. Not only every seat but every inch of space inside the theatre was filled and so many sat on the stage itself that very little room was left for the action of the play. Artisans and the *vile plebeo* were excluded; they were disappointed but many climbed up the outside and watched through the windows.

While this discrimination was not, perhaps, quite in accordance with modern democratic taste, the *Penulo* can reasonably be said to have been performed in public. The Pope and his noble guests, together with members of the papal court, the government and other privileged people, saw the whole entertainment again the next day, behind the closed doors of the Vatican palace, but they had all been present, too, at the public performance. It is interesting to read that at the end of the first performance of the play the actors took a curtain-call when the effect of the costumes, seen assembled together, was described as magnificent.[19]

Admission of members of the public to a drama produced in a building specially erected for the purpose was a move towards the establishment of a theatre in the modern sense and since play-producing companies and confraternities already existed all over Europe, only buildings reasonably accessible to at least the graver members of society were wanting. In the meantime a new type of intellectual was appearing – the academician. The Platonic academy of the Medici circle of the second half of the fifteenth century was responsible for an eruption of academies in most parts of Europe in the sixteenth century, and if this seems an over-simplification it can, perhaps, be corrected by pointing out that the new centres for the enjoyment, discussion and practice of the arts not only had, in most cases, their roots in earlier organisations – the Chambers of Rhetoric in France and the Netherlands, for instance – but were not infrequently simply transformations, with little alteration, of organisations that already existed. Discussion of the arts led inevitably to the search for rules by which they could be assessed (and finally produced) and some at least of these deliberations found their way into print.

Since most of the academies were concerned with music, poetry and the purity of language, the theatre, by its nature, was bound to be affected by their conclusions. Discussions on the theatre naturally turned to the question of the unities but occasionally its architectural aspects were also mentioned. The first writer to occupy himself with the actual production of plays, however, seems to have been Giraldi Cinthio whose *Discorso sulle tragedie* was published in Venice in 1554.[20]

Giraldi stressed the importance of scenery – *l'apparato* – which, he pointed out, gave the action a real locality as a setting; he also considered that the costumes worn by actors should not only suit the theme of the play but also their own situations within it. More important than individual character, however, was the nature of the drama itself. Whereas, that is to say, actors could suitably appear in a comedy dressed as private citizens, this would be most improper in tragedy, in which they should always be presented in costumes that were lordly and magnificent – *grandi e magnifici*. They should also, wherever possible, appear in the dress of people from distant countries because, in the theatre, costumes that are novel not only arouse the admiration of the audience but, in addition, help them to follow the play with more attention. Most important of all, the characters represented should appear real, both to clarify the plot and to arouse the sympathies of the audience.

The views expressed by Giraldi Cinthio on the attention that should be devoted to costume in the theatre do not go very far, but they are important in that they must have been shared by contemporary connoisseurs. The next writer to consider the production of plays, Leone de' Sommi, viewed the whole subject from a more professional angle and discussed it in far more detail in his *Quattro dialoghi in materia di rappresentazione sceniche.*

Yehuda Sommi di Portaleone seems to have been born between 1525 and 1527 in Mantua. In 1562 he was appointed *scrittore* to the academy *Degli Invaghiti* founded by the Duke of Mantua, Cesare Gonzaga, in that year, with headquarters in his own palace. Anywhere but in Mantua, in a century when in Italy the Inquisition was at its most active, it would have been remarkable that a Jew should have been admitted to an academy at all, let alone permitted to hold office in one. In Mantua, however, as earlier in Ferrara, Jewish companies had played an important part in the development of the theatre and especially in Mantua dispensations of many kinds were allowed to Jews, whose artistic gifts were understood and appreciated by the Gonzagas. Far from attempting to hide his nationality therefore, among his other activities de' Sommi composed, on the popular subject of the ladies, a poem in which verses in Italian alternated with those in Hebrew[21] and although he was so closely associated with the Gonzaga court he continued to identify himself with the Jewish community on whose behalf he presented, from time to time, petitions to Cesare Gonzaga. There existed, in the sixteenth century in Mantua, a Jewish university which provided much of the music and drama performed at the Gonzaga court and Leone de' Sommi himself wrote plays of the fashionable kind not only for the Gonzagas but for the Jewish theatre as well. The first of these plays which can be given a more or less definite date was *Drusilla*, dedicated to Cesare Gonzaga and probably produced in 1575, the year in which Cesare died. In the same year de' Sommi wrote a prose comedy, *Gli Sconosciuti* as well as *intermezzi* to be played between its acts, *Amor e Psichi*. There is some reason to believe, however, that a tragi-comedy, *L'Hirifile*, was considerably earlier and may have been written before the *Quattro dialoghi*, the date for which is usually assumed to be 1565 or 1566. De' Sommi was still alive in 1590 but probably died a year or two later.[22]

The four dialogues which take the form of conversations between Massimiano, Santino and Veridico are introduced by a note to the reader followed by the dedication to the duke, a short philosophical meditation in which the life of man is compared to the brief appearance of an actor on the stage, a theme to be explored later and with more panache in the forest of Arden. At the end of the dedication de' Sommi identifies himself as the Veridico of the dialogues. Members of sixteenth-century academies, like those of the humble Rozzi of Siena, assumed pseudonyms which expressed in open or in hidden metaphor, their views of themselves but the name Veridico sounds too arrogant for an academician and is more likely to have been invented purely as a device for laying down the law in the *Quattro dialoghi*.

These open with an almost theatrical presentation of the approach of Santino and Massimiano to the house of Veridico, the embroiderer, to see whether some work ordered by Massimiano is ready. Satisfied by Veridico's promise that it will be done tomorrow, Santino then asks what the extraordinary garment to which Veridico is putting the finishing touches can be, for, he remarks, besides being made of the richest gold, it looks as though it were cut in a completely new style. Veridico explains that it is a costume for a rainbow who will lead the gentle knight into the lists at next Sunday's tournament. After discussing the knight's motto, the two visitors then enquire whether a bizarre head-dress they can see is also for a tournament or whether it might be for a masquerade. It is for neither, they are told, but will be worn by the actress who will play Costantina, a Greek, in the play, and this leads them into the real matter of the dialogue, the nature of drama.

A play, says Veridico, is none other than an exemplary picture of human life in which vice is condemned and virtue applauded. Plato, he continues, imitated the ancient writings of the Hebrews, in which various characters were shown reasoning together and, after pointing out that the story of Job has exactly the correct number of characters for a model drama, the discussion turns to ideal forms of tragedy and comedy.

The second dialogue, expanding the same theme, attempts to arrive at the perfect number of characters for a play, the correct number of appearances each should make and the division of the action of the play into three acts, while in the third dialogue the three friends discuss the deportment of the actors on the stage, both as regards speech and movement; they then turn to the way the actors should be dressed.

By now it is the third day and, compliments having been exchanged, Massimiano and Santino are welcomed by Veridico who asks them to sit down. When they object that they may be disturbing him he assures them that he is only making a list of properties and costumes for the next production. As might have been expected, in speaking of costumes their thoughts – or rather Veridico's – turn first to the theatre of the ancients where it had been the custom for old men to wear white, the young varied colours, prostitutes yellow and parasites cloaks twisted and pleated. But, since those days were forgotten, it was now important to dress all actors in as *noble* a fashion as possible, remembering always that a proper relationship between the various characters must be observed. Sumptuous costumes greatly enhance a comedy and still more a tragedy and there is, indeed, no reason why a servant should not be dressed in velvet or satin provided that his master wears cloth of gold and rich embroideries. There is no need to dress a maid-servant in an ugly frock nor a man-servant in a shabby waistcoat; the former should wear a fine gown and the latter an elegant jacket. Even a miser or a peasant, so long as the correct social relationship is maintained within the play, can be richly dressed.

In Veridico's opinion it was also extremely important to vary the design of the costumes of the actors so that they could be easily recognised – as the ancients had realised in distinguishing them by colours. If you have four servants, give one a cap, another a hat, a third a livery of various colours and the fourth sleeves of mail. The three friends agreed on the importance of this point as it would otherwise be impossible to follow the plot of the play.

Veridico then goes on to point out that exotic forms of dress are always attractive in the theatre, which is the reason for setting the play to be produced on the following Thursday in Constantinople. This will enable him to introduce, both for the ladies and for the men, costumes which will be quite unfamiliar to everybody here. The spectacle will be far more effective if it includes these strange people than if only the sort of citizens to whom everybody is accustomed were to be presented. It is well known, he repeats, that this practice suceeds very well in comedy but infinitely more in tragedy. In tragedy, indeed, one should always follow this principle and never allow it to be presented in modern costume, it should, on the contrary, be dressed in costumes which follow the styles of antique sculpture, or those which are to be found in paintings representing the antique, where mantles and garments which approximate to those of the times of antiquity are to be found. And there is no doubt at all that the most successful and beautiful productions are those in which, in the company of kings and captains, there are always to be found some soldiers and gladiators dressed in the antique style.[23]

These principles present no difficulty for, when it comes to presenting a tragedy, the wardrobe of a prince is never so ill equipped that it is impossible to find material that will serve for mounting a grand tragedy. One can find pieces of stuff that can be used exactly as they are for making mantles, stoles and over-garments without cutting or spoiling them in any way at all. Costumes of this kind should simply be belted and knotted in imitation of the antique and the same thing applies in staging a comedy or a pastoral play. Naturally if the poet has introduced some God or other one must follow his intention but as for shepherds, the main thing is to make them look as different as possible from each other.

To begin with it is essential to cover their legs and arms with flesh-coloured material unless they are very young indeed in which case their legs and arms may be bare but never their feet; these should be covered by very light *socchi*. They must then be clothed in a *camicia* of the lightest possible stuff, or perhaps some other drapery of a nondescript colour but always sleeveless. Over this should be draped two skins (in the style described by

Homer as being worn by the shepherds of Troy) either of leopard or some other wild animal, one crossing the chest, the other the back, the legs of the skin being allowed to hang down at one end and being passed over the shoulders at the other. And vary the way they are put on; sometimes, for instance, over one shoulder only, at others fastened on the shoulders and at the hips. The hair of shepherds, whether natural or false, should be ornamented with sprays of laurel or ivy and, just as they should wear skins of different animals, so the arrangement of the hair should be varied. But all this should be done according to one's taste and good judgment.

Turning to the subject of costumes for nymphs Veridico says it is important to follow the descriptions of the poets. They should wear feminine *camicie*, embroidered and varied in style but always sleeved and he, personally, would use a little starch. They should be girded with coloured silk to make them puff out a little and appear to be very light and airy and they should be short, so that they do not reach the ankle. Nymphs should wear a *socco*, gilded *all'antica*, fitting the leg elegantly. Some of these might be of leather stained with the leaves of the sumach-tree. Over their chemise they should wear a sumptuous mantle which passes round one hip and is gathered up on the opposite shoulder. Their coiffure should be blond and, in some cases, allowed to fall over the shoulders with a garland round the head, alternatively it can be held by a golden filet tied across the forehead or, again, it can be knotted up with ribbons and thin veils. Usually, in fact, veils, which catch the breezes, serve to show at their best every other hair ornament that can be worn by a lady. Nymphs should carry a bow and wear a quiver at their hips unless, as an alternative, they carry a single dart.

Surely, objects Santino, you do not include all ladies who may appear in dramatic spectacles under the general name of nymph, nor all men in the category shepherd? No indeed, replies Veridico, for the poet may introduce, for example, an enchantress whose costume must follow his description of her; there may, on the other hand, be a ploughman among the characters in which case his dress must, of course, be rough and countrified.

In Veridico's opinion the actor's face was not of great importance since it could be altered by means of make-up so that art would supply what was lacking in nature. A beard, for instance, could be dyed, a scar could be added, a face could be made pallid, yellow or rubicund. But he could never agree to the use of either a mask or a false beard because both impede the actor. If a young man is to play the part of one who is old he must paint his shaven chin with a beard and add a few touches to the forehead with a paintbrush to give an appearance of age.

In the fourth dialogue the friends discuss the setting of the scene and the problem of inventing *moresche* of the fantastic kind usually associated with banquets, as well as the actual serving of dishes which is sometimes performed by mummers who may include a buffoon. The whole thing stops abruptly; there is no ceremonious leave-taking which may indicate that de' Sommi had planned, one day, to continue these dialogues which were not published but which survived, until comparatively recently, in two manuscripts: one was destroyed in the fire in the library at Turin; the other is at Parma.

There is nothing particularly new about de' Sommi's instructions as to the dressing of nymphs and shepherds: Giulio Romano is described as having designed almost exactly the same kind of costumes for them twenty years earlier. His shepherds wore thin green *camicie* together with flesh-coloured hose and some sort of over-garment; their boots were of Spanish cat-skin and they wore skins of wolves, one over the chest and one across the back. Over their wigs they wore wreaths of laurel and on their faces masks, but these were made so that they stopped short above the mouth in order that the music of the *moresca*, which they performed on various instruments, was not interfered with.[24]

Nor was Giulio Romano by any means the inventor of this convention, as we have seen; nevertheless the dialogues of de' Sommi mark a new point in theatrical history. The precepts they laid down, even though they were not published, must have been those which were by then generally adopted all over Italy and which certainly spread thence to France, if not (which is most unlikely) further abroad. In discussing possible inspirations for the design of stage costume de' Sommi recommended that, especially for tragedy, they should be based on clothing to be found in the works of painters and sculptors, although he does not speak of the sources used by painters who were his contemporaries. Twenty-five years later, in 1589, Cesare Vecellio, publishing a book of annotated engravings of ancient and modern fashions, offered some useful guidance to artists in this respect. In his section devoted to fashions of the past he not only based his engravings on earlier works of art, those by Carpaccio, for example, but he actually pointed out in a caption accompanying an engraving of them that the porphyry figures of tetrarchs on the exterior of St Mark's Basilica in Venice would be useful as models for those who wished to portray classical dress.[25]

Descriptions of comedies and their *intermezzi* performed in the courts of Italy during the later sixteenth century have survived in such numbers and the detail in them is so minute that they soon become wearisome reading. Classical myths, their casts enlarged to include numerous nymphs and shepherds formed the theme of most of them, but side by side with these were simple stories that certainly owed their existence to the *Orlando Furioso* and *Gerusalemme Liberata* which were sometimes used as subjects for *intermezzi*. In considering these stories it has to be remembered that whereas the north of Europe instinctively thought (and still thinks) of Crusaders in Gothic armour – often rather late – it is clear from Italian painting that they were thought of there as wearing armour *all'antica*, which always meant a theatrical version of Greek or Roman dress.

As for the sacred drama in Italy during the sixteenth century, numerous enthusiastic descriptions of this, too, have survived, but the costumes, although they evidently aroused interest, were seemingly too familiar to be described in detail. Typical accounts relate that a young girl dressed in whitest of white – *bianchissima* – represents Faith: the Queen of Heaven is dressed and adorned very suitably – *aptissimamente*: a David with his psalter is clothed regally: Susannah, Daniel, the two Elders and quantities of angels still carried scrolls – *brevi* – and mottoes. Here and there a new piece of information such as a little hat *alla greca*, black, made in papiermâché for a philosopher[26] slips through; sometimes a particularly spectacular invention such as a *trionfo* loaded with devils dressed in red with red hair and masks, appears. In this procession the writer goes on to tell us that the masks were made with open mouths to look as though they were groaning and that the devils were accompanied by twelve standard-bearers mounted on horses disguised as dragons. From what appeared to be a cavern in the bowels of the triumphal car flames shot forth and strident voices could be heard within.[27] Nebuchadnezzar was attended by gentlemen – *signori* – of diverse nationalities, variously dressed according to the custom of their countries: there were Turks, Barbarians, Tartars, Arabs, Greeks and Moors, a clue to the ability of the contemporary audience to recognise the clothing of the variety of pagans and heretics considered as suitable escorts for Nebuchadnezzar.

When, however, it came to speaking of the actual dress of these characters the writer contented himself with explaining that some wore hats, others head-dresses and others again, turbans.

Forbidden from time to time in one place or another in Italy as in the north of Europe, religious drama continued, nevertheless, to be produced somewhere throughout the century. Both Reformers and Counter-Reformers were, not unnaturally, made uneasy by the buffooneries that had been interpolated in so carefree a spirit during the fifteenth century and both sides made efforts to abolish Fools and over-boisterous, not to say indecent, *intermezzi*. But it appears to have been difficult to banish completely either the great religious dramas or the Fools who crept in and out of them: in Italy the sixteenth-century Inquisition certainly lacked either the will or the means to do so.

CHAPTER 8

The Sixteenth Century in the North of Europe

It is difficult to trace the origins of the relationships which existed in the Netherlands, and in some parts of France, between shooting-companies and Chambers of Rhetoric but by the middle of the sixteenth century a close connection between the two can be clearly seen. At least in some places similarly close connections still survived in the seventeenth century but during the sixteenth century the practice was wide-spread and festivals in which shooting-contests were combined with dramatic entertainments are very well documented. They seem to have been particularly well suited to the political outlook of the Low Countries.[1]

Like the *brigate* of youths in Italy, Chambers of Rhetoric gave themselves fanciful names often, though not always, of flowers. They differed from the *brigate*, however, in stressing the writing and speaking of poetry which meant that their members, who sometimes included poets and artists of distinction, were not confined to the very young. During the fifteenth and sixteenth centuries several Chambers of Rhetoric often existed in a single town and there seems to have been at least one to every village. Rhetoricians did not share their names with the shooting-companies with which they were connected, the latter tended to be named after appropriate saints, particularly St Sebastian and St George. Since names were often duplicated, the name of the town was usually attached to the name of the company for the sake of clarity; the same applied to Chambers of Rhetoric.

The character of the Chambers of Rhetoric belonged essentially to the Low Countries and although similar institutions existed in parts of Germany and in those districts of France nearest to the Netherlands, they did not serve quite the same purpose. In spite of the fact that during the fifteenth century Netherlandish Chambers were encouraged by the rulers of the House of Burgundy they really belonged not to the court but to the community. At the same time, though democratic, they were far more fastidious than the popular companies of Fools and *Sots*. Their entertainments did include both satire and the intervention by the Fool attached to each Chamber, but their aim was neither satire nor buffoonery: it was the nourishment of the poet and the perfection of poetic expression. The Chambers of Rhetoric were thus the forerunners of the academies of Italy and France and it is not surprising that in the seventeenth century some of them transformed themselves into academies on the Italian model. Princes were often their patrons and sometimes joined them as members, but even so the Netherlandish Chambers of Rhetoric, however modified in other ways, remained throughout their history, academies not of princes but of the people.

All the same, the importance of the Rhetoricians may be considered to lie not so much in their democratic spirit as in their practice of holding regular competitive festivals on, from time to time, so great a scale that whole Chambers travelled from one end of the Netherlands to the other in order to take part in them.[2] The magnificence with which they presented themselves on these occasions, both on and off the platform, provoked the admiration and respect of local rulers as well as the ordinary public. More important still, they must themselves have been constantly refreshed by hearing each other's poems and dramas and by watching the behaviour of their rivals from distant places. They paved the way for the touring companies of professional actors which were to grow up in the second half of the sixteenth century.

Descriptions of many of the important reunions of Rhetoricians have survived; one of the most detailed is an account of the festival – *landjuweel* – in Ghent in 1539 where many poets expressed Lutheran views. These, far from passing unnoticed by the municipality, led to the banishment of several poets (many of whom fled to Holland), the restriction on future performances and finally, in 1566, to the closing of all Flemish Chambers by the Duke of Alba.[3] But although thorough, the Inquisition did not crush the spirit of the Rhetoricians in the South Netherlands, for with the Pacification of Ghent in 1576 many Chambers reopened. A year later great festivities were arranged there for the visit of William of Orange, three temporary open-air stages were erected on which plays on allegorical themes were performed [69]. In 1584, however, the reign of terror closed the Chambers of Rhetoric in the South Netherlands completely. In 1598 the first floor of the Hôtel de Ville in Ghent was arranged as a permanent theatre; it opened with a performance by a visiting Italian company.[4]

The story of the North Netherlandish provinces was different, and in spite of the inevitable suppressions at the end of the sixteenth century, Chambers of Rhetoric remained vigorous enough to be able to re-establish themselves as soon as the worst of the danger was over. They became, early in the seventeenth century, the structure on which both the Dutch academies and the remarkable seventeenth-century Dutch theatre were based while, at the same time, some Chambers continued to maintain a separate existence in more or less their original form.

The description of the entry of the competing Chambers of Rhetoric into Antwerp in 1561 gives some idea of the state they maintained. Fourteen Chambers took part which meant that about eighteen hundred poets and

69. A temporary stage erected for the Rhetoricians' festival at Haarlem in 1606

their supporters were gathered together. One contingent of three hundred and forty poets and actors was mounted on horseback, each man wearing the livery of his Chamber, crimson silk and velvet *casaques à la Polonoyse*, bordered with silver braid. Beneath these their *pourpoints*, like their boots, were white and so were the feathers in their red head-dresses made in the form of antique helmets. They were accompanied by seven cars on which stood divers personages representing the finest men of antiquity. On this occasion the prize of a Silver Salamander went to one of the Chambers of Brussels but it was usual for every Chamber to receive a prize of some kind, even if it were only a wreath of natural roses.[5] Apart from the major prize given for the best poem, others were awarded for delivery and deportment. The contest ended, members of the Chambers rode back carrying their prizes to their respective centres where they were greeted with a wine of honour at the expense of the municipality.

Chambers of Rhetoric provided a valuable continuity in the development of drama in the Low Countries, but a similar continuity was not established in most other parts of the north of Europe where, although companies of *Enfants*, *Sots* and *Fous* continued to perform on various intellectual levels throughout the sixteenth century, there was no inter-city communication on the Netherlandish principle. Here and there really magnificent religious dramas were staged from time to time which drew together many of the institutions that existed in the same centre, but these were spasmodic happenings. Accounts of some of these ambitious productions have survived, one of them, a detailed description of the costumes worn in Bourges in 1536 in a drama based on the Acts of the Apostles, suddenly brings some reason into the apparently irrational though indisputably decorative clothing that northern eclectic painters of religious scenes chose to set against the marble, crystal and gilded carvings of their backgrounds.

The *Mystere des SS Actes des Apostres* at Bourges, was presented by the clergy, the magistrates and the citizens as a united effort. More than four hundred and ninety characters appeared in it. After Mass, attended by the mayor and aldermen at six o'clock on the opening morning, the traditional triumphal procession through the city was undertaken by the whole cast, wearing their costumes for the drama, some on horseback, others on foot or on triumphal cars, according to the status of the characters they represented. Apart from the dramatis personae actually required by the text, a large number of colourful heathen and pagan potentates, accompanied by their wives and servants, were added to the story. The costumes of all of them, as well as details of the scenic effects, were carefully recorded at the time by Jacques Thibout, 'sieur de Quantilly, secrétaire du roy, élu de Berry.'[6]

The play itself had been written nearly a hundred years earlier (though the original text does not now survive), and had already been performed in several places including Le Mans and Angers. In 1541, five years after its performance in Bourges, it was done in Paris. The production in Bourges was staged, according to Thibout, in the Roman arena over which, as an amphitheatre, a stage and a two-storey auditorium were built for the occasion. A canopy shielded the audience from the intemperate rays of the sun and the whole structure was 'excellently painted in gold, silver, blue and other rich colours'. The performances continued for forty days, they were presided over by the mayor, *noble homme* Claude Genton, provost of the king's household and native of the Ile de France.

After the roll-call of the cast, the parade through the city on the opening morning – the *Cri* – was headed by the official representatives of the King and the Queen of Navarre, mounted on mules. They carried, as did each of the twelve sergeants who followed them, a white wand, a fact which recalls the producer included by Fouquet in his *Martyrdom of St Apollonia*. Rather surprisingly, this little band of officials was followed by five trumpeters, two fifers and then two infernal furies, nude men with 'long beards' on various parts of their bodies, long hair and eyebrows reaching their chins. Between the tufts of hair were 'gashes and mouths' from which fire appeared to issue. After these followed four little devils wearing cloth of strange colours and wings that fluttered incessantly. After more devils there came a dragon twelve feet long which moved its head perpetually from side to side; it was the mount for Satan himself who was seated between its wings. Then came *Bélial*, official representative of Hell, dressed in tan-coloured velvet embroidered with various beasts; attached to a chain worth three hundred crowns which he wore round his neck was a large live tortoise. Baal is described as wearing a *chaperon à borlet*,[7] that is to say, a rolled-hood, fashionable in the middle of the fifteenth century but, by 1536, confined to official dress and therefore a recognisable symbol of his official standing. But he also wore wings of shot taffetas – *taffetas changeant* – embellished with embroidery. Cerberus followed and then, again surprisingly, Proserpine, wrapped in a bear-skin, her pendulous breasts dripping blood. It was certainly a long way from Bourges to the court of Mantua.

After the inhabitants of Hell came the sick, the maimed and the mad, all of them, commented Thibout, better dressed than their condition deserved. These were the people to be cured by the miracles related in the Acts, twenty-four in all. They were followed by Jews and Jewesses as well as

pagans and satraps all clothed according to *la mode antique* in velvets and
satins. There followed the good Jews and then the Apostles themselves, led
by St Peter wearing a gown of crimson satin brocaded in gold enriched with
diamonds and large pearls, over which was a mantle in the form of a scarf —
écharpe — (presumably a toga) of cloth of gold. St Peter's costume set a
standard that was followed, with variations, by the other Apostles. St James
the Greater, for instance, wore shot taffetas closely embroidered in silver
thread in an 'antique' pattern, covered by a mantle of crimson which was
embroidered in its turn with cockle-shells, attached to each other by inter-
laced cords.

The Three Marys, who followed, were also exceedingly grand in their
dress and they were followed by the Holy Kindred wearing costumes in the
Jewish fashion, made in blue and white velvet and white, yellow and violet
damask bordered at the hem with gold fringe; their tall hats matched their
gowns and were covered with strings of beads — *paternostres* — and gold
chains.

The next group, walking in simplicity, one after another, consisted of
sixty-two Disciples wearing velvet and red satin, some gowns embroidered,
others trimmed with ribbons of silk or gold, all of them in *la mode ancienne*.
Among the Disciples were Aquila, Drusiana and Platilla, also wearing the
mode ancienne.

An enormous company representing the Synagogue followed. Annas, the
high priest, rode a mule caparisoned in velvet *semé* with great golden nails
done in *ouvrage antique*, but the dress of these highly-placed characters,
magnificent though it was, was overshadowed by the supporting tyrants
who followed after them. King Dampdeomopolys, for example, wore a
gown with a collar cut into points from each of which hung a golden tassel;
his hat, which was very tall indeed, was made in cherry-coloured velvet
enriched with chains and rings. From its summit hung a great tassel of pearls
and the whole hat rose above a thick padded roll of the same cherry-
coloured velvet, beneath which the king wore a long *perruque* somewhat in
the Jewish style.[8] The King of India was accompanied by two squires
dressed in a 'strange' fashion which included large and wide collars sewn all
over with little tassels. Chains of gold, especially hanging from hats, fringes,
tassels and pendant jewels as well as linings of great richness were everywhere.

224

Herod-Antipas wore azure tablets, in front and behind, suspended from blue silk bands. On them in letters of gold, was inscribed, *Satis est si hoc habemus, ne quis nobis malefacere possit.*[9] With him was Herodias who wore a head-dress in the Italian fashion, consisting of a golden coif sewn all over with pearls and edged with precious stones. Set behind the coif was a bonnet of black velvet, trimmed with goldsmiths' work and gold buttons and, at the back of this was a cupid worked in pearls.

Herod-Agrippa wore orange velvet in the Jewish style; Marc Anthony, in boots and a yellow hat, wore a gown of the same colour and a long beard; Tiberius, Emperor of Rome, had a red satin hat; the King of Egypt, a Moor, wore his arms and legs bare, encircled with gold chains. Thibout described him as being dressed *à la Turque* with a collar cut into points. Towards the end of the account (from which the extracts quoted above are mere fragments) Thibout comes to the angels and archangels, Powers, Thrones and Virtues who brought up the rear, but he was either too exhausted to say more than that the wings of the angels waved incessantly and that the Virtues were *richement habillées,* or else the costumes worn by these good characters were less spectacular than the rest.

Thibout's invaluable description raises the question as to what his contemporaries in the north of Europe understood by a costume *à la mode ancienne* and *à la mode antique* – expressions which may or may not have been interchangeable. They are used not only in reference to the cut of clothes but also in several instances to the patterns embroidered upon them. In spite of their scarf-like mantles, only the embroidery on the clothes of the Apostles is described as 'antique'. The description of Marc Anthony's appearance comes as a shock – although he wore boots he also wore a hat and a long beard so that in his case *la mode antique* could not be equated with the Italian *all'antica.* Since, however, the velvet housings of the High Priest Annas's mule, with its *orfèvrerie,* is described as *faits d'ouvrage antique* this must surely refer to fifteenth-century France and not to classical Rome; to, in other words, the olden days.

This supposition is borne out by an observation made by a Spaniard who described a banquet given in August 1549 in the grand salle in the Palais de Binche to celebrate a meeting between the Emperor Charles V, Mary of Hungary and Philip II of Spain. Drawings both of the specially designed decorations and *apparati* of the grand hall itself and of an entertainment (either a masque or a *moresca*) performed there, have survived.[10] These, apart from a few minor details, correspond to the description of the proceedings by Calvete de Estrella, one of the Spaniards present.

The drawing of the theatrical performance shows a group of women wearing steeple head-dresses from the points of which hang long veils; their skirts, which are cut open in front to reveal an underskirt, trail on the ground behind. Accompanying the women are men who seem to wear tight jackets and long hose. Although the costumes of the women cannot be said to reproduce with absolute fidelity the fashion of the 1460s on which they were obviously based, they are certainly a good theatrical representation of the 'Burgundian' style that was current in that decade. In describing this episode in the entertainment Calvete speaks of the ancient head-wear of the women – tall and pointed with jewelled white veils – and their skirts *ala antigua* of crimson satin. This dress recalls the rather more accurate version of the same fashion recorded in the *Freydal* drawing of the Monkey *moresca* performed at the court of Maximilian, Charles V's grandfather. Both the dress of the ladies in the Monkey *moresca* and that worn in the Palais de Binche in 1549 were examples of historical costume, a fact which illuminates the use in at least some circumstances of the term *ala antigua* and, presumably, *à la mode ancienne* but which, in the history of the European theatre, has far more important implications as well.[11]

The account of the sumptuous costumes used at Bourges in 1536 may not be explicit in regard to the terms discussed above, but they certainly make it clear that stage costumes must have corresponded closely to the rich clothing which painters of the north of Europe were choosing, at almost exactly the same time, as appropriate for religious subjects. Earlier Netherlandish painters had made careful records of brocaded silks, damasks, furs and jewels – the crown worn by the Virgin in the Ghent altarpiece, for instance, combines goldsmiths' work with natural flowers to produce a very rich effect – but the dress in the middle of the fifteenth century looks restrained when it is compared with the extraordinarily complicated garments to be found in northern works of art of a hundred years later. Attributions of the various paintings that belong to the category 'Antwerp Mannerism' have not all been finally agreed by art historians, but although the work of obviously different hands varies stylistically, the clothes that appear in the paintings share, as do the paintings themselves, the same spirit. This dying explosion of the northern Gothic style combined a terrifying naturalism in the recording of detail with an exaggeration in the choice of furnishings and costume as wild as the choice of brightly coloured velvets and satins for the dress of lepers, hunchbacks and blind beggars in the Bourges *Acts of the Apostles.*

In some of these elaborate paintings of religious subjects the dress has manifestly been copied from similar garments in other works of art, a practice that is not difficult to recognise since the construction of the clothes is almost always weak and unconvincing and the detail misunderstood. In other paintings, however, it is impossible to believe that the dress was not the result of observation of existing garments for it is recorded in a manner that only an understanding of actual dress of extremely exotic design could have made possible. The behaviour of the brocaded velvet and the ornamental trimmings of the dress of the middle-aged Magus in the von Groote *Adoration of the Magi*[12] is an example of observation of this kind [70]. The distribu-

70. Master of the von Groote altarpiece. *Adoration of the Magi:* detail. The hat of the mature Magus is oriental, but the gown is purely theatrical

tion of the pattern of the brocade on the sleeve and on the slit-up skirt of the gown is painted with due consideration for the shape of the garment when it was laid flat on the tailor's table – a feat virtually impossible to the *pasticheur*. Equally convincing is the behaviour of the fringe that edges the gown. Although this fringe is just sufficiently weighted by its own edging of hanging golden drops to prevent it from flying out horizontally with the natural motion of the wearer's body, it is not weighed down so heavily that its own movement is purely an extension of that of the gown itself. And even the gold drops have a life of their own as they swing together and away from each other as a final variation of the movement of the whole skirt.

But the dress of this man bears no relation to the current fashion. In design it is rather prosaic 'fancy dress' but it must have been painted from life. The slit of the tunic is held together by a jewelled ornament, not only a decorative but also a functional device for preventing the slit, if exposed to strain, from splitting further. The slit itself is edged with a trifling little trimming, which extends to the bottom of a wider decorative border with which the gown is edged. But the trimming does *not* extend to the edge of the fringe, to have done this would have been easy for the painter but too difficult a feat for the tailor. The costume of this Magus is certainly *étrange* and perhaps *à la mode ancienne*, though this is impossible to determine.

Almost certain to have been described as *ancienne* or *antique* is the decoration on an equally strange costume painted with equal conviction in a work ascribed to the Master of Frankfurt, a Fleming whose late paintings seem to have been done in the first half of the sixteenth century. The costume in question appears on one of two detached wings of an altarpiece, both of which are in the Netherlands State Gallery; the centre panel is in Liverpool. On each wing stands a female saint, St Catherine on the left, St Barbara on the right, both are richly dressed in a style which, while it could have been produced nowhere but in the Netherlands, is not the dress of Netherlandish ladies of the early middle of the sixteenth century [71]. Some traces of the contemporary fashion are, however, apparent in the dress of these saints, especially in the general bulk of the silhouette, in the position both of the waistline and of the head-dress as well as in the proportion of the head, encased in its head-dress, to the body. In its character the dress, particularly

71. Master of Frankfurt. *St Barbara:* detail. This dress, too, is a theatre-costume and certainly one which had existed

oño diſapuli m montem
aſcenxxrunt ſic ꝗ moxo fixe
les anme xxum amantes
ꝗ tommu diligentes : regna
celeſtia reſixrantes. dñm
ſemper ſequentes : poſt do
mmum m illu celeſte mon
tem aſcenxunt audientes
aplm dixentem : Que ſurſu
ſunt ſapite : ubi rps eſt m

72. North European School. Two borders from the *Grimani Breviary* ornamented with bells

of St Barbara who occupies what was the right-hand wing of the altarpiece is, and is meant to be, exotic. Her little close-fitting brocade coat is edged with what must almost certainly have been what Thibout meant when he spoke of *ouvrage antique*. This edging consists of a band of metallic braid from which hang a row of large pear-shaped drops which correspond, in their design, to the bells that decorated the housings of horses used in tournaments of the fifteenth century. Described in detail by chroniclers such as Olivier de la Marche, these bells were reported as being sometimes round and sometimes pear-shaped.[13] This is the kind of ornamentation which, already out of fashion even as the wear of tournament chargers, was still, at the beginning of the sixteenth century, used to embellish the borders of late manuscripts – the *Grimani Breviary*, for instance [72].[14] Like the gown of the Magus in the von Groote altarpiece, the dress of St Barbara is carefully recorded and includes details which add little to the aesthetic effect of the painting. The white sleeves which emerge from beneath two layers of over-sleeve appear, at first sight, to be striped with black but a closer look shows that the stripes are not a woven pattern belonging to the stuff of the sleeve but are fine cords which lie over it and which are attached to a little tasselled band belonging to one of the over-sleeves.[15] Near the hem of the saint's dress are two narrow 'scarves' which terminate in tassels very carefully drawn. From the angle at which these scarves hang it is clear that they have nothing to do with two similar scarves, one tied round her waist, the other knotted at the back of her cap. The two tasselled scarves must have been part of an arrangement belonging to the front of her elaborate dress but completely concealed from the spectator. This is too complicated a concept to have been invented by the painter.

St Barbara holds, instead of a martyr's palm, a feather, a not uncommon feature in northern painting. The feather is ornamented, again quite gratuitously from the aesthetic point of view, with a line of small pendant jewels, sewn down the centre rib. They hang as they would in life: some fall freely but others are caught to one side, entangled in the fronds of the feather.

It is impossible to interpret Thibout's description of the 'Italian' head-dress of Herodias in the Bourges *Acts of the Apostles*, but he wrote of it as being placed over a coif which was sewn all over with pearls and edged with precious stones whilst the bonnet 'behind it' was trimmed with goldsmiths' work and gold buttons. The head-dress of St Barbara has nothing in common with any Italian style of the period but neither is it really Netherlandish. Although now, after four hundred years, its similarity to the normal dress of its day can be recognised, it must certainly have been thought of at the time as completely fanciful. The bow of the scarf knotted at the back of the cap is placed exactly where the embroidered cupid that decorated the cap of Herodias at Bourges must have sat.

Paintings by the group of artists who made use of this kind of stage costume

231

belong to the first, or the early second, half of the sixteenth century. Their choice of dress was soon to change in favour of much simpler, looser garments that were nearer to the Italian versions of the clothes of classical antiquity. Both types can be found in paintings by Scorel whose work bridged the middle of the century.

It is improbable that the extravagance of the costumes used at Bourges were surpassed anywhere else. It would have been difficult to load more embroidery, tassels, brocade and velvet, more pearls, gold fringe and precious stones on to the persons of those supposed to be citizens of a colony of the Roman Empire, but richness and strangeness of design were commented on by all who wrote about productions of religious dramas throughout the fifteenth and sixteenth centuries. The difference, therefore, between these great public spectacles and the private entertainments held in the princely courts must have been of theme rather than of degree of splendour. The gusto with which Jacques Thibout attacked the formidable task of listing and describing the costumes at Bourges is in marked contrast to the querulous account of a royal entertainment hurriedly put on in Paris twenty-two years later.

In 1558, to gratify the *Prévost*, the merchants and the aldermen of Paris, and, at the same time, to honour the Duke of Guise who had been ultimately responsible for the recapture of Calais, Henri II informed the municipality that he and the Duke would sup at the Hôtel de Ville on Thursday February 17th (referred to as *jeudi gras*) which was probably no more than a week ahead. Being carnival time, the Paris corporation clearly had no choice but to put on an ambitious entertainment and, in addition, to decorate the Town Hall in a suitably elegant and sophisticated manner. There was manifestly no municipal officer fit to undertake the necessary arrangements and so the distinguished poet, Jodelle, was asked whether he had on hand some tragedy or comedy that would do. Etienne Jodelle replied that he had several of both.[16]

In the event Jodelle found himself providing not only the script of an appropriate play but also designs for works of art and practical plans for the whole affair, including the decoration of the banqueting hall. Paris, he reported, was either too stupid or too indifferent to realise the importance of the occasion whereas he, on the contrary, would rather God had given him an elephant in his eye than a stain on his honour. The grand hall he divided into alcoves in the form of arbours contrived of interwoven sprays of ivy and enclosed in each alcove a painting. There were also statues with poetic Latin inscriptions.

The entertainment began with a triumphal entry of Argonauts in a ship (Jodelle had to see that its mast rose and lowered itself as required and that the rocks in which it was set were not too long). The Argonauts were led, to give a touch of sweetness, according to Jodelle, by Orpheus playing his lute and singing.[17] There followed addresses by Minerva and by Jason and at that point Virtue arrived, dressed à *l'antique*, her garments sprinkled with stars. The Argonauts themselves wore black and white – the king's colours – made in the fashion of the classical sailors – à *la matelote antique* (sic). Jodelle, who said that he had not slept for nights, described himself as half dead with fury and fatigue. He had been forced, he said, to see to everything, down to the last ivy-leaf. He admitted that he had composed the masquerade itself on the very morning of the party, and if, he asked rhetorically, 'that masquerade over which I have taken so much trouble, as you have read, turned out to be the worst, from the point of view of its recital, that you could possibly imagine, who could blame me?'[18]

However, reading between the lines, it appears that everything went fairly well apart from the fact that Virtue who, it was arranged, should distribute a leafy crown of honour to each of the royal guests, muddled the business so that the king did not get his at the right time but much too late. The king's was of laurel, that of the Duke of Guise poplar, the victor's leaf.

This entertainment, though perhaps more refined, was evidently very different and much less grand than the production of the *Acts of the Apostles* at Bourges, but it represented French entertainment in the Italian style – its theme was classical. What its costumes were like, apart from Virtue's star-sprinkled dress (by then a cliché) made in the antique fashion and the black and white classical matelots, is not recorded. Eight years earlier, in 1550, however, Henri and Catherine de' Medici had made their triumphal entry into Rouen where they were entertained by, besides triumphal edifices in the street and a battle of naked Brasilians on an island in the Seine, a procession of triumphs in the Italian manner, presented by the *Connards*. Since engravings of this have survived we may, perhaps, assume that the costumes they represent were the accepted form of classical dress in France.

The procession, which combined motifs from triumphal processions of ancient Rome with decorated cars of a rather more mediaeval character, shows that the north of Europe was beginning to some small degree at least, to reject the idea that Marc Anthony and the celebrities and deities of his time could be appropriately presented in satin hats and long beards; though both beards and satin abounded at Rouen, hats were avoided. With natural civic pride an illustrated souvenir of the *entrée* was published in Rouen at once and reissued in 1551, the following year.[19] Elephants, or rather, horses *travestis en Elephans* took part in the parade as well as horses disguised as unicorns. Both elephants and unicorns drew triumphal cars.

Among the men on foot – all of them dressed in short tunics or classical armour with wreaths on their heads – some carried trophies in correct Roman fashion but specially designed to suit the occasion. Wearing musculated Roman armour, which, from its shape must have been made in leather, this group of men carried pikes on which were mounted small models of fortresses and strong-points captured by Henri II; as pictorial evidence of the kind of fortifications which were in use at the time they are very interesting.

73. *Entry of Henri II into Rouen, 1550:* detail. Engraving. Men in pseudo-classical civil costume carrying sacrificial lambs

Other men on foot were not armed but were dressed in tunics which were a combination of costume *all'antica* of Italy and *la mode ancienne* of France. The men, who carry live lambs in, the souvenir explained, 'imitation of the ancient practice of offering sacrifices to the gods on occasions of public rejoicing', are all bearded and wreathed. They wear *socchi* and short fairly loose tunics edged with silver tassels. The description that accompanies this wood-cut explains that the tunics were of violet satin and the boots of velvet to match, lined with white satin [73].

The publication of an illustrated 'souvenir' of this *entrée* has provided one of the three most precious pieces of evidence of theatrical costume of the sixteenth century. The description of the clothing is detailed but its value lies, of course, in the fact that it accompanies a series of wood-cuts in which the dress corresponds exactly to the textual accounts. One of the most interesting groups from this point of view, represents musicians and a Fool followed by Flora and her nymphs [74]. Flora's over-garment is called a *surcot* and is described as being made in cloth of gold *frize* on a green velvet

74. *Entry of Henri II into Rouen, 1550:* detail. Engraving. The goddess Flora and her two nymphs, preceded by four musicians and a Fool

ground, edged with a double row of pearls and quantities of tassels in gold thread and green silk. Her *camicia* – called a *cotta ou basquine* – was of cloth of silver and her arm-pieces of silver, with big puffs emerging at the elbow, were cut and fastened with gold buttons, silk crepe being drawn through the cuts. Her head-dress – *cuffion* – was made from drawn-gold wire sewn with pearls. An interesting stage property was the basket of flowers she carried, it was made of figured green velvet. Flora's two nymphs wore cloth of silver.

The costume of Flora and particularly the dressing of her hair is reminiscent of designs for nymphs by Vasari and Buontalenti as well as of exotic dress to be found in Netherlandish painting which was inspired by Italian works of art. It goes a long way to establishing a theatrical origin for all dress of this kind to be found in paintings from both the south and the north

75. *Entry of Henri II into Rouen, 1550:* detail. Engraving. Orpheus, the nine Muses and Hercules. Although the Muses apparently wore white satin and Orpheus blue velvet, the shapes of their costumes are reminiscent of those of classical antiquity

76. *Entry of Henri II into Rouen, 1550:* detail. Engraving. A group of captives wearing costumes *étranges*

of Europe. Orpheus in the Rouen *entrée*, playing a harp in an edifice made in the form of a rocky cave, is described as wearing blue – *pers* – velvet embroidered in gold but the engraving shows that the form of his robe was simple and that, though bearded, he wore no hat [75].

A further theatrical convention to be illuminated by the Rouen engravings is the term *étrange* which is used in the text to refer to the costumes of a group of 'Captives', all of whom wear what the text calls, 'robbes longues de diverses couleurs & facons etranges' [76]. Although varied in their style as

237

77. Hans Mielich. *Outdoor Banquet*. 1548. A group of masked actors wearing oriental costume approach the diners

well as, apparently, in their colour, each of the costumes worn by the captives is familiar as a standard version of oriental dress to be found in paintings of the period.

Whether or not the display mounted by the *Connards* at Rouen, however expensive and carefully designed, set a new standard of classical elegance, it established the fact that when its chronicler spoke of 'un chacun portoit entre ses bras un Agneau vivant a l'imitation de ces Anciens Triomphateurs qui rendent graces a Dieu en offroyent des victimes' he really was referring to ancient Rome and not merely to the olden days. Once the spirit of classical antiquity was established in the theatre of the north of Europe it was exploited all over the place as regularly and with the same monotony of theme and design as its counterpart in Italy. From the middle of the sixteenth century both inside the princely courts and in the more popular amusements of the streets, Minervas, Dianas, Apollos and Muses galore danced, served delicacies to honoured guests, inhabited property caves or rocks and sang songs or recited poems written for them by Rhetoricians or academicians.

When these *divertissements* and ballets were recorded by the pencil of a Callot they appear, however stereotyped, to have considerable charm but, like the rigidity of court etiquette, they must often have seemed wearisome and, however fashionable, they were naturally not the only form of theatrical entertainment that went on.[20] There are hints and even some straightforward portrayals of other performances of a different kind that have survived in a handful of minor works of art of the sixteenth century, some of them remarkably interesting. Among them is a delightful little painting that could only have been a record of an actual event [77].

Seated in the open air in front of an artificial arbour, which must have been a more ambitious version of those assembled by the unfortunate Jodelle, is a little company that dines to the accompaniment of music emanating from five different sources: from a small orchestra, placed in the foreground of the painting, from a choir perched up on one side of the summit of the arbour, from a small brass band nesting on the other, from an aviary of birds on the spectator's left and from another little band almost hidden behind it. The diners are served by a company of masked mummers of oriental aspect, some of them wearing long *postiche* beards attached to their masks. On the lid of the virginals in the foreground is inscribed the date 1548; the dress of those people in the painting who do not wear stage costume accords perfectly with the fashions in northern Italy in that year. A happy chance has preserved so unimportant but intimate a little picture of an occasion that must have seemed, to those who were there, enjoyable or eminent enough to be worth recording on canvas.

In a far more ambitious painting, also of an al fresco music-party grouped round a centre table, Pieter Pourbus assembled his company in an artfully contrived composition but provided them with clothes which were certainly drawn from stage costumes. Pourbus, a Netherlander, was one of the few artists who is recorded as having actually designed costumes for Rhetoricians. Netherlandish and Italian artists appear fairly frequently in documents as designers and painters of decorations for triumphal entries and other theatrical functions. Pourbus was one of about a dozen artists who worked on designs for settings and set-pieces for the entry of Philip II in 1549 but he alone is mentioned as having designed costumes for that event when the organisation, production and acting was undertaken by Rhetoricians.

In his *Allegorical Love Feast* [78][21] Pourbus shows that he knew a lot about theatrical costume. Here is stage dress as it must have looked in the courtly

78. Pieter Pourbus. *Allegorical Love Feast.* The dresses are evidently based on stage costume

masques and pastorals round about 1548; not only, that is to say, at about the time of the joyous *entrée* of Philip II at Bruges but also, from the fashionable clothes it includes, at almost exactly the same date as the little painting of an outdoor banquet discussed above. True, the Pourbus girl who sits behind the table and holds a posy wears inscribed across the bosom of her dress the name *Fidutia* and her lover, on his belt, *Sapientia*, but the dress of these two is in every other respect a careful record of the current fashion. The company is gathered together, it seems, to celebrate a pact between these two; it is witnessed by their guests, three of whom are the Graces who dally with Adonis and Daphnis (a shepherd, of course), *Cordialitas* and *Affection* are equally well disposed.

The Grace Euphrosyne wears over her *camicia* – which is soft and full enough to have pleased even the court of Mantua – a feminine garment widely used in art in the sixteenth century to suggest anything from the dress of classical antiquity to that of Ethiopian Queens, including highly-placed Jewesses of biblical times. A *camicia* alone was too plain for the taste of almost every Renaissance artist with the exception of Mantegna, and descriptions of theatrical nymphs, even those of the fifteenth century, usually refer to an over-garment which was evidently difficult to place, historically, and therefore difficult to describe.

Affection's short jacket, rather like the jacket worn by St Barbara in the wing of the Master of Frankfurt's triptych, (see p. 229 above) is edged with the kind of metal drops that must have been like those used so freely in the great spectacle at Bourges and which appear in numerous Netherlandish paintings that include dress which looks theatrical. The absurd arrangement of feathers which trims the sleeves of *Reverentia*, though too silly to have been invented as a detail in a painting, would be rather ingratiating as the invention of a stage-designer and if, in this instance, Pieter Pourbus had been both, their presence is excusable.

On the right, balancing the Adonis group and manifestly a portrait, is the Fool. His hair is a fascinating piece of recording for, since his eared hood is thrown back, it can be seen to be cut in a triple tonsure, an exact parallel to the tonsure worn by the Fool in the April procession in the *Grimani Breviary* (see p. 113 above). His one sleeve, *a comeo*, runs out of the picture so that its tassel cannot be seen. His clothes are comparatively romantic, to match his intellectually sardonic face. A coarser character in a coarser dress would have

242

broken the pastoral spell, and, in addition, contradicted the tradition of the Rhetoricians that the Fool should behave with a certain harmonious seemliness. From the point of view of correct tailoring no detail in the dress of any of the protagonists can be faulted, though some of it may not have appeared in public in so fragmented a form.

But in a completely different sphere of life masquerades were also being held and some of these, too, were recorded pictorially although, in the middle of the sixteenth century at least, in a less ambitious form than the sophisticated pastoral of Pourbus. While they often combined with other members of the community when they contemplated a big public theatrical function, companies of legal clerks and university students kept Epiphany and Carnival in the traditional manner of their own colleges. The record of one such occasion may have been the subject of a tinted drawing in the Ashmolean Museum in Oxford [79]. The drawing, which may perhaps represent a supper arranged by medical students, must have been executed at about the same time as the two al fresco banquets discussed above.

From the beginning of the sixteenth century onwards, there is no doubt that the design of theatrical costumes showed a growing aware-

79. French School. *Feast of Mummers*. Apart from the serving women, the participants' dress imitates early fifteenth-century fashion

ness of the dress of the historical past. Some of the *Freydal* clothes, as has been seen, were scholarly reconstructions of earlier fashions, but in no work of art is the subtle spirit of the dress of the International Gothic period reproduced with such understanding as in the Oxford drawing of an appallingly unappetising high-spirited feast conducted by a Fool dressed as a professor.

There is no need to dwell on the food being consumed at this ornithological blow-out, for even more surprising is the fact that the mummers who appear not only represent farm-yard fowls but fowls in International Gothic clothing designed and worn with the authentic elegance of the beginning of the fifteenth century itself. From the dress of the three or four serving-women who wear the fashion of their own day the drawing can be dated in the later 1540s.[22]

Wearing a gown and a rolled hood with dagged edges, not of the kind favoured by the International Gothic aristocracy but by a grave citizen represented, as it might be, by Claus Sluter on the *Puits de Moïse*, a grotesque figure – perhaps the 'professor's' beadle – offers a dish at a serving table. The Professor-Fool himself wears, with his doctor's gown, two tasselled sleeves *a comeo*. The masqueraders who make up the procession which arrives in the foreground on the spectator's left, have the heads of ducks, their neck-feathers wittily forming Gothic serrated edges, as though they belonged to hoods. Led by a bearded man with the head of a cockerel, these ducks may actually have been represented by women, since some women guests are present, seated at the banqueting-table and wearing not contemporary hair-styles but the horned head-dresses of the first half of the fifteenth century. Between two of these women (or are they, too, men?) sits the king of the feast (the Professor acts as Chamberlain) dressed slightly differently from the rest. From a musicians' gallery, high up in the raftered hall, a choir, wearing the gowns and conical caps of the middle of the fifteenth century, sings from a huge book.

Costumes based on the fashions of the International Gothic period of the first decade of the fifteenth century and used, a hundred years later, as 'historical' clothing for romantic characters had, evidently fifty years later still, sunk in the social scale to the level of a students' rag although, as will be seen later, they had still not been abandoned completely by the romantic theatre.

From the paintings of the two open-air banquets and the drawing of the carnival supper, it is apparent that in all three not only has the subject of the work of art been purely secular but also undisguisedly illustrative of a theatrical occasion. Nor are these the only surviving records, from the middle of the sixteenth century, of entertainments that must actually have taken place. By this time, therefore, the student of the theatre is no longer compelled to peer beneath the picture's apparent subject – as was the case in the Fouquet miniature – for traces of the theatrical performance that inspired it. Paintings and engravings which partially concealed their theatrical origins did, nevertheless, continue to be executed; north European scenes, which portray, for instance, the prosperous early life of St Mary Magdalene are often partly clothed in archaic style and many of them include a Fool lurk-

80. Lucas van Leyden. *Life of the Magdalene*. Engraving. 1519. St Mary Magdalene wears the current fashion, but on the spectator's right a couple wear costumes based on those of the beginning of the second half of the fifteenth century. A Fool, with tasselled sleeve, appears on the left

ing in a corner of the foreground [80].[23] In paintings or engravings of this particular subject the heroine herself, like the heroines in modern historical films, is usually kept sympathetically close to the current fashion in her dress, which reverses the normal theatrical practice of the time that usually reserved historical costume for the main characters.

At the same time the aristocratic court theatres which patronised, and were served by, academicians steeped in the neo-classicism of Renaissance Italy were confining themselves to pastorals that looked back to Theocritus and Ovid, the massive Gothic spectacles on sacred themes, weighed down not only by brocade and *orfèvrerie* but also by elaborate *ad hoc* machinery for letting down angels from above and ejecting devils from below, were lumbering towards extinction. They included the sumptuous dramas on Magdalene and Prodigal Son themes.

Meanwhile, between these two forms of drama the new theatre of comedy and tragedy was settling into permanent buildings where the machinery could be comfortably grounded into sites prepared to hold it. None of the three forms was unaffected by the others for no court was so isolated that it did not expect to be visited, from time to time, by a company playing a conventional comedy and most of these were still designed to enclose short pastoral interludes or ballets. Only religious drama was often too hot to touch in this century of religious intolerance.[24]

CHAPTER 9

The End of the Period

Advancing towards the spectator with rather artificial bonhomie, the mixed company which illustrates the month of April in the calendar of the luxurious manuscript known as the *Grimani Breviary*, performs a different office from the crowds of varied nationality that follow the three Magi painted by Gentile da Fabriano and Gozzoli (see p. 112).

The Grimani crowd follows no star. Its members exist simply as decorative specimens gathered not from remote lands so much as lifted from earlier times. Together they present a picture as unaesthetic as a fancy-dress dance, always an unpleasing spectacle, for fashions, since they express a fleeting moment, cannot satisfactorily be mixed – indeed it is against nature that they should be for they are the epitome of the moment for which they were created. It is true that the Grimani dancers have not actually been cut out of earlier works of art and pasted together as a *collage* composition and they are, therefore, coated, as it were, with a mild unifying varnish – the artist's vision – but it is transparent.

The Grimani crowd is, all the same, important in the context of the present study for it represents an early and timid move towards the sixteenth century's passionate interest in history and travel which gathered momentum as the century advanced. Not long after the time at which the Breviary must have been painted, Dürer[1] was journeying round Europe with his sketch-book noting with precision the strange local costumes he encountered and at about the same time two south German artists, Hans Holbein[2] and Niklaus Manuel Deutsch[3] were doing the same thing though in a more limited way. All three seem to have been prompted more by curiosity than by a necessity for finding factual information to include in paintings, though they were able, sometimes, to incorporate some dress they had found in a later work of art.

More than fifty years passed between Dürer's last drawings of local fashions and the publication of the first of the costume books to be widely distributed, but enough artistic curiosities have survived from the intervening period to show that when books of engravings devoted to national and historical dress began to appear the study was not an altogether unfamiliar one. So far as is known the earliest book on costume was the *Recueil des habits, qui sont de present en usage, tant des pays d'Europe, Asie, Affrique & Isles savages . . .* of which a copy bearing the date 1562 is in a German collection.[4] It was reprinted in 1567. In 1563, Ferdinando Bertelli published in

Venice, *Omnium fere gentium nostrae aetatis habitus*, which was reissued in 1569. As in most books on costume published in the sixteenth century, although some of the engravings seem to have been taken from life, a good many are manifestly misunderstood versions of existing works of art – most of them impossible to trace. After the appearance of Bertelli's book, the Netherlander, Johannes Sluperius, published *Omnium fere gentium nostraeq. aetatis Nationem, Habitus & Effigies* in Antwerp in 1572 and these were followed by a succession of books, some but not all of which dealt with a limited aspect of the subject of dress – military uniforms of Europe or the vesture of the clergy, for instance. But, until Cesare Vecellio published his *Habiti antichi e moderni* in Venice in 1589, every author and engraver had confined himself to the current fashions of his own country in addition to contemporary foreign fashions.

Vecellio, as the title of his book implies, went further and included historical dress. For this he used works of art of the past as sources, some of which he identified himself in his text and some of which are in any case familiar to us. Others, however, are difficult if not impossible to trace at this distance of time. Although in the short introductions that accompany each engraving (in Latin as well as Italian) Vecellio did not, as a rule, attempt to give specific dates for his historical clothes, in some he clearly looked back not only to the end of the fifteenth century – using Carpaccio, for instance, as a source – but to much earlier works of the middle ages and he naturally included Roman dress of the classical period. For one example of this, which he described as the most ancient dress of the Romans which was also worn by the Trojans and Alexander the Great, he explained that, as we have seen, he had used the porphyry tetrarchs on the façade of St Mark's Basilica. These, he said, had been brought, together with other precious things including works of sculpture of ancient Greece, from very distant parts when 'this most powerful republic of Venice was extending the boundaries of her Empire'.

For an example of the dress of an early member of the Venetian Senate, Vecellio took as his model one of the tiny figures carved on the capitals of the pillars which support the exterior walls of the Ducal Palace. In both the instances quoted above he redrew his sculptured models in different poses; on the capital the Senator is seated – Vecellio draws him standing.

In 1601 Zacharias Heyns, publishing a book of engravings of costumes in

Amsterdam, stated that he had taken his engravings from the designs of Sluperius (who had in turn borrowed them from a still earlier work). Heyns pointed out that the old costumes he reproduced would be useful to stage-designers, the title of his book is, in fact, Theatre Dress – *Dracht-Thoneel.*

A sense of historical chronology was slowly forming itself in the consciousness of both artists and writers. The castle inhabited by Macbeth, the ramparts visited by Hamlet give an indefinable impression of belonging to an earlier architectural tradition than any building that might have housed Orsino's court. It is true that *Macbeth* and *Hamlet* are tragedies whereas *Twelfth Night* is a comedy and therefore, according to Giraldi Cinthio, not compelled to be set in the past or in an exotic land, but furthermore, and for all its textual anachronisms, *King Lear* exudes a primitive barbarism that seems actually earlier than mediaeval Elsinore, and the Rome of *Coriolanus* appears to be earlier than the more sophisticated Rome of *Julius Caesar.*

Although sixteenth-century books on costume with their attempts to explain the dress of foreigners and of those who had lived in the past, were modest manifestations of the prevailing spirit, they were straws in the wind. By the century's end national barriers against the contemporary giants – Imperial Turkey and Imperial Spain – were rising all over Europe. Everywhere eulogies of national heroes long dead and of national victories long past were beginning to appear in works of art of diverse character. Venice, the great day of her Republic already over, commissioned her best painters to cover the walls and ceiling of the hall of her *Maggior Consiglio* with huge canvases which represented the Republic's former importance as victor and arbitrator in the European scene. In the Netherlands, material was gathered together for a history of the House of Burgundy, seen, in retrospect, as the natural and benevolent government once the threat from Spain had become acute.[5] In England, Shakespeare embarked on a sequence of dramas based on English history and leading up to the apotheosis of the House of Tudor at the beginning of the sixteenth century.

Vecellio and Heyns had aimed at providing information for the guidance of painters and stage-designers. In 1597, Robert Boissard took the further step of publishing a book, *Mascarades recueillies*, in which the engravings were not copies or adaptations of earlier works of art but original designs for oriental, fantastic and historical costumes, the latter based on information

81. Title page to the Boissard *Mascarades*. 1597. The name of the artist, *Ianus Jacobus Boissardus*, followed by *inven.* runs along the frieze of the building

gathered from earlier works of art but quite freely interpreted. Together with the *Freydal* drawings and the text and wood-cuts in the Rouen souvenir of the *entrée* of Henri II, Boissard's *Mascarades* are the most valuable surviving source of information on the sixteenth century's attitude to theatrical costume.

Robert Boissard, whose book was published in Valenciennes, was editor and engraver only, the designs themselves were almost certainly all done by a member of an older generation of the family – Jean Boissard born in Besançon [81]. The print room of the British Museum owns a copy of this valuable collection of engravings but since they are bound in with some works by other artists, van Gheyn, for example, the result is a little confusing. The van Gheyn engravings too, represent masquerade costume but although no less fascinating than Boissard's, with one or two exceptions they do not represent the dress of the past. Included with them in this copy are two or three late sixteenth- or early seventeenth-century engravings of somewhat romanticised Italian peasant costumes, quite unconnected with the stage but a part of the period's addiction to pastoral manners.

Boissard had shown as much interest in oriental dress as in that of the past and had already published books on distinguished heroes of Europe and the Near East with engravings that must have been the result of some serious research.[6] Some of his studies seem to have been reused, with great ingenuity and originality, for certain of the clothes that appear in the *Mascarades recueillies*. Only two or three of the Boissard designs, which always show a man and a woman together, are examples of historical dress and these are confined to the fifteenth century, but they are so exquisitely interpreted that their importance outweighs their scarcity. Boissard's attitude to his source-material was imaginative and unique. The engravings are supported by no explanatory text: the Latin couplets, playfully amorous, which are set beneath each of them are merely embellishments. The engravings are unnumbered.

One pair of lovers in the *Mascarades* – 'Blandus amor . . .' – is shown wearing clothes of the International Gothic style, inaccurate from the historical point of view but drawn with a sympathetic feeling for the spirit both of the fashions of the beginning of the fifteenth century and of the deportment of the period, which is very rare [82]. The figures and their clothes, which are obviously drawn by someone who understood the way

82. Boissard. *Mascarades:* 'Blandus amor . . .' 1597. Both figures wear costumes based on dress fashionable in the International Gothic period

that clothes are made, are idealised not according to the accepted taste of the end of the sixteenth century but of that of the early fifteenth whose dandies would, if it had occurred to them, certainly have wished to wear the great rolling curls of hair provided for them by Boissard. Another pair, 'Virtuti est gratus . . .' who wear costumes based on those of the 1450s,

83. Boissard. *Mascarades*: 'Virtuti est gratus . . .' 1597. The costumes here are based on those of the mid-fifteenth century

seems equally free from the influence of the taste of 1597, if indeed we can be sure that we can interpret that taste through other works of art which is not, perhaps, as easy as might be expected [83]. The soft romantic swing in the stance of the nude men who decorate Boissard's title-page is nearer to that of his figures in historical dress than to the posture of sitters in French and

Netherlandish portraits of the time, and so little is known of the Renaissance theatre that the behaviour of its actors may very well be more accurately reconstructed from little works of art like Boissard's than from anything more ambitious.

The unexpected revelation of the conduct of the actors performing their scenes on the two theatrical pageant-wagons in the Maximilian *Triumphzug* may not, after all, be isolated examples. It is possible that the stage-deportment of actors who were contemporaries of the young Shakespeare was reflected with equal clarity in the dance-like postures assumed by the figures who wear theatrical costumes in the engravings of both Boissard and van Gheyn, whose engravings were executed at roughly the same time. It is a theory that is supported by the carriage of the mummers arriving to entertain the diners at the students' orgy, who paraded with their hip-bones thrust forward in correct Gothic style and their heads drooping to balance them. The same long convex curve from breast to instep is assumed by the figures wearing Gothic dress drawn by Boissard and, when he was in romantic mood, also by van Gheyn.

In arriving at an almost objective understanding of the aesthetic qualities of the fashions in dress of the International Gothic period, the engravings of Boissard and the drawing of the students' feast mark the final theatrical phase of this early Gothic revival. Thenceforward dress of this style was to disappear from the stage or, rather, from works of art depicting stage dress, for more than two hundred years. It had lasted long enough to have been available to dress the first production of Shakespeare's *Richard II*, though there is no evidence at all that any English designer either did, or did not, take advantage of it. By the end of the first decade of the seventeenth century its place was taken, temporarily, by the feminine steeple head-dress of the north European 1460s, and the masculine close-fitting jacket and hose of the opening years of the sixteenth century.

Boissard used, apart from Gothic dress, classical armour as an inspiration for his masquerade designs and, treating it with great freedom, sometimes combined Gothic elements such as hanging-sleeves with dagged edges with decorative musculated cuirasses. At other times he introduced oriental details, striped textiles and jewelled head-dresses for instance. In the engraving, 'Qui Genio indulgens . . .' a lady wearing Gothic sleeves and an oriental head-dress is accompanied by a male figure representing Death, whose costume is most elegant [84]. This was, of course, not the last time that Gothic and

84. Boissard. *Mascarades:* 'Qui Genio indulgens . . .' 1597. The couple wear costumes
ornamented with dags; the lady's dress is also oriental in character

257

85. Boissard. *Mascarades:* 'Insanire licet locupleti . . .' 1597. The designer combines a theatrical version of Roman armour with accessories that suggest somewhere further East

oriental motifs were to be mingled in the same work of art : the nineteenth century, which the sixteenth century so much resembled, from the design of the Brighton Pavilion onwards, often did the same thing.

The Boissard pair, 'Insanire licet locupleti . . .' hold masks in their hands ; hints of the contemporary fashion can be discovered in the woman's dress in this and a few other Boissard designs but they are elusive [85]. Although not published until 1597, the drawings may have been executed between the early 1570s and the middle 1580s, not necessarily all at the same time. It is interesting, in the context of Boissard's masquerade costumes, to notice that during the first decade of the seventeenth century wide hanging-sleeves, sometimes with dagged edges, found their way into some English portraits of ladies usually regarded as wearing masquerade dress.

Van Gheyn,[7] whose graphic style was very different from Boissard's and who was not French but Netherlandish, designed costumes mainly for comic characters but he included a few drawings as romantic as any of Boissard's. The masked oriental, for instance, who forms one of a group of three people of which the others are two peasants, a woman making butter and a man with a flail [86]. Of these the woman wears a decorative netted mask of the

86. Boissard. *Mascarades:* design by van Gheyn. 1597. A masked oriental and two peasants

kind worn by most of the mummers in the *Freydal* drawings and considered, perhaps, ridiculous by the end of the sixteenth century. Her companion, with his back turned, wears a solid mask of which only the edge can be seen; it appears, therefore, that the disapproval of masks expressed by de' Sommi, was not shared by stage-designers of the north of Europe. In the van Gheyn group the tunic of the countryman is worn over ill-fitting hose. Its shape is a clumsy version of tunics in fashion at the end of the fifteenth century but its slashed sleeves belong to the beginning of the sixteenth. This dress bears a certain resemblance to some of the costumes that became associated with certain characters in the *commedia dell'arte* and may have been thought of by van Gheyn's contemporaries as the standard stage dress of peasants, the northern equivalent of the *villani* or *contadini* of the Sienese Rozzi plays. Of the engravings by van Gheyn bound in the Boissard volume under discussion none really portrays *commedia dell'arte* costume.

One other pair of masquerade costumes by van Gheyn should be considered here; they can be found in an engraving of a vigorous comic dance performed by two mock-musicians, one of whom uses a grid-iron as a lute, the other a pair of bellows as a violin [87].[8] This engraving must have been very popular, both the musical instruments and the way they are played were borrowed by later portrayers of masquerade or mumming dress. The dancer with the grid-iron wears an early version of one of the two types of fashion of the past to have been newly adopted, in van Gheyn's day, as suitable to represent the old days — it is the style associated with, particularly, the Emperor Maximilian I. Van Gheyn had been a pupil of Golzius, a designer of, among other things, decorations for street pageantry who was known to have owned a collection of works by the earlier artist, Lucas van Leyden.[9] Lucas, a painter and engraver, had not only lived and worked when Maximilian dress was high-fashion but had himself been closely connected with dramatic entertainments so that both Golzius and van Gheyn would have had at hand works of art that could serve as sources for a revival of Maximilian dress as theatrical costume.[10] The appearance of this fashion of the beginning of the sixteenth century in one of van Gheyn's masquerade designs is important if only because as a type of dress it was to be used increasingly by artists of the seventeenth century, including Rembrandt, as romantic costume.

Jacques van Gheyn the younger, the member of the van Gheyn family almost certainly responsible for the masquerade designs, is recorded as

87. Boissard. *Mascarades:* design by Van Gheyn. 1597. Comic dancers wearing half-masks

having acted, in 1594, in a Rhetoricians' play produced in Amsterdam in honour of Prince Maurice of Nassau.[11] It is particularly in the Netherlands that it is possible to trace the careers of a number of artists either connected in some way with a Chamber of Rhetoric or with commissions involving the design or construction of stage-settings erected in the streets to welcome some distinguished visitor. It may be significant that the masquerade costumes designed by Boissard were published not in Besançon but Valenciennes, and if any sense of the historic **past** penetrated the English theatre of the sixteenth century it must have come from the Netherlands rather than from elsewhere.

Although it does not appear in the *Mascarades recueillies*, the other fashion of the earliest years of the sixteenth century to be reintroduced as romantic dress – the close-fitting jacket and hose – was also beginning to make its way into the theatre at about the time of their publication. An early example, though not the first, of the use of this dress to represent the old times,

88. Otto van Veen. *Evening Meal in the Woods*. 1613. On the right, the woman wears a dress of the 1460s, the man a 'Giorgionesque' costume, the woman behind the table wears a misunderstood version of a head-dress of the first quarter of the fifteenth century

appears in a painting of a nocturnal open-air banquet by Otto van Veen [88]. In this picture, painted in 1613, the diners are represented wearing fashions of the past; a lady, the steeple head-dress (badly made) and ermine-lined gown of the later fifteenth century: two men, jackets and hose. Like the figures in the Boissard engravings, these people stand in graceful fluid postures as though pausing in an attitude of dance. Otto van Veen, court painter to the Archduke and Archduchess, Albert and Isabella, was involved, as earlier both van Gheyn and Golzius had been, in designing settings for a joyous entry.[12] Twenty years later, in the 1630s, when Pieter Codde painted actors wearing this skin-fitting type of costume striking theatrical poses in a Dutch drawing-room, it had clearly become a normal part of the stage wardrobe [89, 90].

89. Pieter Codde. *The Ball:* detail. A masked actor wears a costume based on the Italian fashion of the turn of the fifteenth–sixteenth centuries

90. Pieter Codde. *Masked Ball:* detail. Another version of the 'Giorgionesque' costume used fairly frequently in the early seventeenth-century theatre

If the revival of these two past fashions – Maximilian dress and Giorgionesque jacket and hose – was a parallel to similar earlier revivals, then it should be possible to discover that, at the moment at which they were regarded as sufficiently ancient to be adopted as a costume to represent the old times, they still survived, in however modified or humble a form, somewhere. This was, in fact, the case.

The Maximilian skirted tunic had long since sunk down to the level of working-class dress, where it remained, in a rough home-spun form, until the end of the century having been recorded, in the meantime, by Brueghel and his contemporaries and followers. The jacket and hose, which at the time of its first appearance was far more daring and exacting, lingered even longer as the laughable and inappropriate suit which covered the lean and aged shanks of Pantaloon in the *commedia dell'arte* – the dress of his youth still worn in old age. Before their costumes had become entirely formalised, characters in the *commedia dell'arte* wore the kind of dress, perhaps a little exaggerated, which the types of people they caricatured would have worn in real life. The part of Pantaloon in the *commedia* was that of an old and rather seedy upper-class Venetian who was identified by the regulation *toga* of a Patrician of the Republic.[13] Under this open black gown Pantaloon's spindly crimson legs and shrunken torso clothed in the Giorgionesque habit of a fashion sixty years out-of-date were comic but they were a survival rather than a revival. Pantaloon gave his name to the close-fitting trousers which were adopted as high-fashion in the early years of the nineteenth century. By this time Harlequin, another member of the *commedia dell'arte*, had changed his character, losing the traits of a Bergamasque peasant from which his type had originally derived, and assuming a smooth sophisticated cunning which demanded a modified dress. His costume itself became smooth and tight, a change which coincided with the romantic moment at which the dandies themselves were going into Pantaloons. With the addition of one or two extra characters to their original cast and modified a little with the passing of time, the dramatis personae of the *commedia dell'arte* remained, nevertheless, faithful to their original forms of costume and never assumed new types of historical dress. They are, with the chance exception of the costume of Pantaloon, outside the scope of this book.

In the French theatre of the later sixteenth century, the costume is very difficult to study. The extravagant production of the *Acts of the Apostles* at Bourges in 1536 was followed by a presentation of the same text by the *Confrèrie de la Passion* in Paris in 1541, but although this seems to have been successful a repeat performance was opposed by the *Parlement* of Paris which declared that the players had been artisans who knew 'neither A nor B' and who spoke with coarse accents as well as offending by lengthening the text by the introduction of *plusières choses apocryphes* including *farces lascives* and mummeries. Productions of religious dramas finally ceased officially in Paris in 1548.[14]

In addition to visits to Paris of Italian theatrical companies, who first began to arrive in the 1570s and included in their repertoires plays of the *commedia dell'arte* variety, ballets in the Italian taste continued to be performed in the princely courts of France, as might have been expected since not only did the French *ballet de cour* originate in Italy but, where the courtly theatre was concerned Italy was still the leading country of Europe. In France nymphs and shepherds, Muses and Gods, still cavorted, during the last quarter of the sixteenth century, with allegorical characters chosen to flatter the more significant members of the French court. To judge from some of the designs for costumes that have survived from this period, French ballet dress no longer retained the classical forms of its Italian prototypes but had lapsed into unimaginative variations on contemporary fashionable dress, over which a few motifs regarded as 'antique', such as veils and garlands, were thrown.

This decadence belonged to the end of the century; the Valois tapestries, which include theatrical dress, probably reflect the taste of the French court at a slightly earlier period, the 1560s. In these the kings and princes of the French Royal House are portrayed in conventional armour *all'antica* and nymphs are dressed in *camicie vaghe*. Catherine de' Medici, the queen who arranged for the despatch of the tapestries to Florence, had almost certainly been responsible, during her youth, for the admiration felt in the French court for entertainments in the Italian style.[15]

The Italians themselves were more concerned at the end of the century with scenic than with sartorial innovations though their eagerness to describe the costumes of their pastoral casts had not abated. The attitude to nymphs seems to have grown more fastidious for, at the marriage of Bianca Cappello to the Medici Duke, Francesco I in 1582, driads, hamadriads and oreads appeared and were, presumably, distinguished from each other by their dress.[16] On this occasion the shepherds wore, apparently, a type of *biretta*, described as being in *forma strana* but, at the same time, pastoral. These caps, like the rest of the costumes were recorded in minutest detail down to the last yellow ribbon. Satyrs also formed a part of the cast, their legs and hooves were, it was said, covered with hair and their masks were marvellous. The nymphs of various kinds were *superbissima vestite*, their skirts cut into layers of leafy shapes and ending, of course, at mid-calf; their boots were fastened *alla nimphale*. When Virginia de' Medici, three years later, married Cesare d'Este[17] her goddesses could hardly outdo Bianca's nymphs in grandeur while in 1589, when Catherine de' Medici's grand-

91. Cristofano Allori. *Isabella of Aragon before Charles VIII*. Apart from the pages' dress, the costume bears no relation to current fashions

daughter Christina of Lorraine, married the next Medici Duke of Tuscany, both engravings and descriptions of the prolonged festivities show that the costumes were designed in the usual classical style of the Renaissance theatre.[18] It was as a wedding-present for Christina of Lorraine that Catherine de' Medici had sent the Valois tapestries to Florence.

But one remarkable piece of pictorial evidence from the end of the sixteenth or, more likely, the beginning of the seventeenth century suggests that the scope of the Italian theatre was not, perhaps, as limited as might appear. It represents not a classical but a historical drama in progress. The painting, in the Louvre, by the Florentine Cristofano Allori [91][19], is not a work of genius but it is unusual for its period in that it represents an actual event of the historical past being performed on the stage. Isabella of Aragon

– for whose marriage in 1489 Leonardo had designed his *paradiso* – is shown kneeling in supplication at the feet of Charles VIII of France on behalf of her young husband, Gian Galeazzo Sforza, whom we see lying on his sick bed in the background. A not very reliable tradition, no doubt already rife when this scene was recorded, suggested that Gian Galeazzo was slowly poisoned by his uncle, Lodovico il Moro (who had dressed up in Spanish fashion at Isabella's wedding). In the painting a page lifts a curtain, downstage, left, to reveal the dramatic scene. He is dressed in the typical livery of the turn of the sixteenth and seventeenth centuries but both the king and Isabella wear theatrical costume; Isabella's, though certainly stagey, bears no resemblance to the clothes of the period intended, the 1490s. It is, in fact, very much like the type of costume that might have been allocated to an Esther or a Queen of Sheba in a religious drama; in other words it has what the sixteenth century regarded as a biblical character intended, in this case, perhaps, to suggest that Isabella was a Spaniard of the olden time. The dress of Charles VIII is rather different; here an attempt has been made to suggest a definite period of the past, albeit not the right one. The ornate armour is meant to be Gothic and so, no doubt, are the tunic and mantle. The flimsy skirt of the tunic is trimmed with thoroughly theatrical braid, the mantle is embroidered with fleurs-de-lis but too coarsely worked for anything but stage costume. Most interesting of all, Charles wears classical boots or, rather, stage-classical boots, produced by superimposing on to boots of the style worn by fashionable gentlemen at the time the painting was done, an open trellis-pattern cut in thin leather and sewn with jewels. A pair of gilded boots, made in exactly this manner for Charles XI of Sweden to wear with Roman armour in a tournament in 1672, is preserved in the Nordiska Museum in Stockholm. No painter, trying to envisage the event which this picture portrays, could have chosen such a dress. The pedestrian accuracy with which the costume in the painting is executed, however, shows that no imagination was called for – it can only have been painted from life.

Unique as a painting of an Italian (or a French?) production of a historical drama of the period, Allori's picture is significant. The costumes of both Charles and Isabella demonstrate that, as might have been suspected, except for the costume of the classical periods, theatrical dress in the Netherlands must have been far in advance of that of the south of Europe both aesthetically and from the point of view of historical accuracy.

Cristofano Allori was a professionally competent artist; Claus Sluter was much more, but each illuminates the other's work. The costume of Sluter's King David, whose wig fits so badly and the design on whose mantle is so commonplace, is a theatrical reconstruction of a fashion current a hundred years before the date of the *Puits de Moïse*. The dress of his other prophets, on the other hand, is not inspired by a past fashion. While David's costume could only have been worn by an actor, the hat of Zacharias could have belonged to a local Jew and the gown of Isaiah to a citizen of Dijon. It is just conceivable (though even to suggest such a thing may be too bold) that the dress in Sluter's group at the *Puits de Moïse* reflected a transition-stage in theatrical design – a moment when attempts at reconstructions of historical clothing had been, but were ceasing to be, desirable in the theatre. Careful study of earlier works of art, outside the period covered by this book, which include stage dress, the tympanum at Vezelay[20] and the Bodleian *Romance of Alexander*,[21] for example, might reveal patterns of taste not unlike those that can be observed in later centuries.

Sluter worked at the end of a romantic age: Allori in the middle of another. In Sluter's day, and for half a century after it, very few traces of costume based on earlier fashions can be found in works of art and those that can are usually only small details of dress. It was not until the second half of the fifteenth century that a consistent interest in the fashions of the past began to be discernible. This interest became very lively at the beginning of the sixteenth century and thereafter for more than a hundred years serious attempts at historical accuracy, which must have been based on careful research, become more and more noticeable in works of art. Both painters who manifestly used stage costumes as models and those whose clothes are too weak in construction to have been painted from life, were concerned to give their characters appropriate clothing.

The costumes painted by Gentile da Fabriano and Gozzoli, although they include, where suitable, elements of dress that were theatrical, did not pretend to present scholarly reconstructions of past fashions. These painters used instead a formula for the olden times together with a fantasy of their own. They may have been, in fact they almost certainly were, seeking models in the theatre but, seen through their eyes (almost the only eyes of the period we have), it appears that the attitude of the contemporary theatre to its costume was nearer to the eighteenth century's, or to our own, than to that of the sixteenth or the nineteenth centuries' – two centuries which were fascinated by every aspect of the history of the past.

The sixteenth century's preoccupation with historical research provided the right environment in which theorists like Leone de' Sommi could flourish. Although his dialogues were not published until recently they must have been widely known and followed all over Europe. Mantua's theatre was famous and there were few important festivities in the aristocratic courts of Italy or, for that matter, of France, at which a representative of the Gonzagas was not reported as being present; he cannot have escaped being questioned, on such occasions, about the latest innovations at the Mantuan court. Intermarriage between members of the Italian, French and Spanish nobility must have meant, since weddings were always accompanied by dramatic entertainments, that the ingenious scenic inventions in which Italians excelled, were known of, talked about and copied everywhere. In due course they influenced Inigo Jones whose designs for scenery were based on those of the Italian theatre and whose costume designs were always nearer in spirit to those of Vasari and to the instructions of de' Sommi than to Boissard's engravings.

The influence of the Netherlands is more difficult to estimate for it must have penetrated not so much the courtly masque as the dramatic theatre which is so badly documented from the visual point of view. Otto van Veen's *Nocturnal Banquet* is not only more dramatically evocative than any of the numerous engravings of the long drawn out entertainments for the wedding of Christina of Lorraine and Ferdinando de' Medici but it relies much less on an elaborately contrived setting. If Continental theatrical design influenced the English theatre at all, Boissard's should have been the name that became known here. His *Mascarades* were published in 1597; his other publications include a collection of *Icones Diversorum Hominum*, among them portraits of Thomas Challoner, Drake, Humphrey Gilbert, John Hawkins and the Earl of Essex.[22] De' Sommi's dialogues, although probably known of in England, might well have been difficult to translate into visual terms but Boissard's engravings speak for themselves.

Leone de' Sommi was not only an Italian but a child of his time. His warnings that uniformity in costume design should be avoided was not in the tradition of Italian classicism – it was a mild reflection of the sixteenth century's romantic outlook which everywhere penetrated even the most modest forms of artistic expression. The nymphs that danced at Urbino in 1474 and the gentlemen at Lille, in their *orfèvrerie* and gold masks, like their companion ladies who wore Portuguese head-dresses, were dressed in costumes of uniform design, a parallel to the uniform pattern of the liveries of the members of the *brigate* – the festive companies – which Gozzoli placed in groups round the main characters in his Riccardi Palace frescoes. This was an effect that could no longer appeal to de' Sommi in the middle of the sixteenth century and although, naturally, uniform was retained for livery (on parade the Rhetoricians themselves rode out wearing the suits of their own Chamber, identical in colour and cut), in the theatre it had become important to bring out the individuality of each character even though he might be no more than a servant or one among a crowd of shepherds.

Respect for the individual, like the respect for the past, is a part of the romantic idea, and the sixteenth century's reverence for the past is not difficult to account for. A society which is reasonably free from political and religious tyranny can afford to despise its history whereas one which is threatened cannot. The threat in the sixteenth century, of which the whole of Europe was uncomfortably aware, was nowhere graver than in the Netherlands and it was there particularly that the theatre, in its prophetic quality, was both a danger to the oppressors, who attempted to suppress it and often succeeded in shutting it completely, and a solace to the oppressed who struggled constantly to keep it open. When the theatre could not overtly criticise or ridicule the present it could do so by implication in eulogising the past.

Otto van Veen's *Nocturnal Banquet* was not, in fact, a theatrical scene; it was one of a series of twelve paintings depicting the successful revolt of the Batavians – a north Netherlandish tribe – against the Roman occupation, and together with the other eleven paintings was bought by the States General to decorate the walls of their assembly chamber and to remind them of the blessings of freedom. All the paintings deal with the heroic struggle of the Batavians against the Roman invaders; many of them look as though they were based on the drama and in all of them the fashions of the late fifteenth or early sixteenth centuries are used for the freedom-loving Batavians who were seen, throughout this series of paintings, as a parallel to the contemporary Dutch struggling against the domination of Spain. To speak of historical accuracy in reference to the use of later fifteenth-century costume as suitable to an incident related by Tacitus may seem grotesque but

271

although the period chosen for the dress was incorrect, the costumes themselves are not mere stereotyped generalisations, they are varied in design and
must have been copied with care, if with some misunderstanding, from
works of art of their period. To discover authentic source-material on which
to base the clothing of Batavians would be as difficult today as it would have
been for painters and stage-designers in the seventeenth century. By the time
Rembrandt was painting his own majestic *Conspiracy of the Batavians*, commissioned in 1660, stage costume was already hardening into the uniform
which to Rembrandt and his contemporaries represented the old times.[23]

But if politically the Netherlands were particularly vulnerable, religious
controversy threatened every European state during the sixteenth century
and the emphasis on heroic and tragic themes, even when they did not refer
to the current situation, was a sign of the gravity of contemporary thought.
By comparison the eighteenth century, which enjoyed a remarkably stable
political climate until the time of the Revolution, produced, after the death of
Racine, few dramatists tempted to write tragedies. Shakespeare continued to
be played in England, but in versions from which everything that appeared
uncouth was eliminated, and when his tragedies were presented their
grandiose aspect was minimised, as it is today. Until his later years, when the
classicism of the century began to break down, Garrick played in costumes
which made little attempt to look historically accurate. He acted Macbeth
in a well-cut eighteenth-century suit and contented himself with loosening
the hair at the back of his wig in a civilised disarrangement that could
suggest no more than a mildly disturbed state of mind. This was a very different point of view from that held by the sixteenth century, when Giraldi
Cinthio had stressed the importance of further ennobling the tragic drama by
dressing it in costumes that were *grandi e magnifici*.

Leone de' Sommi stated unequivocally that in acting tragedy the leading
characters should introduce their awesome theme with the splendour and
gravity appropriate to it, an argument he pursued to the extent of suggesting
that for preference tragedies should not centre round the common people but
should concern themselves with kings and queens and people of authority
who could speak more weightily. Shakespeare shared this view, which is
the antithesis of the noble savage philosophy. Lear and Hamlet were of royal
blood; Coriolanus was unlikely to have antagonised an Elizabethan audience
by despising the common cry of curs; Macbeth, who had proved successful

in a position of authority, was all the more a criminal for killing not a commoner but a king.

These sovereigns of the sixteenth century's tragic stage were symbols. They had little in common with the royal tragic hero-villains who actually lived their lives in the courts of Europe of the time – Charles IX of France, Mary Stuart, the broken Charles V. The power of the royalty in the tragic drama lay in their remoteness, for all of them had lived in the 'old times'. Leone de' Sommi was aware of the importance of this aspect too for, he explained, as all actors should be attired as nobly as possible, so those who played tragedy should be more sumptuous than any and, imitating that style of dress which sculptors of antiquity understood so well, should emulate those who had lived in ancient times by assuming the draperies which had so handsomely adorned them.

> All suddenly a stormy whirlwind blew
> Throughout the house, that clapped every dore
> With which that yron wicket open flew,
> As it with mighty levers had been tore.
> And forth issewed, as on the ready flore
> Of some Theatre, a grave personage,
> That in his hand a branch of laurel bore
> With comely haveour and count'nance sage
> Yclad in costly garments, fit for tragicke stage
>
> Proceeding to the midst, he still did stand,
> As if in mind he somewhat had to say,
> And to the vulgar beckning with his hand
> In signe of silence as to heare a play
> By lively actions he gan bewray
> Some argument of matters passioned;
> Which doen, he backe retyred soft away,
> And passing by, his name discovered
> EASE on his robe in golden letters cyphered . . .

'The Maske of Cupid', *The Faerie Queen*, book III, canto XI, 1597.

Notes

Full titles and publication details for all works mentioned in the notes are given in the bibliography

Chapter 1 : Introduction

1. The setting in Hogarth's painting of a private performance by children of Dryden's *Conquest of Mexico*, 1731–2. Lord Ilchester collection.
2. But the final word on productions at the Globe is almost certainly yet to come.
3. M. D. Anderson has traced the influence of texts of English mediaeval religious plays on works of art in English churches and, calling attention to sculpture and stained-glass which can only have owed their inspiration to the theatre, has provided valuable evidence which can also be studied from the point of view of costume. *Drama and Imagery.*
4. On a visit to the King's Theatre to view its equipment. '. . . my business here was to see their clothes, and the various sorts, and what a mixture of things there was; here a wooden-leg, there a ruff, here a hobby-horse, there a crown, would make a man split himself to see with laughing. . . . But then again, to think how fine they show on the stage by candle-light, and how poor things they are to look at now too near at hand, is not pleasant at all.' *Diary of Samuel Pepys, 1665–1666*, March 18th–19th.
5. *La Vie de saint Jean Baptiste* at Claremont. From Palm Sunday until the feast of St John *Les Diables* were allowed to go round the town and the nearby countryside in their costumes to announce the Feasts; they were joined by some *sarrasins* who were a part of Herod's *cortège*. Petit de Julleville, *Les Comédiens*, pp. 237 ff.
6. '. . . Les Gens, un personnage couvert d'un masque et marchant à reculons'. Petit de Julleville, *Répertoire du théâtre comique*. Catalogue, p. 177.
7. For discussion of *Roger Bontemps* see Petit de Julleville, *La Comédie et les moeurs*, pp. 129, 179 and passim.
8. 'Au commencement du quinzième siècle l'orientalism parait avoir repris en France une faveur plus particulière encore' – partly due to the disastrous Crusade of the Comte de Nevers, the future Duke of Burgundy, Jean sans Peur who, with his companions, was imprisoned by Bajazet '. . . Et quelle vision de

l'Orient byzantin ne durent pas constituer pour les compatriotes et contemporains du duc de Berry les visites faites à Paris en 1399 et 1400 par les Empereurs de Constantinople de la maison des Paléologues, Andronic IV et Manuel II'. Durrieu, *Les Très Riches Heures.*, p. 98.

9. *A Book of Drawings*, ed. by Dodgson, generally accepted as the work of Marco Zoppo includes men in the dress of the Near East as well as fragments of antique sculpture.

10. Ghirardacci, *Della historia di Bologna*, R.I.S., vol. 33, pt. 1, p. 153.

11. The Sienese chronicler, Allegretto Allegretti (1355–1453) referred to *invenzione* at festivals 'Postevi per diletto de' riguardanti'. Mazzi, *La Congrega dei Rozzi*, p. 29.

12. *S. Michele delle Trombe e dei Trombetti* was given in 1140 to the Bardessa Cecilia di S. Ambrogio who restored it. This was the parish church of the *Trombetti della Signoria* in the district where they lodged ' . . insieme coi pifferari l'accompagnavano nella solennita pubbliche e suonava tutti i sabati nella ringhiera del Palazzo Vecchio'. *L'Illustratore fiorentino*, 1910–12, p. 118. They wore a uniform on the breast of which was a silver plaque bearing in red enamel the Lily of Florence and from their silver trumpets hung a pennant with the arms of the city. *L'Osservatore fiorentino*, 3rd ed., vol. 1, 1821, p. 124.

Chapter 2: The Structure of the Renaissance Theatre

1. The English Order of the Garter, which was certainly in being in 1350 but almost certainly not in 1340, is one of the earliest of its kind (the great Hospital Orders were earlier but different in intention). In 1351 Louis of Taranto and Giovanna of Aragon established the Order of the *Saint Esprit au droit désir*. The Order of the *Etoile* of France came into being at about the same time. By the middle of the fifteenth century knightly orders, often belonging to very small states, could be found all over Europe.

2. In 1381 Adolph of Cleves instituted an Order of Chivalry in memory of thirty-five gentlemen, whose names have come down to us, and called it the *Société du Fou*. Members of this Cleves Order were entitled to use as a crest the head and shoulders of a Fool in motley. The similarity between knightly orders and play-producing organisations can be seen, therefore, to be very close. See du Tilliot, *Mémoires pour servir à l'histoire de la Fête des Foux*.

3. *Ricordanza di Bartolomeo Masi, calderaio fiorentino*, ed. by Corazzini. Masi's relations with all the members of his family and especially his father, provide a

valuable picture of a hard-working and fairly prosperous artisan-manufacturer's household of the time. Bartolomeo was inscribed in, among other confraternities, that of the *Fanciulli di S. Giovanni Evangelista* of which, he says, the 'fratello Giuliano di Lorenzo de' Medici' was a member and provided the company with a fine banquet during the carnival of 1490.

4. The banners – *gonfaloni* – of the Confraternity of the Annunciation of 1467, ascribed to l'Alunno and that of S. Bernardino of 1465 by Bonfigli, are both in the Gallery of Art in Perugia. In the latter painting a procession of the Confraternity in honour of the saint is shown as actually taking place.

5. The Hospital of the Santo Spirito, which still functions in Rome, had, in the fifteenth century, branches all over Europe: the St Anthony hospitals were almost as widespread and there were many others. The branches were governed by local committees of distinguished laymen who accepted certain rules of religious observance and who helped in the day-to-day running of the hospital.

6. After the coronation at Tyre, in August 1286, of Henry II, King of Cyprus, as King of Jerusalem, 'the Court returned to Acre and there they held a fortnight of festivity . . . and in the great Hall of the Hospital pageants were enacted. There were scenes from the story of the Round Table . . . and they played the tale of the Queen of Femenie, from the Romance of Troy . . .' Runciman, *A History of the Crusades*, vol. 3, p. 396.

7. *Le Jeu de Robin et de Marion* is written in couplets and designed to include incidental music using *musettes* and *cornets*. See Petit de Julleville, *La Comédie et les moeurs*, pp. 16, 27, 33 and passim. There is a late thirteenth-century text of this play in the Bibliothèque Méjanes in Aix-en-Provence, ms. 166. It includes a musical score and miniature paintings. Several folios are reproduced by Cohen in *Le Théâtre en France*.

8. Ibid., p. 38. '. . . une lettre de remission', dated 1392 mentions Jean le Begne and five or six 'écoliers, ses compagnons s'en allèrent jouer par la ville d'Angers déguisés à un jeu que l'on dit Robin et Marion . . .' the text adds that the scholars were 'fils de bourgeois'.

9. Petit de Julleville lists and explains the names given to various types of entertainment in France in the fifteenth century, in *Répertoire du théâtre comique*. For types of popular drama produced in Italy see, for instance, Mazzi, *La Congrega dei Rozzi*.

10. Petit de Julleville, *La Comédie et les moeurs*, defines a farce as '. . . une comédie très réjouissante, où étaient retraces, d'une façon plaisante les ridicules et les travers de la vie privée ou de la vie sociale . . .'

11. Petit de Julleville, *Les Comédiens*, p. 64, says that when a magnificent production of the *Acts of the Apostles* was staged in Paris in 1541 rehearsals were held every

day until the production was considered to be perfect and (p. 263) that players in the *Mystère de la Vrai Passion* at Valenciennes in 1547 were fined if they turned up late for rehearsals. Strict rules ensured good behaviour – members of the cast were forbidden, for instance, to band together to drink in taverns after rehearsals and were to be satisfied with the official refreshments provided. Cohen, *Histoire de la mise en scène*, pp. 215–17, devotes a section to the obligations of actors, quoting especially from the *Contrat de Valenciennes*, which states them in great detail.

12. See Petit de Julleville, *Les Comédiens*, pp. 88 ff., for a discussion of the important companies of *Basochiens* which existed all over France.

13. The *Connards* of Rouen are well documented and therefore well known but they were only one of numerous companies of equal importance. Their name was originally *Cornards* from the horns or ears which were an essential part of the hood of the Fool. For Henri II and the *Connards* see p. 233 ff of text.

14. PUY in the *Dictionnaire de la langue française et de tous ses dialectes du IXe au XVe siècle* (Paris 1881), is defined (1) as a height, summit or mountain etc.; (2) *pui* (*puy, puis*) . . . *société littéraire* which awarded a prize for poetry the subject of which, in the earliest times, was required to be a eulogy of the Mother of Jesus. The contributor traces the foundation of a *puy* in Tournai in the year 1375.

15. The formal *ballade* concludes with an *envoi* of four or five lines which addresses a particular personage under a title such as 'sire' or 'Prince' and forms both the dedication and the climax of the poem.

16. The role of a preaching priest in a religious drama is obvious. The *sermon joyeux* was a monologue, the most usual 'un récit burlesque dans lequel un personnage plaisant étale naïvement ses travers ou ses vices . . . Le sermon joyaux est né de la Fête des Fous'. Petit de Julleville. *Répertoire du théâtre comique*, p. 259.

17. A notable exception was the *Jeu du Prince des Sots et Mère Sotte* by Pierre Gringore which supported Louis XII in the claim that he would be justified in making war on the Papacy and in seeking to depose Julius II. The *Prince des Sots* represented the king himself; *Mère Sotte* was described as 'habillée comme l'église'. The play consisted of a 'Cry, Sottie, Moralité et Farce'. See d'Héricault and de Montaiglon. *Oeuvres complètes de Gringore.*

18. Francis I ordered the demolition of the Hôtel de Flandres in 1543 and in 1548 the Confrèrie acquired part of the Hôtel de Bourgogne in the rue Mauconseil. They later, in partnership with the *Enfants Sans-souci*, acquired the freehold of this building and added a *grande salle* and other 'edifices' necessary for the production of plays. See Petit de Julleville, *Les Comédiens*, p. 70.

19. The masons and carpenters of Paris commissioned Pierre Gringore to write the

Vie de Monseigneur Saint Loys, roy de France and it was performed frequently between 1510 and 1515. Petit de Julleville, *Les Comédiens*, p. 56.

20. Fools appear constantly in works of art of the late fifteenth and sixteenth centuries and invariably wear the eared-hood even though it may be pushed back so that it looks more like a collar than a hood.

21. '. . . lequel s'appelloit La Mère Folle. Il avoit toute sa Cour comme un Souverain, sa garde Suisse, et ses gardes à cheval, ses officiers de Justice et de sa maison, son chancelier, son Grand Ecuyer et toutes les autres dignités de la Royauté.' Du Tilliot, *Mémoires pour servir à l'histoire de la Fête des Foux*, p. 109. The official name of the company led by *La Mère Folle* was the *Infanterie Dijonnaise*.

22. Estienne Pasquier commented in 1560: 'Mais surtout me plaist celuy qui composa la Farce de Maistre Pierre Patelin, duquel encore je ne scache le nom, si puis-je dire que cette Farce tant en son tout, que parcelles, fait contrecarre aux comédies des Grecs et des Romains . . .' Quoted in Cons, *L'Auteur de la farce de Pathelin*, who shows that *Pathelin* was probably written between 1464 and 1469.

23. The theatre in Geneva played satires after they were forbidden by Francis I in France. Petit de Julleville, *La Comédie et les moeurs*, pp. 172 ff.

24. The complicated character of most of Shakespeare's Fools is a development of the character that could be assumed by Fools in the satires of the late fifteenth- and sixteenth-century theatre.

25. 'Franc Arbitre . . . habillé en Roger Bontemps', tells 'l'Adolescent' (Man) to 'faits tous ce que tu voudras. . . .' Petit de Julleville, *Répertoire du théâtre comique*, p. 72.

26. See note 23 above.

27. Lucas van Leyden's engraving of the *Dance of the Magdalene*, dated 1519, shows her with a merry company in the open countryside. A Fool rushes into the picture from the spectators' left. (Ill. 80, p. 245.)

28. The same year, 1519, Lucas van Leyden made an engraving of the Prodigal Son, an interior scene in which a Fool looks in through the window. Both this and the Magdalene scene mentioned in note 27 above are reproduced in Hollstein, *Dutch and Flemish Engravings and Wood-cuts*, vol. 10, pp. 114 and 217. The Master of the Magdalene Legend and Cornelisz van Haarlem are among the later painters who treated the two stories in a similar way. Cohen, *Histoire de la mise en scène*, p. 225, quotes a passage from a Passion play by Jean Michel which shows the Magdalene at her toilet-table, applying perfume and make-up before putting on her earrings and her fashionable bonnet. In his sermons preached in the middle of the fifteenth century Michel Menot included lurid and detailed descriptions of the luxurious lives of both the Magdalene

and the Prodigal Son. Gaste, 'Michel Menot', *Mémoires de l'Académie Nationale des Sciences, Arts et Belles-Lettres de Caen*, p. 4 and passim.

29. '. . . une moult belle moralité et farce, ou moult de gens de ville alèrent pour veoir iouer qui moult prisèrent ce qui fut faict . . .' There follows a description of the damage done by the rain. De Troyes, *Histoire de Louys XI*, p. 387.

30. Mazzi quotes Allegretto Allegretti, *Cronaca*, who says that the festival of S. Bernardino was established to celebrate his canonisation in 1450: in a religious play based on the life of the new saint he rose to heaven on a wire from the Campo to the *paradise*. *La Congrega dei Rozzi*, vol. 1, p. 28.

31. Inventories of the *Compagnia del Gonfalone*, who played in the Colosseum include many references to mechanism for ascending to and descending from the *paradise*; e.g., p. 101: 'item, uno ferro longo con la centura et la nuvila appede per la Nostro Donna che salliva a cielo'. Vattasso, *Per la storia del dramma sacro*. The compact shape of the mandorla and the flat, board-like clouds that appear in numbers of fifteenth-century Italian paintings of heavenly beings who float in the sky suggest that these are directly inspired by similar mechanical effects.

32. '. . . frate Raniero Fasani . . . vestito di sacco cinto di fune' with a whip in his hand (*disciplinato*), established the *Disciplinati di Gesu Christo*. See Monaci, *Appunti per la storia del teatro italiano*, p. 19, who quotes R.I.S. (vol. 6, p. 472) on a gathering of more than 20,000 people at the end of October 1260 in Bologna. They, 'coi loro gonfaloni battendosi e cantando Laudes divinas', walked to Modena. Similar processions were reported in Treviso in 1261 and in Rome in 1264.

33. The *Frati Gaudenti* were, among other works, committed to act as peacemakers between contending parties and people: the *Bianchi* (who wore white hoods over their faces from which the Klu Klux Klan took their dress) cried *Misericordia* and sang *Stabat Mater Dolorosa*: the *Laudesi* of Florence met each evening to sing hymns round the image of the Virgin now enclosed in the Church of Or San Michele. Monaci, op. cit., pp. 27 ff., produces evidence that the songs and hymns of these groups of people were dramatic in form and, from the inventories that have survived from the fourteenth century, even delivered in costume.

34. D'Ancona, *Origini del teatro in Italia*, vol. 1, p. 478 n.

35. At the end of a ms. text (dated 1485) of a fifteenth-century play on Abraham and Isaac in the Uffizi Library, Florence, is a stage direction that '. . . tutti insieme fanno ballo cantando questo laude . . .'

36. The *Compagnia di Sta Lucia del Gonfalone* was the result of the union of several

companies of *Disciplinati*. It became, eventually, the *Arciconfraternita del Gonfalone*. See Vattasso, *Per la storia del dramma sacro*.

37. In a play on *SS Giovanni e Paolo* of the fifteenth century:

> ...*e siam pur giovanetti;*
> *Però scusate e' nostri teneri anni*
>
> . . .
>
> *Puramente faremo e con amore*
> *Supportate l'età di qualche errore.*

D'Ancona, *Origini del teatro in Italia*, vol. 1, p. 401.

38. The series of paintings done originally for the Scuola di Sant' Orsola in Venice is now in the Accademia there. In several of the paintings stylish youths with elaborately embroidered devices on a stocking, a sleeve or a cap, appear. Vecellio, in his *Habiti antichi e moderni* of 1589 engraved a figure of a standing boy from Carpaccio's *Miracle on the Canal*, also in the Accademia, as representing a member of one of the companies *della Calza*.

39. For the *Compagnie della Calza* see Venturi on the subject in 'Le Compagnie della Calza', *Nuovo archivio veneto*, 1908–09–10. For the *Compagnie della Gatta* of Florence which had also depended on a stocking for its device see Morpurgo, 'Le Compagnie della Gatta', *Miscellanea fiorentina*, pp. 92 ff.

40. As can be seen, for example, in the *Camera degli Sposi* in Mantua where Mantegna included in his frescoes Gonzaga liveries, with their stockings divided in the Gonzaga family colours.

41. See Pola, *Associazioni giovanili e feste antiche*, vol. 1, p. 449. He says that the Duke of Athens established six *brigate* covering the six districts of Florence for the Festival of St John the Baptist.

42. Ibid, p. 449. Each *potenza* had its own badge and its own coat of arms. The names of the heads of the *potenze* were taken from the locality in which they were recruited, thus, *Duca della Luna*, called after the *Piazza della Luna*; *Re della Graticola* from their district of San Lorenzo, who was roasted on a grill.

43. See Venturi, 'Le Compagnie della Calza'.

44. At a joust in Florence in 1469, in which Lorenzo de' Medici took part, the devices of the *brigate* were worked entirely in pearls and diamonds (the *Diamante brigata* was particularly associated with the Medici family). A shield on the chest, made of pure gold, worn by the *Brigata della Spera*, had as its centre a sphere outlined in pearls – each device cost five ducats. *La giostra di Lorenzo de' Medici*, ed. by Carocci.

45. A banquet given by the Sienese magnate, Agostino Chigi in Rome in 1512 '. . . e nanti si cominciasse a cenare, se fece far una Representatione pastoral, recitata da alcuni putti, e putte senese che molto bene dissero, et fu bella

materia'. The information that young girls were included in the Sienese companies also occurs elsewhere. Quoted by d'Ancona, *Origini del teatro in Italia*, vol. 2, p. 81. Alessandro Ademollo also discusses Leo X and the Sienese players but there are numerous descriptions of Leo's notorious entertainments, especially those of 1518.

46. The *Palio* appears to have originated in the combination of celebrations of the Feasts of two local saints. Horse-races through the streets and squares were a feature of the festivals in most Italian cities. For the *Palio* and its origins see Mazzi, *La Congrega dei Rozzi*.

47. This was typical of the Sienese companies who all affected this deprecating attitude towards themselves. The Rozzi said that the cork tree, rough inside and out, is bitter and tough and well fitted to its nature which is to provide soles for shoes – it teaches us of the hardships we must be prepared to endure in life and that we should not meddle with those things that are beyond our reach. Mazzi, *La Congrega dei Rozzi*, vol. 1, pp. 85 and 103.

48. Ibid., p. 110.

49. Ibid., p. 181.

50. '. . . e lo Sforza, infatti, chiamava a Milano i comici ferrarese: il Gonzaga chiedeva copia delle comedie . . .' d'Ancona, *Origini del teatro in Italia*, vol. 2, p. 126.

51. The *Maggio* was a festival which was observed throughout Europe but it was in Italy that it acquired this name. It was a season when the beauties of the new green of the countryside were celebrated in song and dance but also a time when plays of chivalry and noble conflicts were performed. Pola, *Associazioni giovanili e feste antiche*, vol. 3, pp. 334 ff. but also all writers on the history of the Italian theatre.

52. Pola, op. cit., vol. 3, p. 360.

53. Isabella d'Este, attending the wedding of Alfonso d'Este and Lucretia Borgia described the entertainments in great detail and remarked on the bucolic nature of some of the *intermezzi*. *Diario Ferrarese*, R.I.S., vol. 24, pt. 7.

54. See Luzio, 'Federico Gonzaga ostaggio alla corte de Giulio II', *Archivio della Società Romana di Storia*, vol. 9, p. 543, for descriptions of *moresche* danced at the court of Julius II, but the most scandalous were those at the court of Leo X in 1518.

55. Del Lungo, 'De altre recitazioni di Commedie Latine in Firenze nel secolo XV', *Archivio storico italiano*, ser. 3, vols. 22 and 23, 1875 and 1876, p. 170, says that in 1479 Piero Domizio asked Lorenzo de' Medici for permission to produce a play by Terence in what is now called the Riccardi-Medici Palace.

56. A disciple of S. Bernardino's, Fra Giovanni da Prato, preached a sermon against the production of plays by Terence as early as 1450.

57. For descriptions of the famous banquet see Olivier de la Marche, *Mémoires*, ed. by Beaune and d'Arbaumont, vol. 2, p. 356.

58. *Quattuor libri amorum secundum quattuor latera Germaniae* by Conrad Celtes published in 1502 includes the *Ludus Dianae*. For Conrad Celtes see Forster, *Conrad Celtis*.

59. For Chambers of Rhetoric see Claeys, *Histoire du théâtre à Gand*, van der Straeten, *Le Théâtre villageois*, and Liebrecht, *Les Chambres de Rhétorique*.

60. Several drawings and engravings of street theatres have survived. For anything but the shortest plays special boxed-in areas were provided for those who could afford them.

61. D'Ancona, *Origini del teatro in Italia*, vol. 2, p. 353, in describing the succession of revivals of plays by Plautus and Terence at the Este court says, 'Accorrevano a cotesti spettacoli estensi, principi, artigiani e dotti: nè ai teatri ducali era vietato l'accesso al popolo.' See also examples quoted on pp. 59, 207–8 in the present work.

62. See above, note 53.

Chapter 3 : Stage Costume in Works of Art of the Early Fifteenth Century

1. *Térence des ducs*, Bibliothèque de l'Arsenal, Paris, ms. 664, did not actually come into the possession of Jean de Berry until six months before his death, having previously belonged to the Duc de Guyenne (later the Dauphin), but Jean de Berry had acquired a Terence in 1408. Cohen, *Etudes d'histoire du théâtre* discusses *la comédie latine* in Chapter 5.

2. Various Milanese mss. have survived which describe a semi-circular theatre that remained from classical times finally to be replaced by the church of St Victor 'at Trenum' (otherwise theatrum). Since the detailed description, 'Theatrum fuit edificum semicirculare, altissimum, fenestris in circuitu vallatum, in medio habens pulpitum, super quod Istriones cantavant . . .' reappears almost word for word in the works of various chroniclers of the fourteenth and fifteenth centuries, the concept of such a theatre must have been familiar. One ms. continues, 'et finito cantu, Mimi, idest Ioculatores, in Cytharis pulsabant . . . Populus autem in diebus festivis, in fenestris stans, audiebat. . . .' The complicated question as to the date of the source of these accounts was discussed by Rajna in 'Il teatro di Milano ei canti intorno ad Orlando e Ulivieri', *Archivio storico lombardo*, vol. 4, anno 14, 1887, pp. 5 ff.

3. In his introduction to the *Très Riches Heures* of Jean de Berry, Paul Durrieu pointed out that the apparent revival of orientalism in France at the beginning

of the fifteenth century may have been due in part to the fatal Crusade directed by the future Duke of Burgundy, Jean sans Peur who, kept prisoner by the victorious Bajazet, came into contact with the civilisation of the Near East. But Durrieu also considered that 'quelle vision d'Orient byzantin' must have been inspired by the visits to Paris in 1399 and 1400 of successively the Emperors of the East, Andronic IV and Manuel IV, both members of the Paleologus family. See Durrieu, *Les Très Riches Heures*, p. 98. Emil Mâle thought that oriental clothing in the *Très Riches Heures* was probably inspired by orientals to be found in Venice. See *l'Art religieux*, p. 70. Durrieu's theories seem the more convincing – foreigners were not confined to Venice and visits from foreign embassies from and to all parts of Europe are recorded frequently at this period.

4. Norwich Cathedral roof-bosses. Also the head-dress of the Devil in a Temptation of Christ in a Peterborough boss. See Anderson, *Drama and Imagery*.

5. The drawing at Longleat of a scene from Shakespeare's *Titus Andronicus* is an interesting example of this. The leading characters wear historical costume but the attendants Jacobean dress.

6. St Apollonia was an aged virgin, according to the Golden Legend, who suffered in the persecutions of Christians in Alexandria in 249 under the Emperor Philip. After all her teeth had been pulled out she was ordered to pronounce the required words or be cast into the nearby fire. Asking for a moment to make up her mind she thereupon leapt into the flames, thus showing that she chose martyrdom voluntarily.

7. See, for a discussion on this, Cohen, *Le Théâtre en France*, vol. 2: *Le Théâtre Profane*.

8. In the carved panels of the pulpits of Pisa, Pistoia and Siena, by Niccola Pisano and his assistants, Roman and modified Gothic dress are used together. Had these panels been paintings instead of monochrome sculpture closely based on sarcophagi, the Gothic elements of the dress would have been more apparent.

9. Drawings by Pisanello from classical sculpture or vase-painting are in the museum at Rotterdam: there are others in the Louvre and in Oxford. A group of drawings in the print-room of the National Gallery in Rome, regarded by most people as belonging to the Paduan school of the early fifteenth century, shows some understanding of classical dress. Like the armour of Donatello's St George, most of the armour in these drawings includes Gothic features. Although they belong to the first half of the fifteenth century these drawings are not necessarily as early as has sometimes been supposed. Reproduced by van Marle, *The Development of the Italian Schools of Painting*, vol. 7, pp. 40 ff.

10. The description of this procession by Gualvane de la Flamma appears in R.I.S.,

vol. 12, pt. 4, p. 22. A note on p. 16 describes the placing of a clock on the tower of the Church of St. Eustace in 1306. The clock was, it seems, surmounted by a golden star which suggests that an earlier tableau of the Nativity was already located in that church. An additional entry by de la Flamma describes the Milanese zoo and the aviary which probably provided the animals mentioned in the procession. Inventories of charitable lay-confraternities of the fourteenth century mention a property star, 'Ancho una sedia da sedere e una stella de leno' in 1339 and in 1367 'una stella dai Masgie'. In the same list 'iii paia de guante dai Masgio' are included and in 1386, 'Ancho quactro corone dai Magie'. Monaci, *Appunti per la storia del teatro italiano*, pp. 27 ff. All the inventories belonged to the *Confraternita dei Disciplinati di S. Domenico di Perugia.*

11. Translated from the Greek of Dr Lami. Cambiagi, *Memorie istoriche*, p. 26 n.
12. The *Très Riches Heures* includes a Nativity in which one of the Magi wears a curious head-dress; although unlike the feathered crown in Gentile's painting, it, too, is trimmed with feathers and may have been inspired by Jean de Berry's so-called Heraclius medal and both may have been inspired by or related to an oriental head-dress since a rather similar one is, unexpectedly, engraved by Boissard as a part of the costume of an Indian.
13. The painting is inscribed OPUS GENTILIS DE FABRIANO MCCCXXIII MENSIS MAIO.
14. For correspondence on the commission for the frescoes see, for instance, Thieme-Becker, *Allgemeines Lexicon der Bildenden Künstler* under *Benozzo.*
15. The servant who leads the horse of the rider often identified as Piero de' Medici, father of Lorenzo the Magnificent, wears a tunic with a pleated front on which is embroidered or applied the Medici device of a diamond ring with ribbon streamers. Since the device is distorted and half-hidden in the folds of the tunic it is not immediately noticeable. The ring also appears enclosing the six golden balls of the Medici arms as a part of a repeating border on the harness of the horse of the rider referred to above.
16. *Palle*, the golden balls of the Medici referred to above.
17. Pisanello drawing in the Chicago Art Institute. Reproduced in *Master Drawings*, vol. 3, no. 1, 1965, plates 29 and 34.
18. Italian fifteenth-century paintings usually show angels wearing either albs or short tunics with long skirts beneath.
19. Cohen, *Histoire de la mise en scène*, calls attention to the important part played by music in fifteenth-century drama, pp. 27, 28.
20. The Patriarch, for instance, several priests and some who were presumably attached to the Emperor's court. Most of these drawings are in the Louvre. The

heads of Greek priests are also reproduced in *Master Drawings*, vol. 3, no. 1, 1965, plate 28.

21. Or, for example, in Parma in 1414, 'convennero i tre Re . . .' at the eleventh hour, one from San Sepolchro, one from San Ulderigo, the third from 'San Gervasio, regalmente vestiti' accompanied by a great many youths, men-at-arms and horsemen and followed by drays, loaded with baggage and birds, covered with silk hangings on which were displayed the coats-of-arms [sic] of the three kings. D'Ancona, *Origini del teatro in Italia*, vol. 1, p. 277.

22. The Magi in this panel by Giovanni di Paolo in Cleveland, USA, wear the dress of fashionable men: the two mid-wives have costumes copied from Gentile's dress and so is that of some of the men in the crowd. In this painting the middle Magus removes from his head a simple gold band.

23. Fra Angelico probably often painted dress that was inspired by stage costume but this would be difficult and tedious to prove.

24. Like most painters of the period, Lorenzo Monaco painted several versions of the Adoration of the Magi and did not use the same type of dress in all of them.

25. Mr Vesey Norman, Keeper of Armour to the Wallace Collection, London, has stated verbally that the armour of Donatello's St George must have been taken from an actual model. It is not contemporary in style but it is perfectly functional.

26. Arena Chapel, Padua, *Resurrection of Christ*.

27. The nature and structure of fifteenth-century armour has been thoroughly studied. See, for instance, Blair, *European Armour*.

28. Jan van Eyck's career is reasonably well documented. His noble patrons included John of Bavaria, Count of Holland and, later, the Duke of Burgundy, on whose behalf he visited both Spain and Portugal so that his experience of European dress was wide, and in the Peninsular he must have come across Moorish dress as well. See, for instance, Weale and Brockwell, *The van Eycks and their Art*.

29. This famous sculpture group is about 2 km. out of Dijon at the *Chartreuse de Champmol*.

30. '. . . et li altri zudei . . . chi aveva barbe posticcie, chi senza, con cappelli grandi in testa chi con altre cose . . .' D'Ancona, *Origini del teatro in Italia*, vol. 1, p. 294.

31. See quotation above about Jews in a religious play which was produced in Ferrara in 1489 with a setting which stretched from the Well of the city on one side to the Fountain on the other. The Clerks' Well (Clerkenwell) in London was the site of productions of mediaeval religious plays.

32. Mâle, *L'Art religieux*, p. 71, considers that the *Puits de Moïse* was almost cer-

tainly a 'traduction en pierre' of a scene in a mystery play – the *Judgement of Jesus* – since the scrolls carried by the Prophets are inscribed with quotations from the text of the drama. This fact, says Mâle, had already been observed by other writers on Sluter. See, also, Zarnecki, 'Claus Sluter, Sculptor to Duke Philip the Bold', *Apollo*, January–June 1962, p. 273, who explains that all the Prophets were in position by 1406. They were, originally, painted in naturalistic colours and adorned with metal accessories.

Chapter 4: Stage Costume in Works of Art of the Later Fifteenth Century

1. Vecellio, *Habiti antichi e moderni* (1589) in his description of the dress of his *Antichi gioveni* (who wear bag-like sleeves) calls them *maniche a gomi* but he also discusses the origins of the *manica a comeo* which has the same shape. Among his *habiti antichi* he reproduces a *Dogalina antica* saying: 'or, more properly, wide sleeves used in Venice and other cities.' In this case it is the whole garment that is called, from the shape of its sleeves, *dogalina*. He describes the *Senato antico* as wearing *maniche larghe alla ducale*. All these terms for types of sleeve are common in fifteenth- and sixteenth-century documents. Sleeves called *ducale* can also be called, in Venice, *dogale*. The *Dizionario Etimologico italiano* defines *gozzi* thus: 'gozzo ant. xv sec. moda rigonfiamento delle maniche *cf.* giabo pettorino a volanti.'
2. The simple hood of classical and mediaeval use was adapted in the early fifteenth century into a stylish hat-like head-piece and was usually referred to as a *chaperon* in the north of Europe.
3. This particular panel, separated from the altarpiece, is in the Louvre.
4. The sort of domestic embroidery, used frequently in England at the end of the sixteenth century but comparatively seldom on the Continent, took its designs from borders of illuminated manuscripts of the fourteenth and fifteenth centuries. These religious manuals were no longer acceptable as aids to worship after the Reformation.
5. One of the *brigate* in which members of the Medici family were involved.
6. '. . . le maniche a gozzi ossia sboffi, e sulla sinistra era ricamata in perle una nuvoletta che gettava fiori su pella manica . . .' Conti, *Fatti e anedotti.*
7. See Kott, *Shakespeare Our Contemporary* (2nd ed.), who discusses the Florentine *girl–youth* and *youth–girl* of the fifteenth century as an ambiguous figure, citing works by Verrocchio and Botticelli. Whether this view is valid or not, it supports the appearance, in works of art, of figures taken directly from the theatre where all the parts were played by very young boys. Since this custom had been followed from the earliest days of Christian drama until well into the sixteenth

century it seems difficult to agree that it had specifically homosexual implications.

8. National Gallery, London, catalogue no. 1124, 'apparently under Botticelli's influence. Gamba even thinks that the design is Botticelli's.' Davies, *The Earlier Italian Schools*. In the embroidered orpheries designed by Pollaiuolo (Florence, Opera del Duomo), Salome wears normal fashionable dress when she collects the head of the Baptist but Gothic sleeves with serrated edges when she dances before Herod.

9. There is nothing dramatic about this very conservative dress. Other theatrical implications have, on the other hand, been pointed out by Gombrich in discussing the *Adoration of the Magi* panel in this altarpiece.

10. For reasons for this date see Antwerp catalogue no. 529.

11. When Philippe de Champaigne painted the members of the Parliament of Paris in the seventeenth century its officers were still wearing *mi-parti*. For *mi-parti* worn by the Paris *échevins* at the funeral of Charles VII in 1461 see d'Escouchy, *Chronique*, ed. by du Fresne de Beaucourt, vol. 2, p. 429.

12. In England some vestiges of traditional dress still remained at the time of the Restoration but most official clothing had to be redesigned. For English legal dress designed in *mi-parti* in the fifteenth century, see the Whaddon Folio in the Inner Temple, two miniatures reproduced in Hargreaves-Mawdsley, *A History of Legal Dress*.

13. Borso d'Este's buffoon, Scocola, was made a citizen of Ferrara in 1466. D'Ancona, *Origini del teatro in Italia*, vol. 2, p. 368n.

14. See, for instance, Botticelli's *Adoration of the Magi*, National Gallery, London, catalogue no. 592.

15. Sebastian Brandt's *Narrenschiff*, which lampooned the whole of society in the guise of Fools of various kinds, included 'virorum effoeminato', or 'of the newe fashions and disguised garments'; this engraving bears the date 1494. There are also 'De Externis et infidelibus fatuis', or, 'of strange fooles and infidels as Sarasins, Paynims, Turkes and such like'. In Florence in 1514 a street procession included 'una fusta (barca) piena di Pazzi, cioe buffoni, diavoli . . .' Pola, *Associazioni giovanili e feste antiche*, vol. 1, p. 279.

16. This early sixteenth-century manuscript in the Marciana Library in Venice has always puzzled scholars.

17. The altarpiece is in the Australian National Gallery at Melbourne, catalogue no. 74–76.

18. Notes on the remarkable recording of this detail of dress-making can be found in the thesis, completed in 1967, by Miss Elizabeth Birbari, Courtauld Institute of Art, London, to be published by John Murray.

19. *Edifici* first developed from candles carried in the hand; later, candlesticks grew to immense proportions and were elaborated until in some Italian cities they became enormous wooden structures. In Viterbo, in the nineteenth century, each *edificio* required forty men to carry it through the streets (water-colour drawings of one such procession can be found in the Viterbo art gallery). Smaller edifices, often incorporating statues or sacred pictures are still carried through the streets on saints' days in some cities of Europe. In the fifteenth century, in Florence, on June 23, clergy and members of confraternities and guilds processed in groups, each surrounding an edifice which, when it halted, became the platform for the performance of a religious or allegorical scene. On the edifice of Adam a scene of the Temptation was performed, for instance. See Guasti, *Le Feste di San Giovanni Batista*, p. 20.

20. Davies, *The Earlier Italian Schools*, writes, 'Cosimo Tura . . . was the first important Ferrarese painter . . . much of his work was for the Este court . . . Tura appears to have been influenced chiefly by Squarcionesques, in particular by the young Mantegna' (p. 402).

21. See Tietze-Conrat, *Mantegna*, Introduction, p. 4 and p. 21. Sigismondo Cantelmo, a member of the Este court described the theatre at Mantua saying that at the two sides were colonnades, bringing to mind a building both timeless and antique, full of delights. Within was cloth-of-gold and some greenery and one stretch of wall was ornamented with the six paintings of Caesar's triumphs by the remarkable Mantegna . . . D'Ancona, *Origini del teatro in Italia*, vol. 2, p. 382, quoted from *Lettere artistiche inedite* by G. Campori.

22. *Il carroccio* drawn by two draped bullocks was already recorded as being used at the coronation of the Emperor Frederick Barbarossa in Milan in the eleventh century. See Fondazioni Treccani, *Storia di Milano*, vol. 3, p. 91.

23. The usual prize of a length of expensive silk or velvet, awarded at city festivals in the fifteenth century, was displayed on the *carrozza* before the competition began.

24. In 1491 Lorenzo de' Medici decided to reduce the number of sacred *edifici* in the procession on St John's Eve and replace them by classical cars. See Cambiagi, *Memorie istoriche*, p. 65. He quotes from cod. Strozziana 1396. In 1512 the edifices were further reduced to ten 'e non piu per non tediare'. The classical *trionfi* were retained. See Guasti, *Le Feste di San Giovanni Batista*, p. 26.

25. Florence, Accademia. A *cassone* was a large wooden chest made to hold clothing. Decorated *cassoni*, usually produced in pairs, were made especially for the marriage trousseau.

26. At a banquet and ball in 1487 in Bologna for the wedding of Annibale Bentivoglio and Lucrezia d'Este, a struggle between *Chastity* and *Matrimony* was

staged, during which a young girl 'gentilmente vestita da habito vago', appeared. Zannoni, *Una rappresentazione allegorica*, p. 426. In 1490, at a tournament, also in Bologna, a woman representing the goddess *Wisdom*, was described as seated on a 'carro, vaga e riccamente vestita'. Ghirardacci, *Della historia de Bologna*, R.I.S., vol. 33, p. 258. 'La Vicenza . . . era lodata . . . per la vaghezza degli habiti . . .' D'Ancona, *Origini del teatro in Italia*, vol. 2, p. 451. The word *camicia* was used in Italy both for the male shirt and the feminine chemise.

27. Thick, bushy hair, artificially fluffed out – *la zazzara* – was evidently popular on the stage: the word is often used instead of *posticcia*, a wig. *Zazzare d'oro* were borrowed from Mantua in 1502. D'Ancona, *Origini del teatro in Italia*, vol. 2, p. 378 n.

28. National Gallery catalogue no. 902.

29. Baron Thyssen-Bornemiszia collection, as *Roberti*, no. 92.

30. The frescoes by Mantegna in the Eremitani Chapel in Padua were destroyed by bombing during the Second World War. Efforts are being made to collect the small fragments that were saved and piece them together.

31. *Smeralda Bandinelli* in her portrait by Botticelli or his school, Victoria and Albert Museum, for instance.

32. The roof-bosses are discussed at length in Anderson, *Drama and Imagery*.

33. Cohen, *Le Théâtre en France*, vol. 1; *Le Théâtre religieux, Mystère de la Passion d'Eustache Marcadé*, plates xxii and xxiii.

Chapter 5: Documentary Evidence on the Subject of Theatrical Dress in the Fifteenth Century

1. Castiglione, *Il Cortegiano*, bk. 2, p. 159: '. . . if a gentleman were to pass *con un robba adossa quaratata di diversi colori, overo con tante stringhette e fettuzze annodate e fregi traversati* would he not be taken for a buffoon or a madman? Neither a buffoon nor a maniac said messire Pietro Bembo but one who *vivuto nella Lombardia perche cosi ʋanni tutti* . . . In that case, said her Grace the Duchess, laughing, it would be as proper to them as for the Venetians to *portar le maniche a comeo, e ai Fiorentiani il capuccio* . . .'

2. *I Diarii di Marin Sanudo* in the Marciana Library in Venice, CL, vii, cod. CDXIX–CDLXXVII were published in fifty-eight volumes in Venice between 1879 and 1902. Sanudo, born in 1466, held various high offices in the government of Venice and kept a day-to-day account not only of the affairs of the republic but of communications from its ambassadors to other courts and of visits of important foreigners.

3. Sanudo, vol. 15, p. 327, 5th November 1512: '. . . Questo Curzense [Mathias Lang] . . . Era sopra uno rozineto vestito con una vesta de veluto negro a la todescha, fodrata di pelle negra, con una bareta a la francese di pano . . .'

4. A *paradiso* had already been presented at the Este court in Ferrara so that Leonardo's was not altogether an innovation. The word *paradiso* in such a context probably meant that the apparatus itself was the main entertainment. As a part of religious drama the word *paradiso* was used for the *mansion* inhabited by the Almighty. It could be built high up on the façade of a church or be suspended from the roof inside a church. Both the Este paradise and Leonardo's appeared on their own and were inhabited, as a set-piece, by the gods of antiquity. *Diario Ferrarese*, R.I.S., vol. 24, no. 7, p. 122: 'La festa de Amphitrione . . . con uno paradixo con stelle et altre rode che fu una bella cosa.'

5. Gian Galeazzo Sforza's uncle, Lodovico il Moro, was soon to marry Beatrice d'Este, daughter of Duke Ercole of Ferrara. Beatrice's sister, Isabella, had married the Marquis of Mantua so that for a time the courts of Ferrara, Milan and Mantua were closely linked.

6. Solmi, ed., *La Festa del Paradiso di Leonardo da Vinci e Bernardino Bellincione 13 gennaio 1490*, mainly consists of the letters of Giacomo Trotti, Ferrarese ambassador who was present. The *Relazione della Festa del Paradiso* in the Este Library, cod. ital. h.521 segn a J.4, 21.

7. Olivier de la Marche, *Mémoires*, ed. by Beaune and d'Arbaumont, vol. 1, p. 276: '. . . habillé d'ung pourpoint à gros cul, à la guise de Behaigne, et d'une robe de drap bleu brun et avoit ung chapperon par gorge, dont la patte venoit jusques à la selle et estoit decouppé a grans lambeaulx . . .'

8. Ibid., p. 316: '. . . se paiges estoyent vestuz de satin vert à l'italienne mode . . .'

9. Ibid., p. 319: '. . . et d'abondant avoient iceulx paiges cheveulx crespez a la façon d'Allemaigne, et croy qu'ils furent artificiez . . .'

10. His *Mémoires* provide one of the most important sources for the social history of his period.

11. Ibid., vol. 4, p. 125: '. . . On the Wednesday the first to enter the lists was messire Jehan de Chassa, Seigneur de Monnet, attended by four gentlemen *habilliez de bien riches robes à façon de Turcqs; et estoient devant lui quatre Moriens* and on a great horse carrying two panniers *ung fol jouans de divers instrumens* the said horse housed in violet velvet embroidered with gold letters, and on another horse housed in crimson velvet embroidered with gold knots sat *une pucelle vestue de drap de soie vert royee*, a heavy gold chain round her neck *habilliée à la manière de Turquie*, the said lady led in the said knight *vestu aussy comme Turcq . . .*'

12. Ibid., vol. 2, pp. 349 ff. *Tresse* used here to mean turban. For the complete description of the Feast of the Pheasant see this volume, pp. 341 ff.

13. Devils and *sarrasins*, a part of Herod's train in a series of fifteenth-century plays on the life of the Baptist in Chaumont were allowed to go round the countryside in their costumes announcing the forthcoming performances. See Petit de Julleville, *Les Comédiens*, p. 237.

14. This is another example of the fifteenth century's familiarity with the dress of foreigners: '. . . un atour tout rond à la façon de Portugal dont les bourrelets sont à la manières de roses . . .' Olivier de la Marche, *Mémoires*, vol. 1, p. 372. That Portuguese ladies wore a slightly different variant of European high-fashion can be seen from the (lost) *cassone* painting of the arrival of Leonora of Portugal in Italy for her marriage with Frederick III in 1452. Reproduced S. M. Newton (Pearce), 'Costumi tedeschi e borgognoni in Italia nel 1452', *Commentari*, October–December, 1957.

15. Women did occasionally play speaking parts in fifteenth-century dramas but very rarely. In 1468 a girl played the part of S. Catharine of Siena so movingly that although she was of low birth a gentleman married her at once. The production was at Metz. Petit de Julleville, *Les Comédiens*, p. 276. Several women took part in the *Passion* in Valenciennes in 1547, but by this time their appearance on the stage was beginning to be accepted as the normal practice in Italy. In the fifteenth century women, although permitted to take part in mimes and processions were not, officially, allowed to play speaking parts.

16. The history of Jason included his combat with the Minotaur, represented by artificial bulls blowing fire from their nostrils. In later scenes Jason killed the serpent on Colcos and sowed the dragon's teeth. Olivier de la Marche, *Mémoires*, vol. 2, pp. 356 ff., where he describes these scenes as *entremectz mondaines*.

17. See Cohen, *Etudes d'histoire du théâtre*, p. 166. Milet's play was by no means the first on the subject, representations of the siege of Troy are recorded as having been done in the fourteenth century and were probably often done earlier still.

18. In 45 BC Cicero's speech in defence of Q. Ligarius, tried as an enemy of Caesar, so moved Caesar that he acquitted the accused.

19. Humbert, *La Sculpture sous les ducs de Bourgogne*, p. 76.

20. D'Ancona, *Origini del teatro in Italia*, vol. 1, pp. 313 ff. discusses directions for a production of a *Passion* in Revello which include 'la nota scena de' vaticinj delle Sibille' whose long scrolls indicated in Latin, besides their names, 'l'età loro, gli scritti che dovranno essere ne' loro brevi' (p. 342). For a *Triumph* in Pistoia staged in honour of the city's patron, St James, the Archangel Raphael was followed by Caesar and Pompey both in chains led by a lady with flowing hair, who was identified by a *breve* as *Vanagloria*. She also led two whose *brevi*

showed them to be Socrates and Aristotle. But references to this means of identification are numerous.

21. But Prophets in plays were probably allowed to wear long gowns resembling those of dignified citizens for not only in the *Puits de Moïse* but also in descriptions of Prophets in Italian texts appear, e.g. 'Abraham, senex cum barba prolixa, largis vestibus indutus'. As in the north of Europe costumes for religious dramas became more and more elaborate, in the middle of the sixteenth century the Counter-Reformation seemed to bring in a greater simplicity in Italy. In Modena, in 1551, for instance, for the Feast of Corpus Christi, the *Compagnia de San Pietro Martire*, presented Prophets in a religious drama 'vestiti da sacco, scalzi e a piedi nudi, e ciascuno di essi portava il suo libro latino . . .' D'Ancona, *Origini del teatro in Italia*, vol. 1, p. 357. At a regal banquet given by the Gonzaga cardinal of Mantua on New Year's Day 1476, the Milanese ambassador reported that the cardinal had dressed his *camarero* as king of the feast and placed him at the head of the table wearing 'una turca de zetonio raso cremossino', from the cardinal's own wardrobe. *Archivio storico lombardo*, vol. 5, ser. 2, 1888, p. 194.

22. One of Pisanello's preliminary studies for the head of the Emperor wearing this hat survives (see Ill. 19, p. 83); it was certainly drawn from life.

23. Vigo, *Una Confraternita di giovenetti pistojesi*.

24. Liveries worn by the Bentivoglio and their court are described, for instance, by Ghirardacci, *Della historia di Bologna*, R.I.S., vol. 33, pt. 1, p. 147.

25. Vattasso, *Per la storia del dramma sacro*, pp. 95-6, 98-9.

26. Ibid., p. 99.

27. D'Escouchy describes the veil of *Sainte Eglise* as being 'moult doucement . . . à la guise de Bourgoigne ou de recluse'. Of the male dancers he says, 'ledits palletots brodez de feuillages d'or et chargiez d'orfèvrerie très richement . . . et sy avoient faulx visages d'or', the ladies wore, 'la façon de Brabant et sy avoient leur visages couverts d'un volet sy delie que elles povient bien veoir parmi'. *Chronique*, vol. 2, pp. 153, 226, 228.

28. Olivier de la Marche, *Description*, p. 24: '. . . de velours bleu seme de tout a.b.c.d. etc en brodure d'or'. When Louis XI, entered Paris in 1461, five ladies each wore a letter of the word PARIS on her sleeve: P = paix, A = amour, R = rayson, I = joye, S = seurete. Guenée and Lehoux, *Les Entrées royales*, p. 86.

29. See, for instance, Paris, Bib. Nat. ms. Lat, a. 1156B. fol. 125.

30. 'Non vogl'esser piu monaca'. Mazzi, *La Congrega dei Rozzi*, vol. 1, p. 50.

31. Cohen, *Le Livre de conduite du régisseur et les compts des dépenses*.

32. 'Quando Jesù sarà sopra el monte sia un bacille pulito che faza che l'esplendore dil sole che fere nel bacino venga sopra di Jesù . . . Et si el sole non lucesse,

abiate qualche brandoni o qualche altro lume . . .' D'Ancona, *Origini del teatro in Italia*, vol. 1, p. 322.

33. Cohen, *Historie de la mise en scène*, p. xxxvii.

34. Sanudo, *I Diarii*, vol. 1, 1498, p. 874: '8 homini a modo cavali marini armati da jostrar, con armadure, et atorno altri zoveni vestiti a uno modo con volti inarzentadi. . . . Poi erano molti vestiti da mori, con casache e volti negri . . .'

35. 'Un uomo nudo, dipinto come morto'. D'Ancona, *Origini del teatro in Italia*, vol. 1, p. 342.

36. A letter to Isabella d'Este in 1534 describes a production of a play on the life of St Lawrence, 'Laurentio fusse imprigionato: et cussi fu fatto a il Papa, che fu un homo artificiato cum maschera at cum soi panni e mitra, li in publico fu tagliata la testa cum bellissimo modo', Ibid., vol. 2, p. 435.

37. Cambiagi, *Memorie istoriche*, p. 69: 'La Fama . . . pennuto di penne di pagone, con alia grande e con visi umani per tutta la persona . . . Mida . . . tutto oro, viso, mane, zanche e ogni altra cosa.'

38. D'Ancona, *Origini del teatro in Italia*, vol. 1, p. 225.

39. Gozzadini, *Memorie per la vita di Giovanni II*, p. 17, is one among many others who write of antique armour in, for instance, a tournament in Bologna in 1468: 'factu est tanto apparatu in vestimentum et armorum ut antiquitas Romana videretur . . .'

40. Quoted by d'Ancona, *Origini del teatro in Italia*, vol. 1, p. 225 n.

41. D'Ancona, *Origini del teatro in Italia*, p. 226 n.

42. '. . . quattro fanciulli vestiti a ignudo, havendo sottilissimi rivolti intorno la testa et le braccia, che erano ventilati al soffiar de' venti'. Ghirardacci, *Della historia di Bologna*, p. 258.

43. Ibid., p. 259: 'Certi Minotauri et un griffone et un'aquila negra artificiosamente imitati dal vero'. At a joust at Milan in 1492 a *carro triumphale* was drawn by three horses 'uno come cervo l'altri come alicorni' for the entry of Gaspare Sanseverino into the lists. Mariolo Viscardo had a *cavallo de lione*. Gelli, *Mostra della giostra.*

44. Botticelli, *Judith Returning with the Head of Holofernes*, Uffizi.

45. '. . . una riforma delle feste ricordo Matteo di Marco Palmieri'. *Storia fiorentino*, 1454. R.I.S. Quoted by Guasti, *Le Feste di San Giovanni Batista*, p. 20. Almost a hundred years later at a tournament in Milan in 1553 a knight appeared wearing Samson putting the Philistines to flight as a crest to his helmet and on his shield, Hercules dragging Cacus from the cave. Vianello, 'Feste, tornei, congiure nel cinquecento milanese', *Archivio storico lombardo*, anno. 1, fasc. 1–2, 1936, p. 376 ff.

46. Sacchi, *Antichità romantiche d'Italia*, epoca 2, p. 49.

47. A production of the *Bacchi* at a wedding in Ferrara in 1502, was described by Isabella d'Este as being long because there were no ballets and for *intermezzi* only two *moresche*, one in which eleven men dressed as nudes appeared, wearing diagonal veils. D'Ancona, *Origini del teatro italiano*, vol. 2, p. 884.

48. On their legs were 'stivalletti d'oro per insino a mezza gamba depinti de perle e di gioie' and on their heads, 'capelletto bellissimo'. Luzzatto, *Una rappresentazione allegorica*, pp. 220 ff.

49. 'ornatissimamente in quello abito che ciascuno pianeta o da'poeti o da'strolagi si dipinge con suo segni . . .' Farno, *Il dramma allegorico*, pp. 174 ff.

50. Tabarrini, *Descrizione del convito e delle feste*, p. 22.

51. Faccioli, ed., *Mantova. Le Lettere*, vol. 2, p. 223 : '. . . uno spettacolo singolare [by "Seraphino Aquilano"] . . . una rappresentazione allegorica . . . all'inizio dello spettacolo il poeta . . . assai lascivamente vestito, come a la Volupta si convene, cum il leuto in brazo . . .'; p. 224: '. . . entro in scena . . . il Magnifico Maso Antonio Manzone, ambassadore de l'illustrissimo signor Duca di Calabria, representando la Virtute in abito leggiadrissimo e severo, come a quella si convene . . .'

52. Verdier, ed., *L'Entrée du Roy Loyis XII et de la Reine à Rouen 1508*, p. 10 : 'Le dieu Apollo dict dieu de Sappience, vestu de damas blanc, ayant son arc et sa trousse . . . [*trousse*, quiver]'; p. 11 : '. . . neufs Muses, vestues de damas de diverses coulleurs, chacune différentement habillées l'une en forme de Sybille, l'autre à la mode y talique, et les autres en aultre manière mais toutes gorgiasement . . .'

53. D'Escouchy, *Chronique*, vol. 2, p. 433, devotes a great deal of space to this funeral and describes the clothes of the mourners in detail. He states that the body of the king was carried in 'ung chariot de cuir bouilli', which suggests that decorative cars, used as *triumphs*, may have been made in a similar way.

54. Olivier de la Marche, *Description*, p. 17: '. . . Partit monseigr. le duc à cheval vestue d'une robe à longues manches ouvertes jusques en terre de drap dor fourie de très fines martres sabelines'.

55. *La Sottie de Folle Bombance*, Petit de Julleville, *La Comédie et les moeurs*, p. 229.

56. '. . . trois josnes enffans, paiges', dressed in white 'en manière d'angeles' mounted on fine corsairs 'enharnechiez de drap blanc bien decoppé.' D'Escouchy, *Chronique*, vol. 1, p. 125.

57. Petit de Julleville, *Les Comédiens*, p. 146.

Chapter 6: Entertainments at the Court of Maximilian I

1. Jason and Gideon were both connected with a fleece. Jason was sent to fetch the Golden Fleece in the possession of King Aeëtes in Colchis; Gideon's fleece was miraculously wet with dew when the rest of the earth was dry.

   The pheasant seems likely to have had a close connection with the sacred peacock which appears in the *Romance of Alexander.* For a discussion on the *Voeux du Paon* see Ritchie, *Buik of Alexander,* vols. 2 and 3, which are part of four vols. dealing with the mss. of this accretion to the story of Alexander. Edward III held a Feast of the Peacock and it was to him that the *Romance of Alexander,* now in the Bodleian, belonged. The Burgundian knights at the Feast of the Pheasant at Lille took their vows on the Holy Trinity and *Sur ce faisan.*

2. As well as being crowned poet laureate 'die 18 mensis Aprilis 1487 in arce Norimbergenii a Friderico III imperatore', Celtes was created doctor of philosophy; he was the first German to be given this double honour.

3. The *Ludus Dianae* was published again in 1502 in Celtes's *Quattuor libri amorum,* the frontispiece of which bears Dürer's monogram, the other cuts do not. Copy in the British Museum Library.

4. See Waas, *The Legendary Character of Kaiser Maximilian* both for Maximilian's attitude to himself and for the impression he made on his contemporaries and on later generations.

5. *Triumph Kaisers Maximilian I* (2 vols) *Jahrbuches des Kunsthistorischen des Allerhöchsten Kaiserhauses,* contains reproductions of all the engravings that make up the *Triumphzug.* See also Panofsky, *The Life and Art of Albrecht Dürer,* who states the scheme of the engravings was worked out by Martin Treitsauerwein in 1512: the wood-cuts themselves were done between 1512 and 1518.

6. British Museum ms. Add. 24098 f. 19b.

7. *Narrenschiff* see note 15, Chapter 4.

8. Thirty-one Fools at the court of Burgundy are listed by name between 1380 and 1480; they include such names as *Andrieu de la Plume* and *Hance le geant.* Two Fools, *Jehan le Sage* and *Richard l'Amoureux* travelled with Margaret of York when she set out on her wedding journey. It was arranged that they were to be returned to the King of England after her arrival. Laborde, *Les ducs de Bourgogne,* pp. 452, 538.

9. *Weisskunig,* a pun on the white armour worn by Maximilian, and his wisdom, is a romantic account of the Emperor's youth. Wood-cuts mainly by Burgkmair, Beck and Schaufelein, executed in 1514.

10. *Theuerdank*, 'the noble-minded one', a romantic account of Maximilian's maturity. Begun in 1510, concluded in 1517.

11. *Rennen, stechen, kämpfen* the standard forms of single combat, mounted and on foot, fought at tournaments of the fifteenth and sixteenth centuries.

12. An entry of 1502 in Cod. 13 of the *Gedenkbuche des Kaisers* in the Staatsarchiv reads, 'Meister Martin sol all mummery so K Mt ye gebrancht hat in ain buch mallen lessen'. No Martin appears as a painter in the Maximilian archives but a *Martin Trummer* is referred to several times as *Hofschneider*.

13. *Freydal des Kaisers Maximilian I. Turniere und Mummereien Herausgegeben*, was published in Vienna 1880–2. All the *Freydal* drawings are reproduced in monochrome 'facsimile' except the frontispiece which is in colour. There is a long and interesting introduction by von Leitner. The British Museum print-room has a copy.

14. Some rather primitive paintings of Maximilian's day show workers in the salt mines wearing a rough dress rather like the costumes worn in this mummery which may, therefore, have represented in a glamorised form an important local industry. In the absence of any contemporary text the themes of the Maximilian mummeries can only be guessed at.

15. Costumes of this kind, as masquerade dress, are represented as being worn by artisans in the Nuremberg Shrovetide Carnival (*Nuremberg Stadbibliothek ms. Nor. K444*). Since, however, these drawings which purport to show costumes of the middle of the fifteenth century were almost certainly done at the end of the sixteenth, it is dangerous to use them as evidence of fifteenth-century masquerade dress; in the nature of things redrawing and copying of earlier works of art almost always involves distortion. If, for instance, the original works from which the later drawings were copied did show lacing at the waist this might have been omitted in the copies. See Sumberg, *The Nuremberg Schembart Carnival*, figs 4–7.

16. Wood-cut by Burgkmair for *Weisskunig*, reproduced by Burkhard, *Hans Burgkmair*, plate 125.

17. See Durrieu, *Les Très Riches Heures* and de Champeaux and Gauchery, *Les Travaux d'art exécutés pour Jean de France*. The *Livre des Merveilles* was commissioned by Jean sans Peur, Duke of Burgundy and given by him to his uncle, the Duc de Berry, some time before 1413. For the oriental dress in the *Livre des Merveilles* and Jean sans Peur's captivity, when Comte de Nevers, see Chapter 1, note 8 above.

18. Sumberg, referring to the *Freydal* mummeries in a different connection also notices that, 'In the Freydal each group of mummers is depicted in the same costume'. See *The Nuremberg Schembart Carnival* by this author.

19. During the joust at the *Pas de l'Arbre d'Or*, at the third banquet seven monkeys appeared 'les dits singes estoient moult bien faictz aupres du vif' with mechanism inside which enabled them to perform clever novel tricks. During the course of these one took up a little drum and another played the flute while a third took a mirror and another a comb. The monkey with the drum began to 'jouer une moresque' and, while dancing the *moresca*, made a complete tour of the tower which formed a part of the setting. Olivier de la Marche, *Mémoires*, vol. 3. The monkeys in the *Freydal* must, because of their chains, be live animals. Monkeys were prized as pets, an inventory for the year 1378 includes payment for 'xi papegays et x singes'. Laborde, *Les ducs de Bourgogne*, p. xlviii.

20. British Museum ms. Harley 4425 f. 36.

21. The famous drawing at Longleat of a scene from Shakespeare's *Titus Andronicus* shows the male principals wearing Roman armour, the Queen of the Goths a reasonable attempt at mediaeval (i.e. 'Gothic') dress and the men-at-arms in attendance, uniforms of a Swiss/German pattern of round about Shakespeare's day.

22. For a clear example of this dress when it was in fashion see the *Lit de Justice* by Jean Fouquet, of 1458 (Munich Library). In this painting (of the trial of the Duc d'Alençon), several of the spectators at the trial can be seen from the back, so that the inserted pleats are clearly visible.

23. *Pattens*, overshoes consisting of thick wooden soles and instep-straps beneath which the foot could be slipped. As protective footwear (against snow and mud) they could still be found in the twentieth century but since both Philippe le Bon and the Emperor Frederick III are shown in paintings wearing them on ceremonial occasions they must have been a part of the high-fashion of the middle of the fifteenth century.

Chapter 7: Costume in the Italian Theatre of the Sixteenth Century

1. When, from the third quarter of the sixteenth century, Brantôme looked back to the entry of Cesare Borgia into Chinon to collect his bride at the beginning of the century, the meaning of *mi-parti* had evidently been forgotten. Brantôme repeated the words of a contemporary chronicler on Cesare's dress, 'avec qu'une robe de satin rouge et drap d'or my-party', and adds, 'je ne puis pas bien comprendre quant a moy cest façon d'éstoffe'. Brantôme, *Oeuvres complètes*, ed. by Lalanne, pp. 207 ff.

2. This is often recorded by Italian painters of the fifteenth century. Pollaiuolo's *Martyrdom of St Sebastian* in the National Gallery, London, catalogue no. 292 is a good example.

3. Rembrandt and his contemporaries used this kind of dress to represent the old times.

4. Forty shepherds accompanied the nymphs who appeared on horseback when Bianca Capello was welcomed in Siena in 1582. Saltini, ed., *Di una mascherata pastorale fatta in Siena.*

5. *La Calandra*, the first play of its kind as far as we know, was produced as a part of the festivities to welcome Isabella Gonzaga on her visit to Rome in 1514. Vasari says that Baldassare Peruzzi did some marvellous scenery for it.

6. Leone de' Sommi (see note 22 below) discussed the place and character of the *intermezzi* in the sixteenth-century theatre in *Quattro dialoghi.*

7. A water-festival was among those illustrated in the Valois tapestries (now in the Uffizi) which depict festivities at the French court in the life-time of Catherine de' Medici. See Frances Yates, *The Valois Tapestries.* Another was among the spectacles arranged for the entry of Henri II and Catherine de' Medici into Rouen in 1550, see p. 233 in text.

8. One of the early actions of Leo X after his election to the Papacy was to arrange for the aggrandizement of his brother, Giuliano de' Medici, Duke of Nemours, and his nephew, Lorenzo de' Medici. Both were given the citizenship of Rome and entertained not only with shows and banquets but a theatre in which to produce the *Penulo* was specially built for the occasion.

9. No foreigner or low-born person appeared as an actor. Palliolo, *Le feste per conferimento del patriziato romano a Giuliano e Lorenzo de' Medici*, p. 130.

10. At least two accounts of this festival of 1513 have survived; they do not entirely agree on minor details. Marcantonio Altieri addressed his account to Lorenzo Orsini, a member of one of the oldest families of Rome, *Il natale di Roma nel 1513.* Paolo Palliolo of Fano sent his account to the most noble and virtuous lady Madonna Lucrezia Borra di Zanchini of Bologna, the wife of the Senator of Rome at the time, a Bolognese, *Le feste per conferimento del patriziato romano a Giuliano e Lorenzo de' Medici.*

11. *Il Monte di Feronia nel quale si contengono le cose d'arme fatte in Ferrara nel Carnevale del MDLXI.* Ferrara 1562.

12. Eleanor of Toledo left Naples with an escort of seven ships on 9 June 1539. The first pages of the account of her wedding in Florence describe her clothes and there follows an account of the triumphal arches set up to welcome her on which the reliefs of enlargements of medals of classical antiquity were especially remarkable. In the description of the festivals themselves Apollo and the Nine Muses are described as each carrying a musical instrument and a plaque inscribed with the character's name. A great many other characters also appeared, including *Baccanti*, ten of whom were women and ten Satyrs. The women are

299

recorded as being 'vestivano corte' like ancient bacchante with 'sottilissime tocche d'oro'. Giambullari, *Apparato et feste nelle nozze dello illustrissimo signor Duca di Firenze et della Duchessa sua consorte.*

13. *And buds of marjoram had stol'n her hair.* Shakespeare. Sonnet 89.

14. Brantôme, *Oeuvres complètes*, ed. by Lalanne, vol. 9. Brantôme dedicated his works to Marguerite de Valois, daughter of Henri II and first wife of Henri IV (though her divorce had probably taken place before their actual publication). Brantôme describes himself in his dedication as 'gentilhomme ordinayre de la chambre de nos deux derniers roys, Charles IX et Henry III et chambellan de monsieur d'Alançon'. Marguerite was the surviving sister of Charles IX, Henri III and the Duc d'Alençon.

15. Vincente Alvarez, *grand panetier de Philippe d'Espagne* also wrote of the nymphs that performed at Lyons in 1548 when Philip was there but he dealt with them drily. Eight of them, he wrote, represented nymphs, eight others *Diane chasseresse* and the last eight peasants. 'I will not enter into descriptions of their clothes', he continued, 'for fear of making this account too long.' Dovilée, ed., *Relation du beau voyage fit aux Pay Bas en 1548.*

16. *Patins*, see note 23, Chapter 6 above. At the time of which Brantôme writes, towards the end of the sixteenth century, pattens with very thick soles indeed were an important part of the feminine fashion. In Venice they were worn as high as eight or nine inches, in other fashionable centres as much as three or four inches. Surviving specimens of these high-soled over-shoes can be found in the Ca' Pesaro in Venice and the Museum of Fine Arts in Boston, Mass.

17. See note 12 above.

18. In 1539 the *Confrèrie de la Passion*, which had occupied the Hospital of the Holy Trinity had to quit when the hospital was returned to its proper use. They then established themselves in the Hôtel de Flandres where they played to Francis I who had confirmed their charter. In 1543 the Hôtel de Flandres was demolished by order of the king, whereupon the *Confrèrie* acquired the freehold of the Hôtel de Bourgogne in association with the *Enfants de sans Souci*. They built 'une grande salle et autres édifices nécessaires'. The Hôtel de Bourgogne was, with this move, established as a theatre in the modern sense. See Petit de Julleville, *Les Comédiens*, p. 70.

19. Palliolo, *Le feste per conferimento del patriziato romano a Giuliano e Lorenzo de' Medici.*

20. *Giraldi Cinthio nobile Ferrarese, e segretario all'illustrissimo et Eccellentiss. Duca di Ferrara intorno al comporre e i Romanzi delle Comedie e delle Tragedie, e di altre maniere di Poesie,* pp. 277 and 278.

21. Oxford, Bodleian Cod. 2251. See *Catalogue of the Hebrew Manuscripts in the Bodleian Library and in the College Libraries of Oxford*, cod. 781.

22. Biblioteca Palatina, ms. Parma 2664, is the only surviving ms. of the *Quattro dialoghi*, the other known ms. was destroyed in the great fire in the Library at Turin in 1904. The *Quattro dialoghi* were published for the first time as a separate volume under the editorship of Ferruccio Marotti, who contributed an excellent introduction and notes, in Milan in 1968. They have been extensively discussed by, among others, d'Ancona, who published the greater part of them in his *Origini del teatro in Italia* and Nicoll who included a translation of them in *The Development of the Theatre*.

23. Even as late as the eighteenth century special clothing was worn for tragedy as can be seen from the inventories of the Norwich theatre. They include several items simply called 'A Tragedy Train Cleane'd – blue; a white Sattin Tragedy Dress; A Tragedy Vest scarlet and silver'. These were evidently costumes of a generalised design and may have been in the wardrobe for a considerable time. Eshleman, ed., *The Committee Books of the Theatre Royal Norwich*, p. 144.

24. These designs by Giulio Romano were described in a letter to Don Ferrante, Lord of Guastalla and uncle and guardian to the young Duke Francesco Gonzaga, from Don Ferrante's secretary, Ippolito Capilupi, himself a poet. In the letter Ippolito described the entertainments in Mantua for the carnival of 1542; it is quoted at length by d'Ancona, *Origini del teatro in Italia*, vol. 2, p. 438, where he also discusses a possible maker of the masks of the shepherds.

25. Vecellio, *Habiti antichi e moderni*.

26. Besides 'uno cappelletto alla greca, nero, di cartoni impastati per fare philosophi' (Vigo, *Una Confraternita di gioⱱanetti pistojesi*), there are many other strange descriptions of clothing supposed to be Greek used in dramas. E.g. 'Eran cinti d'un largo drappo di seta versicolore alla Greca . . . In capo haveano capelli alti alla Greca di veluto paonazzo, peloso, attorniato tutto di bellissime piume, carriche di treccie e tremaruole d'oro . . .' Vianello, *Feste, tornei, congiure nel cinquecento milanese*, p. 390.

27. '. . . centocinquanta giovani tutti vestito di rosso, con maschere rosse, et tenevano la bocca aperta a guisa che gridassero . . .'. The account tells of the *carro* on which they were mounted which was a rock with an open crater from which fire was thrown out as it was also from *certe fessure*. Discordant sounds issued from instruments played within. Quoted from San Gallo's *Diario*, by d'Ancona, *Origini del teatro in Italia*, vol. 1, p. 336 n.

Chapter 8: The Sixteenth Century in the North of Europe

1. A considerable number of studies of the Chambers of Rhetoric have been published in Holland and Belgium. The two mainly quoted here are Claeys, *Histoire du théâtre à Gand*, and Liebrecht, *Les Chambres de Rhétorique*.
2. In 1496 competitors travelled to Antwerp from Amsterdam, Zeland and Holland. On this occasion the highest prize was won by the Chamber of the *Fleur de Genêt* of Lierre. The Chamber *La Violette* of Brussels won the prize for their play *La mort de Christ*. Liebrecht, op. cit., p. 53.
3. The *landjuweel* of Ghent was organised by members of the Ghent Chamber of the *Fountain* – the *Fonteinisten*. Nineteen Chambers entered the poetry contest, for which the majority of themes laid down were on some aspect of theology. In 1595 contests were forbidden to treat of religious subjects and forbidden, too, to publish without permission from the civil authorities. Claeys, op. cit.
4. In 1604 an English company played in the Hôtel de Ville in Ghent and again in the years 1607, 1608, 1611, in all cases as a part of a tour which included other Netherlandish towns. Claeys, op. cit.
5. Liebrecht, op. cit., p. 75.
6. The full title of this account by Jacques Thibout, from which extracts are quoted here, is *Relation de l'ordre de la triomphante et magnifique montre du mystère des SS Actes des Apostres par Arnoul et Simon Greban, ouvrage inédit de Jacquest Thiboust, sieur de Quantilly, secrétaire du roy, élu de Berry*. The script of the play had been written in about 1450 by the two Grebans, both doctors of theology. Baron A. de Girardot published an abbreviated account of the event, *Mystère des Actes des Apôtres*. This is less interesting from the point of view of the costumes but includes other matter not recorded by Thibout as, for instance the list of characters which amounted to 494.
7. Olivier de la Marche often mentions a *chaperon à bourrelet* in reference to the rolled-hood which had become the accepted formal male head-wear by the 1450s. In a vestigal form a tiny version of this is still attached to the left shoulder of the mantle of the English Order of the Garter. The *chaperon à bourrelet* had disappeared as a part of fashionable dress by the third quarter of the fifteenth century, so that its inclusion among the costumes at Bourges means that it represented the dress either of the past or of an official or academic kind.
8. '. . . une grosse houppe de perles pendante, et par le bas ung gros bourrelet de meme . . . il avoit une perruque fort longue, approchant à la mode judaique.' Thibout, op. cit., p. 44.

9. Thibout translates as, 'nous sommes a couvert de tout malefice nous n'en voulons pas d'avantage' (p. 51).

10. See the drawings reproduced by Albert van der Put in the *Journal of the Warburg and Courtauld Institutes*, vol. 3, 1939–40, p. 49. The drawing of the masque in progress is (or was then) in the Cyril Drummond collection.

11. A description of the journey of Philip II from Spain to the Netherlands was published in Antwerp in 1552. The author included in his four volumes devoted to the expedition descriptions of all the joyous entries encountered on the way and they were very numerous. At the Fête at Binche, after describing the clothing of some of the male masquers he continued: 'Cada una d'ellos traya una dama por la mano, las quales tãbien trayan mascaras y tocados muy estrãnos antiguos de brocado pelo muy altos en punta, cubiertos de una toquilla blãca listada de plata q hazia de tras un trẽçado largo lleno de oro y pedreria: venia vestidas de unas cotas ò faldillas ala antigua de raso encarnado.' The theme of the mask or *moresca* was a battle between knights and savages – *salvajes* – the latter being defeated, after which 'sobre un ricco carro' covered with green taffetas was dragged in, 'lecho como quadriga antigua con quatro ruedas'. Writing his long account of this occasion, Calvete uses the term *ala antigua* fairly often but never in describing the clothes of the later actors who played scenes which included Diana and her nymphs, naiads, oreads and fauns. Calvete, *El felicissimo ∪iaie d'el muy alto y muy Poderoso Principe Don Phelippe*, p. 200.

12. This is a good example because it includes in one costume so many exotic features of dress but in numerous, in fact in the majority of paintings of the kind at this period similar stagey details of dress can be found.

13. For his coronation in 1461, Louis XI is described as entering Rheims, 'son cheval a grosses rondes campannes d'argent, couvert de couvrechief de plaisance, a quatre pages aprés luy à semblables campannes qui firent grand noise.' Chastellain, *La Chronique de Georges Chastellain*, vol. 2, p. 53. La Marche referred to, 'ung aultre houssie de drap dor velours violet chargie de campanes dargent a maniere de poires grosses' in describing the housings of a horse at a tournament. *Description*, p. 24.

14. Decorators of late manuscripts evidently searched for novelties with which to embellish the borders which surrounded the pictures that had become large and elaborate. The borders of the *Grimani Breviary* include naturalistically painted jewels, bells, both round and pear-shaped, and what appear to be the kind of *orfevrerie* letters of the alphabet used to decorate clothing for festivals.

15. A rather similar arrangement of cords is worn by the young temptress dressed in Italian fashion in the Patinir *Temptation of St Anthony* in Madrid, for which

Quentin Massys painted the figures. Since the device of using cords in this way may have been Italian (though it is difficult to recall other instances), when it was used for the dress of St Barbara it may have corresponded to the reference to the 'Italian' head-dress of Herodias in the Bourges *Acts of the Apostles*.

16. Etienne Jodelle was a friend of Ronsard and one of the seven members of the *Pleiade*. 'Sixteenth century French academism takes its rise in the group round Dorat at the College de Coqueret which is also the well-head of the Pleiade.' Yates, *The French Academies*.

17. Orpheus is said to have lived in Thrace at the time of the Argonauts and to have accompanied them on their expedition.

18. *Estiene Iodelle Parisien Le Recueil des inscriptions, figures, devises et masquerades ordonnées en l'hostel de Ville à Paris, le jeudi, 17 de février 1558.* In a poem expressing his love and admiration of Jodelle, Ronsard included the lines:

> *Un seul point seulement te deffaut, ma Jodelle :*
> *C'est que nostre grand Prince, ignorant ta grandeur,*
> *Ne respond au destin qui hautement t'appelle . . .*

since this was published in 1559, a year after the banquet, Henri may not have been very much impressed by Jodelle's efforts. Ronsard, *Oeuvres complètes*, vol. 10.

19. Two facsimiles of two editions of the souvenir of the *entrée* were published in the nineteenth century. They do not agree as to the details. But the publication by the Société Rouennaise de Bibliophiles clearly reproduces both engravings and text accurately.

20. A good many details and much of the arrangement of the subject-matter in the Valois tapestries derive from drawings by Callot of festivals at the court of Henri II. Yates, *The Valois Tapestries*.

21. Wallace collection, London, catalogue no. 531.

22. These are the women who wear small turban-like head-dresses, a local fashion in Burgundy in the 1540s.

23. See notes 27 and 28, Chapter 2.

24. The Rozzi of Siena ceased to produce religious plays after the first two decades of the sixteenth century. Mazzi, *La Congrega dei Rozzi*, vol. 2, p. 131. In 1582 the *Connards* of Rouen were still in being but all references to religion in their performances were banned. Petit de Julleville, *Les Comédiens*, p. 123.

Chapter 9: The End of the Period

1. Dürer's drawing of a Venetian woman is dated 1497: he painted a bust-length portrait of a girl in north Italian dress in 1505. His sketch-book of the Netherlands (which includes women in German dress) belongs to the end of the second decade of the sixteenth century. His prayer-book for the Emperor Maximilian, which contains some drawings of men in foreign dress seems to date from about 1515. Among the most interesting of Dürer's costume drawings are three of women from Livonia, a province of Lithuania.

2. Holbein drew few women in foreign dress but several in Swiss regional dress and his portraits, which include sitters of German and of English nationality, as well as the French dress in the large *Ambassadors* painting in the London National Gallery, are important as documents.

3. Three drawings on the same page which show an Italian, a French and a Spanish woman in the high-fashions of their respective countries, appear in the Basle sketch-book of Niklaus Manuel Deutsch. The book bears a date, 1521, but there is no need to regard this as meaning that all the sketches were done at that time: the costumes worn by the three ladies mentioned above are certainly much earlier in date.

4. In the Wolfenbüttel library.

5. The collection of drawings known as the *Recueil d'Arras* consists of portraits mainly of members of the House of Burgundy and their court circle. Although the drawings were done in the later sixteenth century, the sitters lived, for the most part, up to two hundred years earlier and, although the drawings are clumsy, they show considerable research into earlier works of art.

6. Robert Boissard was a draughtsman and engraver, born in about 1570: Jean Jacques Boissard was born in about 1533. It is not altogether possible to separate their works. *Habitus Variarum Orbis Gentium* was published in 1581; *Leben und Contraferten der Turkischen und Persichen Sultanen* in 1596; *Icones Diversorum Hominum fama et rebus gesstis illustrium* in 1591, and *Vitae et icones Sultanorum Turcicorum Principum Persarum aliorumq* in 1596.

7. Wilenski's *Flemish Painters* includes brief biographies of sixteenth-century Netherlandish painters from which it will be seen that a considerable number of them, including Jacques van Gheyn the younger of Antwerp, had connections of some sort with theatre design, sometimes directly involved with Chambers of Rhetoric.

8. These two figures reappear (with minor alterations to the costume) in a painting of a *Nocturnal Banquet* by Joos van Winghe (Amsterdam Rijksmuseum catalogue no. 508). Van Winghe died in 1603.

9. Lucas van Leyden's engravings were collected by Netherlandish painters a hundred years after his death and in the intervening period his influence was still felt by the pupils of his own students. Lucas's work often includes oriental and exotic dress and much of it shows connections with the stage.

10. The popularity of the type of dress associated with Maximilian, particularly as he appears as *Freydal*, began to be used as standard old-time costume at the end of the sixteenth century and can be found increasingly during the first sixty years of the seventeenth.

11. See note 7 above.

12. Rubens was for some time a pupil and assistant of van Veen, who was associated in his work at a slightly earlier period with van Winghe, painter of the *Nocturnal Banquet* mentioned above. An example of the scope and magnificence of the pageants arranged for joyous entries can be understood by studying the details of the paintings of the *Ommeganck* procession of 1615 in the Victoria and Albert Museum, London, reproduced in Laver, *Isabella's Triumph*.

13. The republic of Venice boasted of the ancient descent of its citizens. All those who were members of families whose names appeared in the republic's *Libro d'Oro* were required to wear a long gown which was modified a little in design for informal wear indoors. This gown continued to be called a *toga* although it bore no resemblance at all to the toga of classical Rome. D'Ancona, *Origini del teatro in Italia*, quotes Stopparto, *La Comedia popolare in Italia* (Padua 1887, not in British Museum) who in turn quotes a dialogue of *Massimo Trojano*, Venice, 1568: '. . . il celebre musico Orlando Lasso, fiammingo, ma per lunga dimora quasi italiano, fece da Magnifico venetiano col nome di messer Pantalone de' Bisognosi. De' Bisognosi avava un giubbone cremisino [doublet] con calze di scarlatto fatte alla venetiana, et una vesta nero lunga insino ai piedi . . .'

14. Petit de Julleville, *Les Comédiens*, pp. 70 ff., says that taste had become more refined: the new admiration for the antique led to disapproval of the rich mixture of the comic and the religious. Faced with the new earnest Protestantism it was dangerous to allow the mob to laugh at holy scenes and personages. The playing of *mysteries* ceased in 1548 officially, but only in the capital. From this time the *Confraternity of the Passion* declined. An opposition grew up between the 'people' who sided with the Confraternity and the new literary class.

15. The Italian taste in classical stage-dress is already evident in works of art inspired by festivals in honour of Diane de Poitiers, established mistress of Henri II at the time of his marriage to Catherine de' Medici. It was remarkable that when Catherine de' Medici married the future Henri II in 1533, although the bride was dressed *alla francese*, the company danced *a la fogia de Italia*. Ghizoni,

'Ceremonie seguite il 27 e 28 ottobre 1533 in Marsiglia per Matrimonio del Duca d'Orleans con Caterina de' Medici', *Archivio storico lombardo*, vol. 1, 1874, p. 18.

16. Saltini, ed., *Di una mascherata pastorale fatta in Siena*.

17. See *Descrizione de Magnificentissimo apparato . . . Rappresentata in Firenze nelle felicissime Nozze degli' Illustrissimi, et Eccellentissimi Signori, il signor Don Cesare d'Este e la signora Donna Virginia Medici*. Florence 1585. The goddesses representing the Hours wore curly blond wigs adorned with strings of pearls and *tremolanti* (quivering ornaments, probably sequins) of gold; their gowns were shot yellow silk edged with fringe of gold . . .

18. This was probably the most fully recorded of all the Medici marriages, every one of the prolonged festivities, including each intermezzo that appeared between each act of every comedy was described in detail and many of them were engraved. The *intermezzi* were engraved by, among other people, Epifanio d'Alfiani: see, on this subject, Warburg, *I costumi teatrali per gli intermezzi del 1589*.

19. This little-known painting, attributed by some to Alessandro Allori, is catalogued as no. 1119, Louvre, under Cristofano.

20. Even if the exotic figures above the lintel in the central tympanum of the narthex at Vezelay are regarded as representing various pagans and heathen towards whom the missions of the Apostles were directed, the inspiration for their appearance may well have been the drama. A rondel in the same doorway certainly contains an acrobat.

21. The *Romance of Alexander*, Bodleian ms. 264, is only one of the several Gothic manuscripts that decorated their pages with figures wearing masquerade dress. The fourteenth-century Tito Livio (MS. C214) in the Ambrosiana, Milan, includes Italian masquerade dress.

22. See note 6 above.

23. Rembrandt's *Conspiracy of the Batavians* (National Museum, Stockholm) was designed for the new Town Hall of Amsterdam but was removed a short time after completion. The story is from Tacitus, *Historiae*, vol. 4, p. 13. See Bredius, *The Paintings of Rembrandt*.

Notes to Illustrations

1. Rhetoricians' festival at Haarlem, 1606. *Entry of the Hazel-Tree Chamber of Aedwaertswor:* detail. From *Const-Thoonende Juweel, by de lodijcke stadt Haerlem*, Haarlem, 1607.

At the beginning of the seventeenth century religious drama was still represented in the ceremonial entries of competing theatrical companies at Netherlandish festivals. Here even the traditional Hell's Mouth marches between the Devil and Death.

2. Jean Fouquet. *Heures de Etienne Chevalier: Martyrdom of St Apollonia.* Chantilly, Musée Condé.

The martyrdom is shown as being performed as a part of the action in a religious play. Temporary structures have been erected for the occasion partly to accommodate the audience and partly to serve as locations or *mansions* housing special scenes in the play. The manuscript which includes this miniature is not dated but must belong to the first decade of the second half of the fifteenth century.

3. Reverse of the banner of the *Infanterie* of Dijon. From du Tilliot, *Mémoires pour servir à l'histoire de la Fête des Foux.*

Among their activities the *Infanterie* were responsible for festivities connected with the vintage in which members of the upper-classes, disguised as vineyard-workers paraded on decorated cars.

4. Rhetoricians' festival at Haarlem, 1606. The *Cartouche* of the Chamber of Rhetoric at Leyden called the *Orangie Lelie*. From *Const-Thoonende Juweel, by de lodijcke stadt Haerlem*, Haarlem, 1607.

Rhetoricians seem to have hung their *cartouches* in the inn or other interior in which they held their meetings.

5. French School. *Térence des ducs:* frontispiece. Before 1416. Ms. fr. 664. Paris, Bibliothèque de l'Arsenal.

Northern artists evidently found it more difficult to discover sources for Roman civil dress than for Roman armour.

6. French School. *Térence des ducs: The Eunuch.* Before 1416. Paris, Bibliothèque de l'Arsenal.

The working-class dress in this Ms. is regional and definitely French, not Netherlandish.

7. Another scene from *The Eunuch*. Before 1416. Paris, Bibliothèque de l'Arsenal.

In these miniatures the dress of every character is carefully adjusted to the social standing indicated by Terence's text.

8. Andrea da Bologna. Polyptych, *St Catherine*: detail. 1369. Marche, Fermo.

St Catherine of Alexandria, thought of as having been a princess, is always shown to be wearing the latest princely fashions.

9. Andrea Mantegna. *Adoration of the Magi*: detail of orientals. Florence, Uffizi.

At some periods European fashions were adopted by inhabitants of the Near East, who continued to wear them unchanged for a long time; at other periods oriental dress inspired European fashions. In this case the tunic of the man with a Near-Eastern hat and quiver is certainly European, whatever the origin of the hanging-sleeve.

10. Gentile da Fabriano. *Adoration of the Magi*: detail of crowd. 1423. Florence, Uffizi.

Men wearing a variety of oriental dresses were already to be found in fourteenth-century paintings of the Journey and the Adoration of the Magi.

11. Gentile da Fabriano. *Adoration of the Magi*: detail, the youngest Magus. 1423. Florence, Uffizi.

This is probably the first time that the youngest Magus was represented as a boy young enough to have been a member of a *potenza* rather than as a man old enough to pass as an Eastern sage.

12. Gentile da Fabriano. *Adoration of the Magi*: detail, the skirt of the youngest Magus. 1423. Florence, Uffizi.

Even the decorative treatment of the skirt, painted partly on a gesso ground, cannot conceal the naturalism with which both the fringe and the embroidered flowers are rendered. It was usual for the kings to be shown removing their marks of rank – crowns and spurs – before offering their gifts to the Christ child.

13. Gentile da Fabriano. *Adoration of the Magi*: detail, the second Magus. 1423. Florence, Uffizi.

The design of the gold cuffs may be a decorative rendering of ermine. The hair of this man is much too long for the current fashion and may be intended to look Greek or oriental (see Ill. 16). The Magus' crown incorporates in its design the Lily of Florence.

14. Benozzo Gozzoli. *Journey of the Magi*: detail of crowd. Florence, Palazzo Riccardi-Medici.

The careful recording of so many types of foreign dress show the growing interest in the dress of strangers that was to lead to the publication, in the sixteenth century, of books on foreign dress.

15. Benozzo Gozzoli. *Journey of the Magi*: detail, the youngest Magus. Florence, Palazzo Riccardi-Medici.

As in Gentile da Fabriano's painting (Ill. 11) only the hose and the under-sleeves belong to the current fashion. The young Magus is accompanied by six members of a *brigata* wearing uniform livery.

16. Benozzo Gozzoli. *Journey of the Magi*: detail, the second Magus. Florence, Palazzo Riccardi-Medici.

This Magus, too, is accompanied by members of a *brigata*, wearing a different livery from the boys who accompany the younger Magus.

17. Benozzo Gozzoli. *Journey of the Magi*: detail, the third Magus. Florence, Palazzo Riccardi-Medici.

The design of the textile of the gown may have been based on the gold cuffs of the second Magus in Gentile's painting, though the general effect is quite different. Alternatively, both may have some connection with the Orient.

18. Pisanello, or School of. Drawing of the head of a man in a feather head-dress. Paris, Louvre, Cabinet des Dessins.

The shape of the collar of the subject suggests that the drawing was done during the first two decades of the fifteenth century. It seems probable that the head-dress as it appears here was intended to be worn over some super-structure which would conceal the mechanism by which the feathers are held in place.

19. Pisanello. Study for medal of the Emperor John Paleologus. Paris, Louvre, Cabinet des Dessins.

A large group of head-dresses of related but varied design worn by people either actually or supposedly from the Near and Middle East, consists of a dome-shaped crown and a brim of varying width made stiff by the process of quilting the outer stuff (textile or leather) onto a padded lining. The brim, often cut at the sides, can be wide or narrow: the dome of the crown, high or low.

20. Pisanello. Drawings of heads of priests of the Greek Church. Paris, Louvre, Cabinet des Dessins.

Other, perhaps or perhaps not, later versions of this kind of head-dress omit the slits at the sides and have brims which widen as they rise. These may, however, be of different origin rather than versions of the head-dresses seen in this drawing.

21. Giotto. *The Resurrection*: detail, sleeping soldiers. Padua, Arena Chapel.

In contrast to his 'Roman' skirt, the mantle of this recumbant figure is represented naturalistically.

22. Giotto. *The Resurrection:* detail, sleeping soldiers. Padua, Arena Chapel.

Giotto has decorated the torsoes of the armour with acanthus-leaves and arabesques, but the belt and band round the neck are ornamented with cufic characters.

23. Giotto. *The Crucifixion:* detail, Roman soldier. Padua, Arena Chapel.

Giotto had, of course, no difficulty in portraying clothing of the current fashion seen in movement. The clothes being removed by the spectators at the *Entry into Jerusalem* (Arena Chapel), for instance, provide valuable information on the construction of current dress.

24. Claus Sluter. *Puits de Moïse:* the Prophet Zacharias, detail. Before 1406. Near Dijon.

The sculptor has included the necessary seam that runs down the falling end of the hood; the hat is treated with similar naturalism.

25. Claus Sluter. *Puits de Moïse:* King David, detail. Before 1406. Near Dijon.

Orfèvrerie, highly fashionable in the middle of the fourteenth century, was by this time no longer worn as a part of fashionable dress, though still used as decoration on the surcoats of jousting knights, the housings of their horses and preserved in the theatre beyond the beginning of the sixteenth century.

26. Botticelli. *Primavera:* Flora, detail. Florence, Uffizi.

Gothic dagged sleeves are used here to suggest timeless, romantic or old-time dress. Girls surrounding the Car of Love in a painting of Petrarch's *Triumphs* in Fiesole (by Jacopo del Sellaio) wear dresses sprinkled with small flowers similar to Flora's.

27. Filippino Lippi. *Adoration of the Magi:* detail of crowd. London, National Gallery.

The hat on the ground, left, is based on the type worn by the Emperor John Paleologus (see Ill. 19). Some other men wear dress of the current fashion, others again, something intended to be oriental. This variety can be found in paintings of the subject by Gentile da Fabriano and Benozzo Gozzoli among others.

28. Hieronymus Bosch. *Adoration of the Magi:* detail, the youngest Magus. Philadelphia, John G. Johnson Collection.

The design embroidered on the sleeve is closely related to similar designs to be found (often worn by members of a *brigata*) at the beginning of the fifteenth century. The mature Magus, wearing a sword, has a much further debased version of the cut-edged Gothic sleeve and one which approaches the sleeves of *moresca* dancers.

29. Franco-Flemish Ms. *Lovers in a Garden:* detail. Harley 4431 f. 376. London, British Museum.

The dress in the manuscript belongs to the same fashion as that of the fashionable characters in the *Térence des ducs* (see Ill. 6 and 7).

30. Hieronymus Bosch. *Adoration of the Magi*: detail, the youngest Magus. Madrid, Prado.

The tassel which weighs down the sleeve appears, at the time this picture was painted, to have been a theatrical feature. The behaviour both of the sleeve and the tassel suggests that they were painted from life.

31. Master of Frankfurt. *Shooting Contest*: detail, two Fools. Antwerp, Musée royal des Beaux-Arts.

Both bells and tassels were often used in the dress of Fools but neither had been a part of the original fashion from which this sleeve was derived.

32. Master of Frankfurt. *Shooting Contest*: detail, negro drummer. Antwerp, Musée royal des Beaux-Arts.

His sleeve derives from the dagged-edged sleeves of the International Gothic period but had, by this time, greatly altered its character and was used exclusively, apparently, for costume associated with the stage or with musicians.

33. Albrecht Dürer. Wood-cut from the *Narrenschiff*.

The Fool here is not particularised. He wears the kind of standard costume that was probably the livery of most Fools belonging to small companies, as distinct from the livery of a 'court' Fool.

34. Master of 1462. Wood-cut. *Procession with Hunter, Fools and Monkeys*.

An allegory of the world's vanity. If, as is possible, this is based on an incident in a morality play the monkeys may have been men in disguise, which the wood-cut rather suggests.

35. North European School. *Grimani Breviary*: month of April. Venice, Biblioteca Marciana.

The Calendar is a part of the Breviary. The dress here is represented with considerable accuracy and understanding, although it is not absolutely correct in all its details.

36. North European School. *Grimani Breviary*: detail, a Fool. Venice, Biblioteca Marciana.

This is not the only illustration in the *Grimani Breviary* in which a tonsured Fool appears; there is another in a small *bas-de-page* painting in which mummers approach a doorway through which a Fool wearing a tonsure looks out.

37. Flemish School. *Roman de la Rose: Bel-Acueil shows l'Acteur the Rose*. Late fifteenth or early sixteenth century. Harley 4425 f. 36. London, British Museum.

In spite of his girlish appearance here, in the novel *Bel-Acueil* is a man.

38. Andrea Mantegna. *Triumphs of Caesar*: detail, wheel of car. London, Hampton Court.

Roman reliefs showing chariots with elaborate wheels are not uncommon. In these the wheels are treated, of course, three-dimensionally. Mantegna makes no attempt to do this.

39. Andrea Mantegna. *Triumphs of Caesar*: detail, young man. London, Hampton Court.

The hairdressing of this particular youth is so elaborate that it may well have been inspired by a blond wig.

40. Andrea Mantegna. *Triumphs of Caesar*: detail, young man. London, Hampton Court.

The device of holding in the sleeve by ties, fashionable at the end of the fifteenth century, was usually to be found in feminine dress. A painting in the Brera by Bramante shows Democritus wearing sleeves of this kind.

41. Andrea Mantegna. *Triumphs of Caesar*: detail, armour. London, Hampton Court.

The very unmilitary concept of armour cut through at the waist must have been derived from the difficulty encountered on the stage when actors were required to wear armour of more or less Roman design but made not in leather but in metal.

42. Andrea Andreani, after Andrea Mantegna. Sixteenth-century engraving of *Triumphs of Caesar*: detail, buffoon, dwarf and young man. Vienna, Kunsthistorisches Museum.

This part of the Mantegna painting is badly damaged but an engraving made in the late sixteenth century records its original state.

43. Andrea Mantegna. *Parnassus*: detail, Mars and Venus. Paris, Louvre.

The action in this painting takes place in various locations which recall the *mansions* of mediaeval drama, retained, at this period, in the new theatre which presented plays with classical themes.

44. Andrea Mantegna. *Parnassus*: detail, Pegasus. Paris, Louvre.

A pattern of scales is painted on Pegasus's hooves and his coat has been shaved, leaving small florets of hair. The spots on his legs were almost certainly painted on a real horse. A jewelled pendant hangs through the artificial curl in the middle of his forehead.

45. Italian School. *Argonauts*: detail, young men in armour. Thyssen Collection, Lugano.

Although it conforms in general lines to the current fashion the dress of these boys is both fanciful and extreme.

46. Italian School. *Argonauts*. Thyssen Collection, Lugano.

See, for instance, the reference to a ship in the entertainment presented to Henri II in Paris (p. 233, in text).

47. Flemish School. *A Prophet:* detail. Rome, Palazzo Barbarini.

Gowns edged with fringe were not a part of the fashionable wardrobe in the fifteenth or the early sixteenth century when this picture must have been painted. Fringes did trim ecclesiastical dalmatics, but since the dalmatic was a stiff narrow vestment and the fringe which trimmed it was narrow too, it could not have served as a model for this painting since it could not have been persuaded to behave in this way.

48. French School. *Heures de Marguerite d'Orléans:* detail. Ms. Lat. a 1156B. fol. 125. Paris, Bibliothèque Nationale.

Letters of this Gothic style were used as goldsmiths' work on garments and housings for horses.

49. Pesellino. *Triumphs of Petrarch: Triumphs of Love, Chastity and Death.* Boston, Mass., Isabella Stewart Gardner Museum.

A set of xylograph *Triumphs of Petrarch*, printed in Florence in 1488 bears a resemblance to Pesellino's *Triumphs*, which must, of course, have been done considerably earlier. See A. Venturi, 'Les Triomphes de Pétrarch dans l'art représentatif', *Revue de l'Art ancien et moderne*, Paris 1906.

50. Pesellino. *Triumphs of Petrarch: Triumphs of Fame, Time and Eternity.* Boston, Mass., Isabella Stewart Gardner Museum.

The Triumph of Eternity (sometimes called the Triumph of Religion) is occasionally shown as a flat painted set-piece in which the Almighty is enclosed in a circular glory and mounted on a car.

51. Pesellino. *Triumphs of Petrarch:* detail, Triumph of Chastity. Boston, Mass., Isabella Stewart Gardner Museum.

The unicorns were probably based on horses disguised as unicorns by the addition of a horn and a thick mane. Buffaloes were common enough in Italy to be available to draw the car of *Death*.

52. Pesellino. *Triumphs of Petrarch:* detail, Triumph of Fame. Boston, Mass., Isabella Stewart Gardner Museum.

It is normal in paintings of Petrarch's *Triumphs* to find that the Car of Fame is surrounded by men in dresses of various nationalities.

53. Jacopo Bellini. Drawing of a man riding a horse which is disguised as a dragon. Paris, Louvre, Cabinet des Dessins.

Although some horses were almost certainly more completely disguised this drawing must have been taken from life.

315

54. Hans Burgkmair. *Triumphzug*: detail, Linkmen.

The wide-mouthed Gothic sleeves, called in Italy *al ducale* had, for the purposes of stage costume become slashed into ribbons by the beginning of the sixteenth century and had been adopted as a part of the uniform of *moresca* – morris – dancers. Here the *moresca* linkmen wear masks of the kind often to be found in stage costume of the sixteenth century.

55. Flemish School. *Calendar: February; Dance in a Great Hall.* Additional Ms. 24098 f. 19v. London, British Museum.

The leading dancer himself carries a torch in this painting.

56. Hans Burgkmair. *Triumphzug*: Car of Fools.

The base of the car is decorated by a border which includes monkeys, often used in court entertainments. The date engraved on the bottle held by one of the players is 1517.

57. Hans Burgkmair. *Triumphzug*: Car of bucolic mummers.

The player who gesticulates wears the artist's initials on his belt (cf. p. 168). The sleeves of the mouth-organ player are edged with inconspicuous dags, which suggests that although they were no longer theatrically interesting they could hardly be omitted from theatrical dress.

58. German School. *Freydal*: dancers. Vienna, Kunsthistorisches Museum.

This costume may, perhaps, derive from an earlier convention for the dress of Fools.

59. German School. *Freydal*: Hungarian dancers. Vienna, Kunsthistorisches Museum.

'Hungarian' is a loose term to use in this context; the exact difference between some types of Hungarian and some types of Polish dress has been a matter of dispute.

60. German School. *Freydal*: dance of giants. Vienna, Kunsthistorisches Museum.

Their gowns are long enough to hide the stilts on which they walk. Their female companions wear the Bohemian fashion of the second decade of the sixteenth century.

61. German School. *Freydal*: masked 'women' wearing oriental dress. Vienna, Kunsthistorisches Museum.

The oriental dress of the masked 'women' is probably based on manuscript paintings of the early fifteenth century. The pear-shaped bells which hang from their belts frequently appear in costume associated with the theatre (see Ills. 71 and 72).

62. French School. *Livre des Merveilles.* Ms. fr. 2810. Paris, Bibliothèque Nationale.

Marco Polo's report of his travels led to a profusion of versions of his text in the years which followed his first written account.

63. German School. *Freydal:* dramatic scene. Vienna, Kunsthistorisches Museum.

Moresche could include mimed playlets but never, apparently, spoken dialogue. Spectators in the background wear fashions of south Germany, Austria and Hungary of the second decade of the sixteenth century.

64. German School. *Freydal:* a round dance. Vienna, Kunsthistorisches Museum.

The costumes here are reproduced, in many respects, with surprising fidelity.

65. German School. *Freydal:* male dancers. Vienna, Kunsthistorisches Museum.

The dress of the women here is probably based on a German rather than a French or Netherlandish version of the earlier fashion.

66. German School. *Freydal:* enthroned king and queen. Vienna, Kunsthistorisches Museum.

The dress they wear is almost certainly intended to be of very early date and is most remarkable considering the period at which the *Freydal* was done. The scene might possibly represent the court of King Arthur or some early German legend or romance.

67. B. Buontalenti. (Formerly attributed to Vasari.) Designs for costumes of two female performers in the Florentine intermezzi of 1589. London, Victoria and Albert Museum.

Extremely elaborate, these costumes include tassels, fringes, masks of animals and leather work painted to look like jewellery but they still reveal the *camicie* which were an essential part of the costumes of nymphs. The dress of *Flora* in the Rouen *Entrée* of 1550 (Ill. 74) is clearly related in its design to this traditional dress of mythological and allegorical female personages.

68. Andrea Mantegna. *Bacchanale:* detail. Engraving.

The satyr is wearing what is probably an idealised form of stage costume: there are references to nymphs wearing skirts cut into leaf-shapes (see p. 266).

69. A temporary stage erected for the Rhetoricians' festival at Haarlem in 1606. From *Const-Thoonende Juweel, by de lodijcke stadt Haerlem*, Haarlem, 1607.

A temporary stage, set up on trestles, with a lower stage, shut off by front-curtains and an upper-stage in which an orchestra and/or heavenly characters could be accommodated. This is the kind of *edifice* set up in streets on occasions of a 'joyous entry'. The badges and coats-of-arms would represent both the Chamber of Rhetoric responsible for the performance and the city in which they were situated as well as any further complimentary heraldry demanded by the occasion.

70. Master of the von Groote Altarpiece. *Adoration of the Magi:* detail, mature Magus. Ex von Groote collection, Kitzburg: present whereabouts unknown.

The extraordinary detail recorded in the costume of the mature Magus makes it clear that the artist must have used a model for this dress.

71. Master of Frankfurt. *St Barbara*: detail. The Hague, Mauritshuis.

Carefully-recorded goldsmiths' work similar to that which edges St Barbara's upper garment can be found also in sculptured figures of saints who appear as part of the complex of a princely tomb, but never in the dress of the portrait-effigy of the deceased.

72. North European School. *Grimani Breviary*: two borders. F.95v and 101r. Venice, Biblioteca Marciana.

Bells of this kind were used, at this period, the early sixteenth century, only for jousting ornaments or theatrical costumes. The borders of the pages in the *Grimani Breviary* include, among other things, accurate representations of enamelled flowers used in the jewellery of the period as well as precious stones in fashionable settings.

73. *Entry of Henri II into Rouen, 1550*: detail, men in pseudo-classical civil costume. Engraving.

The current fashion shows very clearly in spite of the attempt at classical dress.

74. *Entry of Henri II into Rouen, 1550*: detail, the goddess Flora and nymphs. Engraving.

Inigo Jones, in the early seventeenth century, was still clothing his nymphs in dresses of this kind.

75. *Entry of Henri II into Rouen, 1550*: detail, Orpheus, the nine Muses and Hercules. Engraving.

This group was set into the actual architecture of a specially built triumphal arch. It was not unusual for dramatic scenes to be acted in these set-pieces at the moment when the distinguished personage to be welcomed approached them.

76. *Entry of Henri II into Rouen, 1550*: detail, a group of captives. Engraving.

Etrange may, in this case, mean foreign.

77. Hans Mielich. *Outdoor Banquet*. Hartford, Connecticut, Wadsworth Atheneum.

This extremely interesting and unique little oil painting is rather dark and therefore difficult to reproduce. It is important if only for the fact that it proves that men and women instrumentalists could play together in a small band.

78. Pieter Pourbus. *Allegorical Love Feast*. London, Wallace Collection.

Almost all the dress is fanciful but its structure is so meticulously recorded that it could not have been painted without models. The three Graces and two or three allegorical Virtues attend the banquet given by the two lovers seated behind the table.

79. French School. *Feast of Mummers*. Oxford, Ashmolean Museum.

The Ashmolean owns another painting of a dance in a raftered hall in which women wearing antique head-dresses appear. It is signed J. Verbeech and dated 1560. Ill. 78 here is also sometimes ascribed to Verbeech but the two drawings do not appear to be by the same hand.

80. Lucas van Leyden. *Life of the Magdalene*. Engraving, 1519.

In the background the Magdalene can be seen again, riding to hounds.

81. Boissard. *Mascarades:* title page. 1597.

The title page makes it clear that Robert Boissard was editor and engraver but not the designer of the costumes which appear in the book. The engravings themselves are not signed.

82. Boissard. *Mascarades:* 'Blandus amor . . .'. 1597.

The dags are cut into the sleeves correctly, unlike the dags that ornament the sleeves of the Magus in Bosch's painting (Ill. 28).

83. Boissard. *Mascarades:* 'Virtuti est gratus . . .'. 1597.

The costumes here are consistent in their attempt to recreate a fashion of the past but this is true of only one or two engravings.

84. Boissard. *Mascarades:* 'Qui Genio indulgens . . .'. 1597.

The figure representing Death may be compared with the Actor belonging to a Chamber of Rhetoric, in Ill. 1.

85. Boissard. *Mascarades:* 'Insanire licet locupleti . . .'. 1597.

An attempt to represent 'barbaric' rather than true Roman armour was often made; much of it is reminiscent of the Dacian or Scythian armour preserved in Bucharest.

86. Boissard. *Mascarades:* design by van Gheyn. 1597.

A few designs for stage costumes by van Gheyn are bound in with the Boissard designs in the British Museum copy. Since in these the pages are numbered, they must originally have belonged to another collection. Here the hanging-sleeve used in their paintings of the Magi by Gentile da Fabriano and Gozzoli, and by Mantegna for an oriental, still persists.

87. Boissard. *Mascarades:* design by van Gheyn. 1597.

The actual group as it appears here, can be found in at least two later works of art.

88. Otto van Veen. *Evening meal in the Woods.* Amsterdam, Rijksmuseum.

One of a series of twelve pictures illustrating the insurrection of the Batavians against the Romans. Purchased by the States-General in 1613.

89. Pieter Codde. *The Ball:* detail. The Hague, Mauritshuis.

The painting can be dated from the dress of the women which is of the 1630s.

90. Pieter Codde. *Masked Ball:* detail. Althorp, Earl Spencer Collection.

Pieter Codde seems to have been directly involved with the theatre in Amsterdam, he is mentioned in connection with the production of a play and also as having written love songs.

91. Cristofano Allori. *Isabella of Aragon before Charles VIII.* Paris, Louvre.

The coarse workmanship which shows in the embroidery and the jewelled borders of the costumes has been carefully recorded by the painter.

Bibliography

of works referred to directly or indirectly in the text

For: *Il Breviario Grimani della Biblioteca Marciana di Venezia*
  see: MORPURGO, SALOMONE.
Les Heures d'Etienne Chevalier du Musée Condé, Chantilly
  see: MALO, HENRI.
Le Livre des Merveilles ms. fr. 2810. Bibliothèque Nationale, Paris
  see: Bibliothèque Nationale, Bertrand frères. Paris. n.d.
Le Térence des ducs ms. fr. 664. Bibliothèque de l'Arsenal, Paris
  see: MARTIN, HENRY.
R.I.S. = *Rerum italicarum scriptores. Raccolta degli storici italiani dal cinquecento al millecento.* Edited by L. A. Giosue Carducci. Città di Castello and Bologna 1900–.

ADEMOLLO, A. *Alessandro VI, Giulio II e Leone X nel Carnevale di Roma. Documenti inediti 1499–1520.* Florence 1886.

ALTIERI, MARCANTONIO. *Il natale di Roma nel 1513.* Rome 1881.

AMIENS, M. M. J. R. D'. *Monnaies inconnues des évêques des Innocens, des Fous et de quelques autres associations singulières du même temps.* Paris 1837.

ANCONA, ALESSANDRO D' (ED.). *Sacre rappresentazioni dei secoli XIV, XV e XVI.* Florence 1872.

ANCONA, ALESSANDRO D'. *Origini del teatro in Italia.* 2 vols. Turin 1891.

ANCONA, ALESSANDRO D'. (ED.). *Documenti sulla Università di Pisa nel secolo XV.* Pisa 1897.

ANDERSON, M. D. *Drama and Imagery in English Mediaeval Churches.* Cambridge 1963.

ARCO, CARLO D'. *Raccolta di cronisti e storici lombardi.* Vol. 2: *Cronaca di Mantova di Andrea Schivenoglia dal MCCCCXLV al MDCCCCLXXXIV.* Mantua 1857.

ARCO, CARLO D'. *Istoria della vita e delle opere di Giulio Pippi Romano scritta da Carlo d'Arco.* Mantua 1838.

AUSSTELLING KAISER MAXIMILIANS I (Maximilian Exhibition). *Katalog.* Innsbruck 1969.

BARCLAY, ALEXANDER. *The Castell of Labour.* Translated from the French of Pierre Gringoire by Alexander Barclay. Reprinted in facsimile from Wynkyn de Worde's edition of 1506 with the French text of 31 March 1501, and an introduction by Alfred W. Pollard. Roxburgh Club. Edinburgh 1905.

BARTOLI, ADOLFO. *Scenari inediti della Commedia dell'Arte. Contributo alla storia del teatro popolare italiano.* Florence 1880.

BASKERVILLE, CHARLES READ. *Pierre Gringoire's Pageants for the Entry of Mary Tudor into Paris.* From the British Museum ms. Cot. Ves. B.II. Chicago 1934.

BAYONNE. *Li grandissimi apparati e reali Trionfo per il Re e Regina di Franza nella città di Baiona, nell'abboccamento della Regina Catholica di Spagna.* Padua 1565.

BELTRAMI, L. *Gli sposali di Galeazzo Maria Sforza.* Milan 1893.

BERTELLI, FERDINANDO. *Omnium fere gentium nostrae aetatis habitus.* Venice 1563, 1569.

BIBLIOTHEQUE NATIONALE. *Le Livre des Merveilles.* Bertrand frères. Paris. n.d.

BLAIR, CLAUDE. *European Armour.* London 1958.

BOCCHIA, EGBERTO. *La drammatica a Parma 1400–1900.* Parma 1913.

BOISSARD, JEAN JACQUES. *Habitus Variarum Orbis Gentium.* Some plates engraved by Golzius. Mechlin ? 1581. (There is some doubt about the place of publication.)

BOISSARD, JEAN JACQUES. *Icones Diversorum Hominum fama et rebus gesstis illustrium.* Metz 1591.

BOISSARD, JEAN JACQUES. *Vitae et icones Sultanorum Turcicorum Principum Persarum aliorumq. illustrium heroum heroinarumq. ab Osmane usq. ad Mahometem III. Ad vivum ex antiquis mettalis effictae.* Engr. Th. de Bry. Frankfurt-am-maine 1596.

BOISSARD, ROBERT (ED.). *Mascarades recueillies et mises en taille douce.* Valenciennes 1597.

BOURDIGNE, JEHAN DE, COUNT DE QUATREBARBES (ED.). *Chroniques d'Anjou et de Maine.* Angers 1842.

BOYSSE, ERNEST. *Le Théâtre des Jesuites.* Paris 1880.

BRANTOME, PIERRE DE BOURDEILLE, SEIGNEUR DE. *Oeuvres complètes de Pierre de Bourdelle Seigneur de Brantôme,* edited by Ludovic Lalanne. Paris 1876.

BREDIUS, A. *The Paintings of Rembrandt.* Vienna and London 1937.

BRUCHET, MAX. *Le Château de Ripaille.* Paris 1907.

BRUYN, ABRAHAM DE. *Omnium pene Europae, Asiae, Aphricae atque Gentium Habitus.* Cologne 1577, enlarged ed. Antwerp 1581.

BURKHARD, ARTHUR. *Hans Burgkmair d.Ä. Meister der Graphik.* Berlin 1932.

CALVETE, JUAN CHRISTOVAL DE ESTRELLA. *El felicissimo viaie d'el muy alto y muy Poderoso Principe Don Phelippe, Hijo d'el Emperador Don Carlos Quinto Maximo desde España à sus tierras dela baxa Alemañia con la descripcion de todos los Estados de Brabante y Flandres. Escrito en quatro libros.* Antwerp 1552.

CAMBIAGI, GAETANO. *Memorie istoriche . . . per la Natività di San Giovanni Batista.* Florence 1766.

CAROCCI, CESARE (ED.). *La giostra di Lorenzo de'Medici messa in rima da Luigi Pulci.* Bologna 1899.

CASTIGLIONE, BALDASSARE. *Il Cortegiano.* Venice 1574.

CASTIGLIONI, CARLO (ED.). *Gualvanei de la Flamma Ordinis Praedicatorum Azone, Luchino et Johanne Vicecomitibus.* R.I.S., vol. 12, pt. 4. Bologna 1938.

CELTES, CONRAD. *Ludus Diane in modum Comedie coram Maximiliano Rhomanorum Rege Calendio Martis 9. Ludis Saturnalibus in arce Liusiana Danubu actus. Clementissimo Rege. Regina ducibusqui illustribus Mediolani Totaque-Regia curia spectatoribus.* Nuremburg 1501.

CELTES, CONRAD. *Conradi Celtis Protucci Primi inter Germanicos imperatoriis manibus Poete Laureati Quattuor Libri Amorum Qua Germanie Feliciter incipiunt.* Nuremburg 1502.

CELTES, CONRAD. *Petri Tritonii Melopoeia Augustae Vindelicorum* . . . Nuremburg 1707.

CHAMBERS, EDMUND KERCHEVER. *The Elizabethan Stage.* 4 vols. Oxford 1923.

CHAMBERS, EDMUND KERCHEVER. *The Mediaeval Stage.* 4 vols. Oxford 1903.

CHAMPEAUX, A. DE, *and* GAUCHERY, P. *Les Travaux d'art exécutés pour Jean de France, duc de Berry.* Paris 1894.

CHARTROU, JOSEPH. *Les Entrées solennelles et triomphales à la Renaissance.* Paris 1928.

CHASTELLAIN, GEORGES. *La Chronique de Jacques Lalain.* Paris 1825.

CHASTELLAIN, GEORGES. *La Chronique de Georges Chastellain,* edited by Baron Kervyn de Lettenhove, Brussels 1863.

CINTHIO, GIRALDI. *Giraldi Cinthio nobile Ferrarese, e segretario all' illustrissimo et Eccellentiss. Duca di Ferrara intorno al comporre e i Romanzi delle Comedie e delle Tragedie, e di altre maniere di Poesie.* Venice 1554.

CLAEYS, PROSPER. *Histoire du théâtre à Gand.* 3 vols. Ghent 1892.

CLAUSSE, GUSTAVE. *Les San Gallo.* 3 vols. Paris 1902.

COGGIOLA, GIULIO. *Il Breviario Grimani della Biblioteca Marciana de Venezia.* Leyden 1908.

COHEN, GUSTAVE. *Le Livre de conduite du régisseur et les comptes des dépenses pour le Mystère de la Passion joué à Mons.* Paris 1925.

COHEN, GUSTAVE. *Histoire de la mise en scène dans le théâtre religieux français du moyen âge.* Paris 1926.

COHEN, GUSTAVE. *Le Théâtre en France au moyen âge.* 2 vols. Paris 1931.

COHEN, GUSTAVE. *Etudes d'histoire du théâtre en France au moyen âge et à la renaissance.* Paris 1956.

COHN, ALBERT. *Shakespeare in Germany in the Sixteenth and Seventeenth Centuries.* Paris 1865.

COLLAS, EMILE. *Valentine de Milan, Duchesse d'Orléans.* Paris 1911.

COLLIER, J. PAYNE. *The History of English Dramatic Poetry to the time of Shakespeare and Annals of the Stage*. 3 vols. London 1831.

COLVIN, SIDNEY (ED.). *A Florentine Picture Chronicle*. London 1896.

CONS, LOUIS. *L'Auteur de la Farce de Pathelin*. Elliott Monographs. Princeton and London 1926.

CONTI, GIUSEPPE. *Fatti e anedotti di storia fiorentina*. Florence 1902.

CORVISIERI, C. 'Il trionfo di Eleonora d'Aragona nel giugno del 1473'. *Archivio di Società Romana di Storia Patria*, vol. 1, no. 10. Rome 1877–8.

COX, TRENCHARD. *Jehan Fouquet, Native of Tours*. London 1931.

DAVIES, MARTIN. *The Earlier Italian Schools*. National Gallery, London 1951.

DENIS, FERDINAND. *Une Fête Bresilienne celebrée en Rouen en 1550*. Paris 1850.

DIARIO FERRARESE. See Pardi, Giuseppe (ed.).

DIEULAFOY, MARCEL. 'Le Miracle de la Femme que Nostre-Dame garda d'estre arse'. *Bulletin de la Société de l'Histoire du Théâtre*, 2nd. ann., no. 8. Paris 1903.

DODGSON, CAMPBELL (ED.). *A Book of Drawings*. British Museum, London 1923.

DODGSON, CAMPBELL. 'Die Freydal-Holzschnitte Dürers'. *Repertorium für Kunstwissenschaft*, vol. 26. Berlin 1902.

DOVILEE, M. T. (ED.). *Relation du beau voyage fit aux Pays Bas en 1548, le Prince Philippe d'Espagne, Nôtre Seigneur*. Brussels 1964.

DRESCHER, KARL. *Das Nurnbergische Schönbartbuch nach der Samburger Sandschrift*. Weimar 1908.

DURRIEU, PAUL. *Les Très Riches Heures de Jean de France, duc de Berry*. Paris 1904.

ESCOUCHY, MATHIEU D'. *Chronique de Mathieu d'Escouchy*, edited by G. du Fresne de Beaucourt. 3 vols. Paris 1864.

ESHLEMAN, DOROTHY (ED.). *The Committee Books of the Theatre Royal Norwich. 1768–1825*. Society for Theatre Research, London 1970.

FACCIOLI, EMILIO (ED.). *Mantova. Le Lettere*. Vol. 2. Istituto Carlo d'Arco, Mantova 1962.

FARIN, F. *Histoire de la ville de Rouen*. 3 vols. Rouen 1668.

FARNO, ENRICO. *Il dramma allegorico nelle origini del teatro italiano*. Arpino 1915.

FELIX, J. (ED.). *L'Entrée à Rouen du Roi Henri II et de la Reine Catherine de' Medicis en 1550*. Société Rouennaise de Bibliophiles, Rouen 1885.

FLEURY, EDOUARD. *Origines et développements de l'art théâtrale dans la province ecclésiastique de Reims*. Laon 1881.

FONDAZIONI TRECCANI. *Storia di Milano*. Milan 1954.

FORSTER, LEONARD. *Conrad Celtis, 1459–1508*. Cambridge 1948.

FRIEDLANDER, MAX F. *Die Altniederlandischer Malerei*. Berlin 1924–37.

GASTE, ARMAND. 'Les Drames Liturgiques de la Cathedral de Rouen'. In *La Revue Catholique de Normandie*. Evreux 1893.

GASTE, ARMAND. 'Michel Menot. En quelle langue a-t-il prêché? Son genre d'élo-quence. Essai de restitution, en français du commencement du XVI siècle, des sermons "sur l'Enfant Prodigue" at "sur la Madeleine"'. *Mémoires de l'Académie Nationale des Sciences, Arts et Belles-Lettres de Caen.* Caen 1897.

GELLI, JACOPO. *Mostra della giostra anno 1492.* Codici Morbio, Brera, Milan. Nozze Fumagalei/Sagui 1892.

GHIRARDACCI, R. P. M. CHERUBINO. *Della historia di Bologna*, ed. by Albano Sorbelli. R.I.S. vol. 33, pt. 1. Città di Castello 1929.

GHIZONI, P. 'Ceremonie seguite il 27 e 28 ottobre 1533 in Marsiglia per Matrimonio del Duca d'Orleans con Caterina de'Medici'. *Archivio storico lombardo*, vol. I. Milan 1874.

GIAMBULLARI, M. PIER FRANCESCO. *Apparato et feste nelle nozze dello illustrissimo signor Duca di Firenze et della Duchessa sua consorte con le sue stanze, madriali, comedie e intermedij in quelle recitati MDXXXIX.* Florence 1539.

GIRARDOT, A. DE. *Mystère des Actes des Apôtres représenté à Bourges en avril 1536.* Paris 1854.

GIRAUD, P. E. *Composition mise en scène et representation du Mystère des Trois Doms joué à Romans le 27, 28 et 29 mai, aux fêtes de Pentecôte de l'an 1509.* Lyons 1848.

GODEFROY, THEODORE. *Le Cérémonial françois.* Paris 1649.

GOMBRICH, E. H. 'The Evidence of Images', in *Interpretation Theory and Practice*, edited by C. S. Singleton. Baltimore 1969.

GOZZADINI, GIOVANNI. *Memorie per la vita di Giovanni II Bentivoglio.* Bologna 1839.

GRUYER, F. A. *Les Quarante Fouquet.* Chantilly, Notices des Peintures. Paris 1900.

GUASTI, CESARE. *Le Feste di San Giovanni Batista in Firenze.* Florence 1884.

GUENEE, BERNARD *and* LEHOUX, FRANCOISE. *Les Entrées royales françaises de 1328 à 1515.* Paris 1968.

GUGLIEMO EBREO. *Trattato dell'Arte del Ballo. Testo inedito del secolo XV.* Bologna 1873.

GUICCIARDINI, FRANCESCO. *Ricordi, politichi e civile di Firenze Del Governo Popolare di Firenze 1494–1512*, edited by A. Civellucci. Florence 1877.

HALLAM, HENRY. *Europe during the Middle Ages.* London 1818.

HARE, CHARLES. *Isabella of Milan. Letters of her Lady-in-Waiting.* London 1911.

HARGREAVES-MAWDSLEY, W. N. *A History of Legal Dress in Europe.* Oxford 1963.

HERICAULT, D. D and MONTAIGLON, A. DE. *Oeuvres complètes de Gringore.* Paris 1858.

HEYDE, W. VON. *Geschichte des Levante Handels.* 2 vols. Stuttgart 1879.

HEYNS, ZACHARIAS. *Dracht-Thoneel.* Amsterdam 1601.

HEYNS, ZACHARIAS. *Const-thoonende Juweel, by de lodijcke stadt Haarlem ter versoecke van Trou moet blijcken in'tlicht gebracht.* Haarlem 1607.

HOLLSTEIN, F. W. H. *Dutch and Flemish Engravings and Wood-cuts, c. 1450–1700.* Amsterdam 1949.

HUMBERT, ANDRE. *La Sculpture sous les ducs de Bourgogne 1361–1483. Paris 1913.*

HYMANS, HENRI. *Le Livre des peintres de Carol van Mander.* Paris 1884.

IDELFONSO, F. DI S. LUIGI. *Delizie degli erudite toscani. Matricole dell'arte della seta 1225–1257,* etc. 24 vols. Florence 1770–9.

ILLUSTRATORE FIORENTINO, L'. Florence 1910–12.

JODELLE, ETIENNE. *Estiene Iodelle Parisien Le Recueil des inscriptions, figures, devises et masquerades ordonnées en l'hostel de Ville à Paris, le jeudi, 17 de février 1558.* Paris 1558.

JULLEVILLE, L. PETIT DE. See PETIT DE JULLEVILLE.

KINDEMANN, H. *Geschichte Europas Theater.* Salzburg 1957.

KONIGSON, ELIE. *La Représentation d'un Mystère de la Passion à Valenciennes en 1547.* Paris 1969.

KOTT, JAN. *Shakespeare Our Contemporary.* 2nd ed. London 1967.

KURTH, WILLI. *The Complete Woodcuts of Albrecht Dürer.* London 1927.

LABORDE, LE COMTE DE. *Les ducs de Bourgogne, étude sur les lettres, les arts et l'industrie pendant le xv siècle.* Paris 1849.

LA MARCHE, OLIVIER DE. *Mémoires d'Olivier de la Marche,* edited by Henri Beaune and J. d'Arbaumont. 4 vols. Paris 1883–8.

LA MARCHE, OLIVIER DE. *Description inédite des fêtes celebrées à Bruges en 1468 à l'occasion du mariage du duc Charles-le-Téméraire avec Marguerite d'York,* edited by Auguste Dufour and François Rabut. Dijon 1877.

LAVER, JAMES. *Isabella's Triumph.* London 1947.

LECOCQ, GEORGES. *Histoire du théâtre de Saint-Quentin.* Saint-Quentin 1874.

LEITNER, QUIRIN VON (ED.). *Freydal des Kaisers Maximilian I. Turniere und Mummereien Herausgegeben ... Franz Grafen Folliot de Crenneville von Quirin von Leitner.* Vienna 1880–2.

LIEBRECHT, HENRI. *Les Chambres de Rhétorique.* Brussels 1948.

LIPPERHEIDE'SCHEN KOSTUMBIBLIOTHEK. *Katalog der Freiherrlich von Lipperheide'schen kostumbibliothek.* 2 vols. Berlin 1896–1905.

LUNGO, ISADORO DEL. 'De altre recitazioni di Commedie Latine in Firenze nel secolo XV'. *Archivio storico italiano,* ser. 3, vols. 22 and 23. Florence, 1875 and 1876.

LUZIO, ALESSANDRO. *Leandro Arrivabene alla Corte di Caterina de'Medici 1549–1559.* Bergamo 1902.

LUZIO, ALESSANDRO. 'Federico Gonzaga ostaggio alla corte di Giulio II in Roma'. *Archivio della Società Romana di storia,* vol. 9. Rome 1887.

LUZIO, ALESSANDRO. *Isabella d'Este di fronte a Giulio II.* Milan 1912.

LUZZATTO, LEONE. 'Una rappresentazione allegorica in Urbino nel 1474'. *Atti e memorie della R. Accademia Petrarcha di scienze, lettere ed arti in Arezzo*, n.s., vol. 1. Arezzo 1920.

MAGNIN, CHARLES. 'Teatro Celeste (Les comédiens en Paradis). Les commencements de la comédie italienne en France'. *Revue des Deux Mondes*, n.s., vol. 20, ann. 17. Paris 1847.

MALAGUZZI VALERIE, FRANCESCO. 'Ricamatori ed arazzieri a Milano nel quattrocento'. *Archivio storico lombardo*, ser. 3, vols. 19 and 20, 1903.

MALE, EMILE. 'Le Renouvellement de l'art par les "Mystères" à la fin du moyen âge'. *Gazette des Beaux Arts*. 3rd période, no. 31. Paris 1904.

MALE, EMILE. *L'Art religieux de la fin du moyen âge en France*. Paris 1925.

MALO, HENRI. *Les Heures d'Etienne Chevalier*. Paris 1946.

MANDER, CAREL VAN. *Het Schilder-Boeck*. Haarlem 1604.

MARLE, R. VAN. *The Development of the Italian Schools of Painting*. The Hague 1931.

MAROT, CLEMENT. *Oeuvres satiriques* and *Oeuvres lyriques*, edited by C. A. Mayer. London 1964.

MARTIN, HENRY. 'Le Térence des ducs et la mise en scène au moyen âge'. *Bulletin de la Société de l'Histoire du Théâtre*, no. 1. Paris 1902.

MARTIN, HENRY. *Le Térence des ducs*. Paris 1907.

MARTIN, HENRY. *Les Joyaux de l'Enluminure à la Bibliothèque Nationale*. Paris and Brussels 1928.

MASI, BARTOLOMEO. *Ricordanza di Bartolomeo Masi, calderaio fiorentino, dal 1478 al 1526*, ed. by Guiseppe Odoardo Corazzini. Florence 1906.

MASTER DRAWINGS ASSOC. INC. *Master Drawings*, vol. 3, no. 1. New York 1965.

MAZZI, CURZIO. *La Congrega dei Rozzi di Siena nel secolo XVI*. 2 vols. Florence 1906.

MEISS, MILLARD. *French Painting in the Time of Jean de Berry*. London 1968.

MELLENCAMP, EMMA H. 'A Note on the Costume of Titian's Flora'. *The Art Bulletin*, vol. 51, no. 2. New York 1969.

MERVAL, L. DE. *L'Entrée d'Henri II à Rouen*. 2 vols. Société des Bibliophiles Normands. Rouen 1868.

MICHEL, JEAN. *Le Mystère de la Passion. Angers 1486*, edited by Omer Jodogue. University of Louvain, 1959.

MIGNON, MAURICE. *Etudes sur le théâtre français et italien de la renaissance*. Paris 1923.

MILSACK, G. *and* ANCONA, A. D'. *Due farse del secolo XVI riprodette sulle antiche stampe*. Bologna 1882.

MONACI, ERNESTO. *Appunti per la storia del teatro italiano*. Imola 1874. Reprinted from *Rivista di Filologia Romanza*, vols. 1–2. Imola 1872. With renumbered pages.

MONTFAUCON, BERNARD DE. *Les Monuments de la monarchie française qui comprennent l'histoire de France.* 5 vols. Paris 1732.

MORICE, EMILE. *Histoire de la mise-en-scène depuis les mystères jusqu'au Cid.* Paris 1836.

MORPURGO, SALOMONE. 'Le Compagnie della Gatta: i suoi capitoli e le sue tramutazioni', in *Miscellanea fiorentina di erudizione e storia.* Florence 1886.

MORPURGO, SALOMONE. *Il Breviario Grimani.* Leyden 1903–8.

MORTENSEN, JOHAN. *Le Théâtre française au moyen âge.* Translated into French by Emmanuel Philipot. Paris 1903.

MOTTA, EMILIO. 'Musici alla Corte degli Sforza'. *Archivio storico lombardo*, ser. 2, vol. 4, ann. 14. Milan 1887.

NARDI, JACOPO. *Le historie della città di Fiorenza, 1494–1531.* 4 vols. Lyons 1582.

NEWTON, STELLA MARY (PEARCE). 'Costumi tedeschi e borgognoni in Italia nel 1452'. *Commentari.* Rome, October–December 1957.

NEWTON, STELLA MARY (PEARCE). 'Costumi tedeschi e borgognoni nel Libro di Marco Zoppo'. *Commentari.* Rome, June–September 1958.

NICOLL, ALLARDYCE. *The Development of the Theatre.* London 1927.

OSSERVATORE FIORENTINO, L'. *L'osservatore fiorentino sugli edifizi della sua patria, per servire all storia della medesima.* 3rd ed., vol. 1: *Teatro della Pergola, ed origini dell' Opera.* Florence 1821.

PALLIOLO, PAOLO DA FANO. 'Le feste per conferimento del patriziato romano a Giuliano e Lorenzo de' Medici'. *Scelta di curiosità letterarie e rare dal secolo 13 al 17*, no. 206. Bologna 1885.

PANOFSKY, ERWIN. 'Conrad Celtis and Kunz von der Rosen: two problems in portrait identification'. *The Art Bulletin*, vol. 24. New York 1942.

PANOFSKY, ERWIN. *The Life and Art of Albrecht Dürer.* Princeton 1955.

PARDI, GIUSEPPE (ED.). *Diario Ferrarese, dall'anno 1409 sino al 1502.* R.I.S., vol. 24, pt. 7. Bologna 1933.

PASTOR, L. *History of the Popes.* London 1894.

PETIT DE JULLEVILLE, L. *Les Comédiens en France au moyen âge.* Paris 1885.

PETIT DE JULLEVILLE, L. *La Comédie et les moeurs en France au moyen âge.* Paris 1886.

PETIT DE JULLEVILLE, L. *Répertoire du théâtre comique en France au moyen âge.* Paris 1886.

PETIT DE JULLEVILLE, L. *Le Théâtre en France, histoire de la littérature dramatique.* Paris 1889.

PICOT, EMILE *and* NYROP, CHRISTOPHE. *Nouveau recueil des farces françaises des XV et XVI siècles.* Paris 1886.

POLA, GIUSEPPE C. *Associazioni giovanili e feste antiche.* 4 vols. Milan 1943.

POLIZIANO, ANGELO. *Stanze per la Giostra, Orfeo, Rime*, edited by Bruno Maier. Novara 1969.

POTTIER, A. *Révue de Rouen*. Rouen 1835.

RAJNA, PIO. 'Il Teatro di Milano ei canti intorno ad Orlando e Ulivieri'. *Archivio storico lombardo*, vol. 4, anno 14. Milan 1887.

RITCHIE, GRAEME. *Buik of Alexander*, vols. 2 and 3. Scottish Text Society, 1921 and 1927.

RONSARD, PIERRE DE.*Oeuvres complètes*, edited by Paul Laumonier. Paris 1939.

ROSSI, VITTORIO. *Il Quattrocento*. Milan 1938.

ROUEN, BIBLIOTHEQUE MUNICIPALE, *C'est la déduction de sumptueux ordre, plaisantz spectacles, et magnifique théatre, dressés et exhibites par les citoiens de Rouen, Ville Metropolitaine du pais de Normandie. faictz à l'entrée de la sacrée Majesté du très chrestien Roy de France, Henry second, leur souverain seigneur, Et à tresillustre Dame, Madame Katherine de Medicis la Royne, son espouze. Qui fut es jours de Mercredi et jeudi, premier et second jour d'Octobre. Mil cinq cens Cinquante. Et pour plus expresse intelligence de ce tant excellent triumphe, Les figures & pourtraictz des principaulx aornementz d'iceluy. On les vend à Rouen au portail des librairer à la prochaine boutique. La Rue sa Jean Dugort 1551*. Rouen 1551. An original edition which can be seen at the Bibliothèque Municipale.

RUNCIMAN, STEVEN. *A History of the Crusades*. 3 vols. Harmondsworth 1965.

RUPRICH, HANS. 'Das literatische Werk Kaiser Maximilians I'. *Ausstellung Kaiser Maximilians I, Katalog*. Innsbruck 1969.

SACCHI, D. *and* SACCHE, G. *Antichità romantiche d'Italia*. Epoca 1, 2. Milan 1828, 1829.

SALTINI, G. E. (ED.). *Di una mascherata pastorale fatta in Siena per la venuta della Granduchessa Bianca Cappello la sera del 22 febbraio 1582*. Florence 1882.

SANTORO, CATERINA. *Milano d'altri Tempo*. Milan 1938.

SANUDO, MARIN. *I Diarii di Marin Sanudo*. 58 vols. Venice 1879–1902.

SAVIOTTI, ALFREDO. 'Una rappresentazione nel 1474'. *Atti e memorie della R. Accademia Petrarca di Scienze, Lettere ed Arti in Arezzo*, vol. 1. Arezzo 1920.

SENN, WALTER. 'Maximilian mid die Musik'. *Ausstellung Kaiser Maximilians I, Katalog*. Innsbruck 1969.

SLUPERIUS, JOANNES. *Omnium fere gentium nostraeq. aetatis Nationem, Habitus & Effigies*. Antwerp 1572.

SOLERTI, ANGELO. *La rappresentazione della Calandria a Lione nel 1548. Estratto dalla Raccolta di Studii critici dedicata ad Allesandro d'Ancona festegiandosi il 40 anniversario del suo insegnamento*. Florence 1901.

SOLMI, EDMONDO, *La Festa del Paradiso di Leonardo da Vinci e Bernardino Bellincione 13 gennaio 1490*. Extract from *Archivio storico lombardo*, fasc. 1. Milan 1904.

SOMMI, LEONE DE'. *Quattro dialoghi in materia di rappresentazione sceniche*, edited by Ferruccio Marotti. Milan 1968.

SOZZINI, MESSER ALESSANDRO DA SIENA. *Mascarata villanesca recitata nel mese di maggio 1586*. Siena 1879.

FONDAZIONE TRECCANI DEGLI ALFIERI PER LA STORIA DI MILANO. *Storia di Milano*, vol 3. Milan 1954.

STRAETEN, EDMUND VAN DER. *Le Théâtre villageois en Flândre*. 2 vols. Brussels 1881.

SUMBERG, SAMUEL L. *The Nuremberg Schembart Carnival*. New York 1941.

TABARRINI, M. *Descrizione del convito e delle feste fatte in Pesaro per le Nozze di Costanzo Sforza e di Cammilla d'Aragona 1475*. Florence 1870.

THIBOUT, JACQUES. *Relation de l'ordre de la triomphante et magnifique montre du mystère des SS Actes des Apostres par Arnoul et Simon Greban, ouvrage inédit de Jacquest Thiboust, sieur de Quantilly, secrétaire du roy, élu de Berry*. Paris 1838.

THIEME-BECKER. *Allgemeines Lexicon der Bildenden Künstler*. 1907–50.

TIETZE-CONRAT, E. *Mantegna*. London 1955.

TIETZE-CONRAT, E. *Dwarfs and Jesters in Art*. London 1957.

TILLIOT, LUCOTTE DU. *Mémoires pour servir à l'histoire de la Fête des Foux*. Lausanne and Geneva 1751.

TIVIER, H. *Histoire de la littérature dramatique en France depuis ses origines jusq'au Cid*. Paris 1873.

TROYES, JEAN DE. *Histoire de Louys XI, roy de France et des choses memorables advenues de son Regne depuis l'an 1460 iusques à 1483. Excrite par un Greffier de L'Hotel de Ville*. Paris 1620.

VAN DER PUT, ALBERT. 'Two drawings of the Fêtes at Binche for Charles V and Philip II 1549'. *Journal of the Warburg and Courtauld Institutes*, vol. 3, 1939–1940.

VARCHI, BENEDETTO. *Storia fiorentina*. Florence 1721.

VARCHI, BENEDETTO. *Storia delle Cose de Firenze*. Florence 1730.

VASARI, GIORGIO. *Lives of the most Eminent Painters, Sculptors and Architects*, edited by William Gaunt. London 1963.

VATTASSO, MARCO. *Per la storia del dramma sacro in italia*. Rome 1903.

VECCHIETTI, GIROLAMO. *Una mascherata mitologica a Ferrara, 1443*. Brescia 1895.

VECELLIO, CESARE. *Habiti antichi e moderni*. Venice 1589.

VENTURI, A. 'Les Triomphes de Petrarque dans l'art représentatif'. *Revue de l'Art ancien et moderne*. Paris 1906.

VENTURI, LIONELLO. 'Le Compagnie della Calza'. *Nuovo archivio veneto*. Venice 1908–09–10.

VERDIER, P. LE (ED). *L'Entrée du Roy Loyis XII et de la Reine à Rouen 1508*. Société des Bibliophiles Normands. Rouen 1900.

VERDIER. P. LE. *Le Puy Souverain Amour par Pierre du Val.* Rouen 1920.

VIANELLO, C. 'Feste, tornei, congiure nel cinquecento milanese'. *Archivio storico lombardo*, ann. 1, fasc. 1–2. Milan 1936.

VIEL-CASTEL, H. DE. *Statuts de l'Ordre du Saint Esprit au Droit Désir ou du Noeud, institué à Naples en 1352.* Paris 1852.

VIGO, PIETRO (ED.). *Francesco Ricciardi di Pistoia detto Ceccodea. Riccordi storici dal 1494 al 1500.* Bologna 1882.

VIGO, PIETRO. *Una Confraternita di giovenetti pistojesi al principio del secolo XVI.* Bologna 1888. (Copy in the Bodleian Library, Oxford.)

VILLANI, GIOVANNI. *Cronica*, edited by F. Dragomanni. Florence 1844–45.

WAAS, GLENN ELWOOD. *The Legendary Character of Kaiser Maximilian.* New York 1941.

WAETZOLDT, WILHELM. *Dürer and his Times.* London 1950.

WARBURG, A. *I costumi teatrali per gli intermezzi del 1589.* Florence 1895.

WEALE, W. H. JAMES and BROCKWELL, MAURICE W. *The van Eycks and their Art.* London 1912.

WILENSKI, R. H. *Flemish Painters.* 2 vols. London 1960.

YATES, FRANCES A. *The French Academies of the Sixteenth Century.* London 1947.

YATES, FRANCES A. *The Valois Tapestries.* London 1959.

ZANNONI, GIOVANNI. *Una rappresentazione allegorica a Bologna nel 1487.* Rome 1891.

ZARNECKI, GEORGE. 'Claus Sluter, Sculptor to Duke Philip the Bold'. *Apollo*, London January–June, 1962.

Index

Confrèrie. *See* Companies
Connards of Rouen. *See under* Companies:
  Individual
Cordonniers of Paris. *See under* Companies:
  Individual
Cords. *See* Ties
Coriolanus, 251, 272
Cornelisz van Haarlem, 279 n28
Corpus Christi, procession on Feast of. *See under*
  Feast: Of
Cortegiano, Il, 135, 290 n1
Corvinus, Mathias, 153
Costume, Costumes: at a joust, 291 n11; at
  Bourges (1536), 223, 224; as symbols, 21,
  30; books on, 137, 249, 250, 251, 253;
  their fragility, 24
  Attitudes to:
    Cinthio, Giraldi, 209; Italian, 70; painters',
    32, 75, 81, 85, 88, 117; Sommi, Leone de',
    209–14
  Garments:
    camicia, 26, 120, 121, 159, 200, 212, 213,
    226, 236, 242, 266, 289 n26; *casaques à la
    Polonoyse*, 221; chemise, 130, 156, 157,
    159, 161, 200, 202; coat, 195, 230; *cotta*,
    236; *dogalina*, 287 n1; doublet, 178, 195;
    écharpe, 224; epaulettes, 200; *farsetto, farset-
    tino*, 195; farthingale, 200, 201; *giubbone*,
    306 n13; gown, 98, 186, 191, 200, 263,
    265; hose, 100, 147, 176, 178, 195, 197,
    200, 306 n13; *houppelande* (spelt variously),
    98; jacket, 122, 195; jacket and hose, 195,
    197, 256, 262, 263, 265; liotard, 177;
    mantle, 76, 92, 146, 147, 162, 163, 195,
    200, 212, 213, 268; *manto*, 147; over-dress,
    131; *palletot*, 148, 293 n27; pantaloons,
    265; *pourpoint*, 163, 195, 221, 291,
    n7; shirt, 120, 121, 129, 130, 195, 200,
    see also camicia and chemise above; skirt,
    75, 164, 176, 177, 196, 197, 204, 205,
    226, 268; *stola*, 156; *surcot*, 235, 236;
    tabard, 195; toga, 224, 265; *tonicelli*,
    147; tunic, *tunica*, 75, 81, 120, 172, 176,
    177, 186, 195, 197, 200, 235, 260,
    264, 268; *turca*, 143, 293 n21; *veste*,
    147
  Garments for:
    Christ, 147; nymphs, 213; rainbow, a, 210;
    shepherds, 213; tragedies, 212, 272, 273;
    Virgin, the, 146, 147

Of:
Adam and Eve, 25; angels, 27, 81, 285 n18;
  antiquity in north Europe, 64; Apollo, 162,
  295 n52; Apostles, 70, 140, 224; Argonauts, 129; *bacchanti*, 299 n12; Saint Barbara, 230, 231, 242; Belial, 223; *brigate*,
  77, 79, 100; Duke of Burgundy, 295 n54;
  captives, 237; Castor and Pollux, 161;
  Charles VIII, 268; Chastity, 156; Christ,
  70, 150, 151; classical periods, 160, 211,
  212; *l'Eglise*, 278 n17; Death, 156, 256;
  Devils, 223, 275 n5, 301 n27; Fame, 152,
  294 n37; Fame's company, 157; Flora,
  101, 235; Fools, 27, 99, 108, 172, 174,
  240, 242; foreigners, 136–8; Frederick III,
  138; a giant, 140; Grand Vizirs, 68; Greeks,
  162, 301 n26; Harlequin, 265; Hebe, 162;
  Herod, 65; Herod-Antipas, 225; High
  Priests, 70; the Hours, 307 n17; Mathias
  Lang, 136, 291 n3; Iris, 161; Isabella of
  Aragon, 268; Janissaries, 178; Jews, 92,
  286 n30; King David, 92; knights, 140;
  ladies, 140; *landsknechts*, 168, 174; lawyers,
  109; Magi, 33, 73, 74, 76, 77, 82, 84, 99,
  100, 103, 104, 106, 227, 228, 231, 285 n10,
  n12, 286 n21, n22; Marc Anthony, 225;
  Maximilian, 197; *Mère Sotte*, 278 n17;
  Midas, 152; minority groups, 131; Modesty,
  161, Moors, 294 n34; *moresca* dancers,
  170; municipal dignitaries, 109; Muses,
  153, 162, 202–4, 295 n52; nun, 140, 150;
  nymphs, 130, 161, 164, 192, 202, 204,
  266, 303 n11; Orient in northern Europe,
  64, 65; Orpheus, 162, 237; page, 268;
  Pantaloon, 306 n13; Penelope, 161; Greek
  philosophers, 144; Pilate, 70; Planets, 161,
  295 n49; *potenze*, 53, 77, 100; Prophets,
  143, 144, 293 n21; Rhetoricians, 221;
  Romans, 162; *Sainte Eglise*, 141; Saracens,
  139, 181; satyrs, 205, 266; shepherds, 42,
  266; squire, 75; Sybils, 143; tetrarchs, 215;
  Time, 155; torch-bearers, 168; torturers,
  27, 65; Turks, 139, 181; Venice, 135; the
  Virgin Mary, 76, 146, 147; Virtue, 233;
  women in late fifteenth-century Italy, 130
Types of:
  à la nimphale, 204, 205, 266; *alla Greca*,
  160; *all' antica, ala antigua*, 153, 158, 202,
  204, 225, 226, 303 n11; antique, 121, 199;
  Biblical, 131; Bohemian, 138, 291 n7;